THE
TIMBER-FRAME
HOME

THE TIMBER-FRAME HOME

second edition
revised and updated

Design · Construction · Finishing

Tedd Benson

Illustrations by Brian Smeltz

The Taunton Press

COVER PHOTOGRAPH: BRIAN SMELTZ

PUBLISHER: JON MILLER
ACQUISITIONS EDITOR: JULIE TRELSTAD
EDITORIAL ASSISTANT: KAREN LILJEDAHL
EDITOR: THOMAS MCKENNA
LAYOUT ARTIST: CHRIS CASEY
PHOTOGRAPHERS, EXCEPT WHERE NOTED: AUTHOR AND BRIAN SMELTZ

TYPEFACE: STONE SERIF
PAPER: 70-LB. PATINA
PRINTER: QUEBECOR PRINTING/KINGSPORT, KINGSPORT, TENNESSEE

for fellow enthusiasts

First printing: 1997

Printed in the United States of America

A Fine Homebuilding Book

Fine Homebuilding® is a trademark of The Taunton Press, Inc.,
registered in the U.S. Patent and Trademark Office.

The Taunton Press, 63 South Main Street, PO Box 5506,
Newtown, CT 06470-5506

Library of Congress Cataloging-in-Publication Data

Benson, Tedd
      The timber-frame home : design, construction, finishing /
  Tedd Benson — 2nd ed., rev. and updated.
          p.   cm.
      Includes bibliographical references and index.
      ISBN 1-56158-129-1
      1. Wooden-frame houses — Design and construction.   I. Title.
  TH4818.W6B464   1997
  690'.837 — dc20   96-44276
                                             CIP

To the memory of my brother, friend, and business co-founder,

Stephen Clare Benson (1950-1974).

Partner in the beginning, partner to the end.

ACKNOWLEDGMENTS

A book such as this is not created by a single individual. I did not think, write, learn, research, or create alone. I will fail to acknowledge all of those family members, friends, clients, associates, and others who have contributed to the information and effort contained in these pages. For the fact that your name does not appear here, you have my apologies; for your contributions, you have my undying gratitude.

My writing, my professional work, and my personal life do not have walls to separate them. I like it that way. All of the things I do—this book included—are really about trying to improve the quality of lives. I first must thank a few people for their lifetime of gifts to me. *Christine:* As I have been married to Christine longer than I have been timber framing, I could not have walked this difficult path were it not for her unconditional love and would not still be treading here were it not for her conditional partnership. *Emily and Corona:* My daughters—women now—still keep me rich in love. I have built and accomplished nothing that gives me such joy and pride as simply being a part of the lives of these two ladies. *Mary Lou and Ted Benson:* My parents set standards of integrity, love, and commitment that are sure to keep me humble but pushing onward. I thank them for finding the grace and wisdom to both accept me as I am while, by example, leaving the bar higher. I will always be their loving and grateful son.

These people I must especially thank for their direct contributions to the content and appearance of this book. Your contributions have clearly made it better, but responsibility for the information and content within is still mine alone. *Dr. Robert L. (Ben) Brungraber, P.E.:* I am not the only one with a debt of gratitude to Ben. His editorial input and suggestions made this book better, but more than this, Ben has contributed mightily to the improvement of timber framing in North America. His enthusiasm, energy, and knowledge seem a bottomless well. My years working in association with Ben have been the best and happiest. *Dr. Leonard Morse-Fortier, P.E.:* Len graciously agreed to review the "Skins and Frames" chapter (5). For his thoughtful suggestions and guidance, I am extremely grateful. *Brian Smeltz:* My associate and friend could not be credited enough for his contributions to this edition. His illustrations speak for themselves, but he also was co-photographer and helped me throughout the process to improve the quality and accuracy of this book. *Laura Tringali:* When this book was first created, Laura, my editor, was the force behind it. She pulled, pushed, and cajoled every part and piece into being and then she plied her considerable skills to make the whole better. This edition has changed substantially, but Laura's efforts remain. *Associates at Benson Woodworking Company:* Together we have agreed that our central mission statement is "Through process and product to improve the quality of lives." I thank you for the grandness of your purpose and for the fun we all have pursuing it. *The Taunton Press staff:* Julie Trelstad for her leadership, guidance, and patience; Tom McKenna for his watchful editorial eye; Chris Casey for his layout and design expertise; and Karen Liljedahl for keeping all the pieces connected.

If this book has heroes, they are the people who built the timber-frame homes that are featured here. My thanks for your faith, for your commitment, and for helping us take another step forward. I also thank the owners of those houses for allowing us to invade your homes to take the photographs featured in this book.

CONTENTS

INTRODUCTION   2

1   EVOLUTION   4

2   THE STRUCTURE   23

3   FRAME DESIGN   50

4   HOME DESIGN   68

5   SKINS AND FRAMES   91

6   GETTING OUT
     OF THE GROUND   116

7   WIRING AND LIGHTING   136

8   PLUMBING   157

9   FRAME DETAILS   172

10   FINISH DETAILS   203

     APPENDIX   228

     BIBLIOGRAPHY   231

     SOURCES OF SUPPLY   232

     INDEX   233

INTRODUCTION

I am one of the fortunate. When I began to timber-frame in the early 1970s, I had no plans to dedicate my life to the building profession, not to mention a career so obscure as the craft of constructing buildings using ancient wooden joinery and heavy timbers. It was a naive youthful yearning that, without plan or preparation, grabbed my life. So I am surprised to be reporting to you now—these many years later—that I'm just as engaged, just as enthusiastic, and still very much at the beginning of a journey, not at the end.

My good fortune is severalfold: first, to have stumbled upon my calling; second, to find myself surrounded by a remarkable group of people who have also been drawn to this work; third, to find in timber-frame construction satisfaction in both the built accomplishments and the constant, beckoning enticement to strive for improvement in each next effort.

As a young builder, I wanted to try timber framing as part of my quest for a better process and product in the construction of homes. It disturbed me that carpentry, once an exalted trade, could be seen as an occupation without challenge, often becoming the last refuge for the unmotivated and unskilled. Driving nails is not craft. Further, I found the average American home to be a sterile, drywalled box without an ounce of aesthetic merit. I couldn't understand why either the builders or the occupants submitted to their fates.

Having become enamored with the magnificent timber-frame barns and houses of New England, I became determined to try it in new construction. Eventually, I found a project, then another, and... Before I knew it, 15 years had gone by, I owned a company that had built several hundred timber-frame houses, and I was publishing my second book about timber framing. Now it is almost 25 years since that youthful flight of fancy, an appropriate milestone to be releasing this second edition of *The Timber-Frame Home*.

The standards and procedures for timber-frame construction are evolving rapidly. Though the fundamental precepts about timber framing are quite old, its integration into the contemporary North American building environment is still young. In an attempt to catch up with some of the developments of the last 10 years, in this edition you will find new joints that make frames stronger, better foundation- and deck-framing details, and some very important information about securing the frame to its underpinnings. Information about foam-core panel exterior insulation has been updated to reflect a more mature manufacturing industry and advancements in the installation procedure. The design discussion is oriented more toward adaptability, with less emphasis on integration. I especially want to note that this book is much more beautiful and easier to read, with completely new illustrations by Brian Smeltz, lots of new photographs, and a great layout job by the good people at The Taunton Press.

An ageless craft practiced worldwide

I am convinced that this is the finest of times to practice timber-frame construction. It is a craft and building style that has been in active use for well over 2,000 years in all parts of the world. In most of the forested areas, some form of timber framing was (or still is) the dominant method of construction. But for most of history, the sharing of knowledge and information among timber framers was haphazard or nonexistent. Now we are lucky enough to be living in a period in which boundaries of time, distance, and nationality have been torn down. We are the first generation of timber-frame builders who have been able to easily learn from the masters in any part of the world and at any time in history. It is thrilling.

When we build a timber-frame home in North America today, it is quite possible that a single frame will employ joinery or frame details from Japan, England, France, Holland, Germany, early America, and turn-of-the-century California. The tools employed probably will have come from at least three different countries, some very modern and some old. The structure will have been subjected to an engineering analysis using test results from high-tech laboratories from around the world and employing powerful computers. Where, then, do these modern timber frames come from and to which time and place do they belong? Why would we deny the best aspects from Japan in favor of that which would make the product purely English or authentic early American? The only reason I can imagine to be so restrained is for the purpose of a reproduction of a style or time period, because to otherwise ignore extant superior knowledge is clearly a shortsighted and unnecessary compromise.

Modern buildings with historical interpretations

Our timber-frame construction does not specifically replicate any particular timber-frame style or tradition; instead, it has grown out of our learning and interpretation from many cultures and environmental contexts. How we make our buildings is a product not only of what we have gleaned about timber-frame methods and details from throughout the world, but it is also hugely affected by modern engineering, architectural influences, local climatic conditions, and all the glittering amenities of our contemporary lifestyle. After all, timber framing is completely useless unless the resulting home is found to be attractive, comfortable, utilitarian, and affordable. In the end, it is the living space for people that matters most, not the method of construction, and certainly not the timbers. It is important that the focus of the work be on the space that's created, not on the components of the structure. In that light, this book is really about how to make timber-frame dwellings efficiently and effectively while creating spaces that are good for habitation—in short, it's about making good homes.

Which gets me back to the beginning. My first imaginings about the potentials of timber framing in residential construction were fired by the desire to improve the quality of houses and the manner of their construction. For my part, little has changed. I still feel strongly that there is a world of work to do toward achieving these goals. The current building standards are too low. I am also still convinced that modern timber-frame construction has enough inherent attributes and potential benefits to be a constantly improving model of the kind of beauty, integrity, and durability that will better represent the best intentions of our society.

Tangible rewards

Those who make good buildings are always both rewarded and humbled. When the work is done, or even when pieces of it are completed, more often than not we stare in wonder at our own creation because our best work always contains more intelligence, beauty, and nobility than we ourselves can summon. When we strive for the most durable architecture and the highest order of construction, we come closest to accomplishing those goals when we lean heavily on the shoulders of the many millennia of builders who have preceded us in the long march of civilization. We recognize the characteristics of beautiful and timeless architecture only because dedicated craftspeople who preceded us have left them on display in surviving buildings both modest and monumental. In our best work, we often emulate without knowledge and remember instead of discover. So, even as we sometimes stand in awe of the fruit of our own labor, there is little room for contentment or smug satisfaction. Good buildings are built by the ages, not just the teams that came together for their construction. What is built by the ages is judged by the ages. It is never "good enough."

Onward...

Tedd Benson

Alstead Center, New Hampshire
Dec. 23, 1996

A properly designed and built timber-frame house is an intriguing mix of an ancient building system with modern technology. Simple, classic architecture yields exciting living spaces.

CHAPTER 1
EVOLUTION

There are two important challenges for those who build timber-frame homes today. Both should concern all those associated with the building project, for the timber-frame house design and construction processes are more like a chorus line than a solo dance, requiring all parties to play an active role. The first challenge is to cherish and nurture the values and standards set centuries ago, to understand in both spirit and substance the legacy of durable, classic timber-frame building that we have inherited from our forefathers. What is it that makes a structure so fine that it survives numerous centuries? Is it the construction, the architecture, or both? What makes people love a building enough to repair and restore it? To give direction to our modern efforts, it's necessary to first investigate the historical precedents. To know where we should go, we need to know where the craft has been.

The second challenge is to bring the timber-frame house into the 20th century, which requires a careful analysis of the limitations and opportunities inherent in the building system. Then we need to take a fresh look at modern home-building requirements, picking carefully from current standards and materials, and casting off conventions when necessary to create the highest-quality work.

In this chapter, we'll look at both challenges, beginning with an exploration of the development of the timber-frame house through history and the attributes that give it timelessness. You won't find a chronicle of each event in the evolutionary path here, just some of the high points. I wish only to capture a sense of the fine thread that united timber buildings through so many centuries and in so many parts of

the world, for it is just this thread we should weave into the fabric of our contemporary houses. We'll be taking a brief look at the evolution through time and across continents. I'll conclude the chapter with a discussion of the goals, problems and opportunities in timber framing today.

THE LEGACY

What is apparent through even a cursory look at the history of building is that dwellings always clearly reflect the relationship of people to their world. Instead of following a single course, timber-frame buildings therefore evolved simultaneously with rising and falling civilizations on several continents. They responded to technological advances, the availability of resources, and to social prejudices (always a mirror of the people who built them). Despite this, out of the history of timber framing emerges a continuity of architectural patterns and styles, and a consistency in human values. There are, for instance, many more similarities than differences between an oriental structure like the Great Buddha Hall in

Japan and a European structure like Westminster Hall in England (see the drawings below). Each building was constructed as a monument to a religious ideal, and the timbers in each were both structural and decorative. Each building demonstrates mastery of a complex craft in a simple rectilinear form with a steeply pitched roof. The focal point in the framework of each building is the cantilevering of forces from the roof to the walls; the finely crafted roof timbers not only draw the eye upward to the heavens, but they also create a sense of balance and mystery, reflecting the forces of God and the universe. One more thing they both have in common: Though over six centuries old, they both still stand.

A 2,000-year history begins

The first timber-frame buildings appeared at about the time of the birth of Christ. They probably evolved from skeletons of tied-together poles around which skins or mattings were wrapped. Such dwellings were usually the homes of nomadic peoples. When permanent settlements became desirable, pole skeletons slowly gave way to more stable and durable timber structures. If

Over the years, the Great Buddha Hall (above) has remained a monument to durability and resilience. (Adapted from The Way of the Carpenter by William Coaldrake, with permission of Weatherhill Press.)

Westminster Hall (right) arose from similar construction restraints and requirements as the Great Buddha Hall. It also has survived because of its inherent strength and durability.

EARLY TIMBER-FRAME STRUCTURES

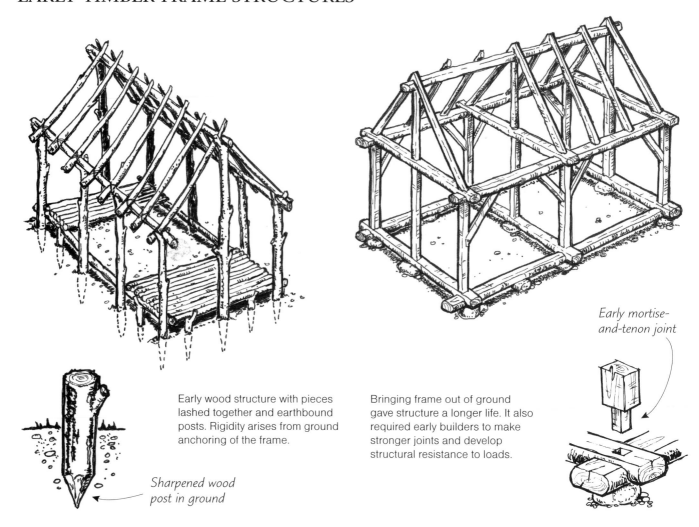

Early wood structure with pieces lashed together and earthbound posts. Rigidity arises from ground anchoring of the frame.

Bringing frame out of ground gave structure a longer life. It also required early builders to make stronger joints and develop structural resistance to loads.

Early mortise-and-tenon joint

Sharpened wood post in ground

we define a timber frame as a self-supporting network fastened with wooden joinery, then there are two significant events in its evolution. The first was the creation of the mortise-and-tenon joint between 500 B.C. and 200 B.C., which meant the tools and technological sophistication existed to work the wood (see the right drawing above). The second event occurred in the 10th century, when a framework was developed that was rigid enough to support itself on top of the ground. Prior to this, the posts of a house were stuck directly in holes and stabilized by compacted earth, a technique that allowed a minimum of interconnection between timbers and caused the posts to rot (see the left drawing above). Seemingly a small achievement, building a self-supporting structure was actu-ally quite revolutionary, as it required that timbers be organized so posts would remain rigid while supporting the beams. Joinery had to become more sophisticated to serve both binding and supporting functions. Constructed in this way, buildings became more durable and expressive, and demanded greater skill to create.

Available resources guide the way

The development of timber-frame buildings differed from region to region, depending on many factors, such as the availability of material. In Egypt, Persia, and Greece, where timber was limited, early temples were built with wooden columns and lintels; their forms were the basis for later stone temples. The scholar Vitruvius, writing at the end of the first century B.C., apparently saw the last of the wooden temples. He described the Temple of Ceres as a timber building with brick and terra-cotta infilling and decoration. Because of the scarcity of material and fear of fire, later temples and public buildings were built of masonry when possible, but timber framing had evolved into an accepted building method and was used for dwellings and less significant public buildings. According to Hansen, editor of *Architecture in Wood,* Vitruvius described the construction, calling it *opus craticiom,* or "timber framing."

Vitruvius also wrote that the best building timbers in his day were oak, elm, poplar, cypress, and fir—surprisingly similar to our contemporary opinion.

Some of these were occasionally imported from Africa, Syria, and Crete, but importation of lumber was expensive and reserved for only the most important buildings. In addition, knowledge of new woods tended to make local builders less satisfied with what they had at hand. Palm trunks did not make good timbers after all, and other readily available woods were worse, as Martin Briggs describes in his book, *A Short History of the Building Crafts*: "Sycamore is neither very strong nor supple; and of acacia and tamarisk, it can only be said that they are the least unsuitable of native trees for building purposes." Not surprisingly, since a growing understanding was combined with a growing scarcity of wood, timbers began to be replaced by masonry in the Middle East.

Timber framing and log building converge, then separate

By contrast, in parts of northern Europe that were heavily wooded, a building style emerged around the 9th century in which the timber frame was vertically infilled with thick wooden planks or more timbers, making a veritable fortress of wood. Also in heavily wooded areas, timber framing was occasionally used with log building—for example, some Swiss chalets have horizontal logs laid between the joined timbers. Where log construction was dominant, timber framing was still used for the roof system (see the drawings at right).

The skills and tools required for log building were certainly similar to those for timber framing, but in other ways the differences were vast. Early log building was rudimentary, with simple corner joints and the natural length of the logs used to determine building dimensions. Stacking logs is a much more basic means of creating a structure than joining vertical and horizontal timbers into a rigid skeleton, and the aesthetics and feel are significantly different. Log walls look massive and earthbound; as the weight of the wood and gravity keep the structure together,

LOG HOME

Stacking logs is a more basic means of creating a structure, yielding a massive and earthbound look.

TIMBER-FRAME HOME

Timbered buildings in heavily wooded areas seemed to rise out of ground with more of a vertical statement and to demand use of complex joinery and geometry.

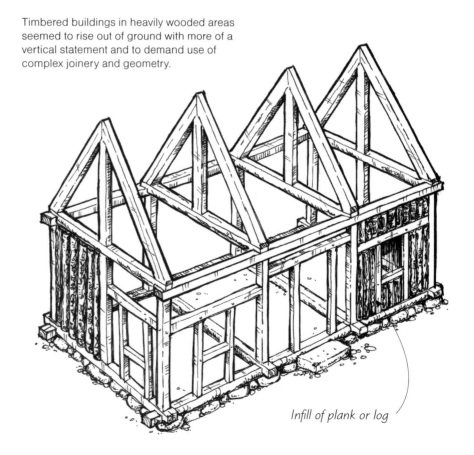

Infill of plank or log

This German building was constructed with both brick and plaster infill. The timber frame was pragmatic and restrained but still graceful.

In this German village, where plaster infill predominates, the use of timber is extravagant—a social statement.

so the heavy horizontal lines seem to hold it snugly to the ground. The feeling of early log buildings, usually built over pits and with few penetrations in the walls, was probably somewhat like a cave of wood, a decided hindrance to the advancement of people as they were working their way out of the dark and dirty habitat of pits and caves.

Where log buildings excelled at creating solid walls, timber frames defined openings. The web of timbers invited light into the living environment—a novel but appealing notion. Timber framing also allowed early builders to use fewer pieces of wood and required greater intelligence and ingenuity. It was a trick to support the loads and keep buildings erect. Demanding the use of some complex joinery, sophisticated geometry, and a thorough understanding of forces, timber framing forced the mind of man to expand.

In the less-forested areas of Europe and for buildings of grand purpose, timber framing dominated log building by the Middle Ages. The ancient use of skins to cover the frame gave way to infilling with wattle-and-daub (a mud-and-plaster system) or later, with brick (see the top photo at left). In both cases, the structure was visible to both the interior and exterior, instead of just to the inside. The architects and inhabitants of these buildings found the structure fascinating and, in an effort to keep up with the Joneses, made the frames fancier and denser with timbers. Through the centuries wood became scarcer (especially in the British Isles), but still frames displayed more and more timbers, not as a requirement of the structure, but to trumpet the wealth of the occupant (see the bottom photo at left). Over the years frames have become more conservative in their use of timbers but only because vanity has found other forms of indulgence.

It is easy to understand why, at any time previous to modern time, local resources had significant impact on construction techniques. People simply did not settle where there weren't sufficient building materials, and when they built they presumably used the handiest material. Structures thus naturally reflected the landscape—bricks were used to a greater degree when there was clay in the soil, stone was used when the shape and quantity of rocks allowed, and timbers were used when there were sufficient trees. In the limestone areas of Great Britain, timber framing was never fully practiced because there just wasn't enough wood to make it practical. Here, as in many other parts of the world, masonry and timbers were used together, the massive stone walls supporting soaring timber-frame roofs (see the drawing at right). Stone protected the timbers from the ground, and timbers made the great spans. Most of the great halls and cathedrals were a mix of the two materials.

The craft reaches an apex of development in the Middle Ages

By the Middle Ages, the craft of timber framing was fully developed, and by the standards of the time, timber-frame homes required the least amount of labor. Timber was therefore preferred, even when it was relatively scarce, and the condition and variety of available trees often determined the shape and style of the frame. According to Martin Briggs, "The feature of Lycian carpentry was the short lengths of timber employed, for the trees that grow on the steep Lycian slopes have gnarled boles and twisted trunks." William the Conqueror's Domesday Book of 1086, an inventory prepared for taxes, indicates that England, although once almost completely forested, was by then only 15% forested. (Three centuries later, the figure was closer to 10%.) Medieval buildings often displayed crooked, twisted timbers, which are now practically a definition of that period's architectural style (see the photo at right). But it wasn't a fad propagated by some early rendition of *House Beautiful*—it was all they had.

TIMBER-FRAME STRUCTURE OF THE MIDDLE AGES

Some of the greatest carpentry of all times is evident in timber-framed roofs of Middle Ages. As European forest resources became depleted, masonry was commonly used for exterior walls.

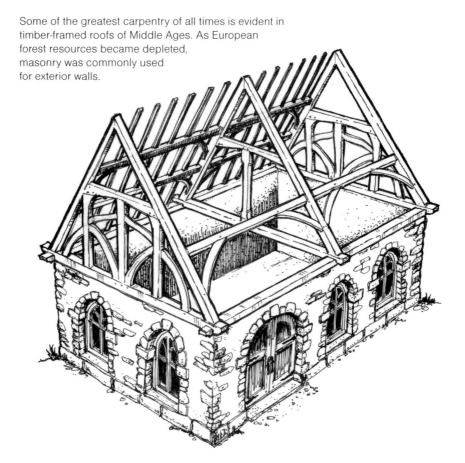

The gnarled and twisted timbers common in medieval buildings were indicative of the available resources.

When timbers became scarce in Europe, tall buildings were constructed by stacking successive stories using short posts and overhanging beams.

During this period, English carpenters developed ingenious systems for spanning great widths without long timbers and created an almost astonishing array of scarf joints to splice timbers longitudinally. Scarce resources sparked creativity, and partly because of this, some of the greatest carpentry of all time is evident in the timber-framed roofs of the Middle Ages. Still, it should be noted that the open-trussed roofs would be stronger with a timber locking the walls together; a scarf joint is not as strong as a timber that doesn't need one (see the top drawing on the facing page).

In France, long timbers were unavailable by the second half of the 14th century, and so multistoried, jettied building became common. Here successive stories were stacked upon short posts rather than being joined to continuous posts—those passing through all the floor levels (see the photo at left). (While horizontal beams can be scarfed, this is a problem in vertical posts because of the extreme compression loads they bear.) To keep the structure rigid, these buildings required bracketing as well as bracing to secure posts to beams. For joinery considerations, horizontal beams would project beyond vertical posts at the outer walls; a timber bracket (much like a shelf bracket) was used in the corner between the post and the projecting beam to reinforce the connection (see the drawing at left). In a later outgrowth of this type of construction, the jetties were cantilevered. Especially popular in the cities, this architectural style accentuated the building's lines and created more space in the floors above the narrow street. But because it resulted in unsanitary conditions in the darkened streets below, jettied construction was ultimately outlawed.

Resources, social structure, memory, and the development of residential style

As surely as timber limitations influenced building design, so did timber abundances. When the colonists came to this country, Europe had been de-

BRACING THE STRUCTURE

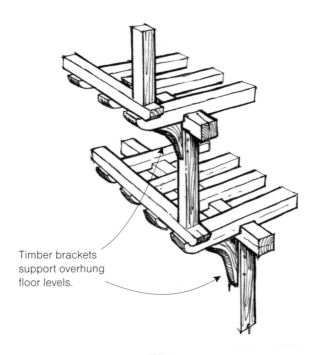

Timber brackets support overhung floor levels.

OLD ENGLISH-STYLE FRAME

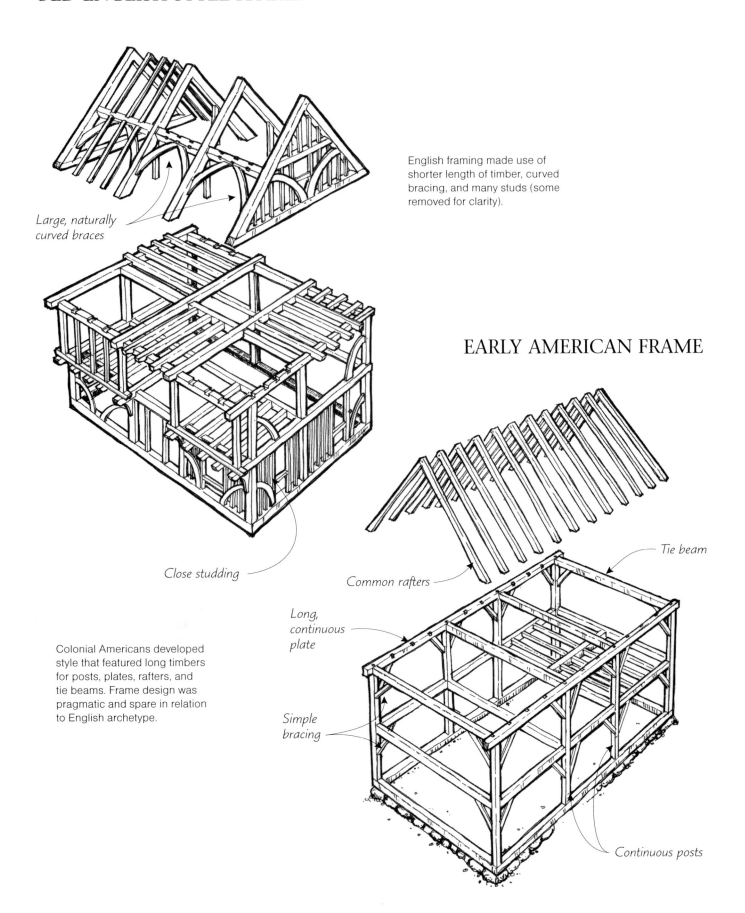

English framing made use of shorter length of timber, curved bracing, and many studs (some removed for clarity).

Large, naturally curved braces

EARLY AMERICAN FRAME

Close studding

Colonial Americans developed style that featured long timbers for posts, plates, rafters, and tie beams. Frame design was pragmatic and spare in relation to English archetype.

Tie beam

Long, continuous plate

Common rafters

Simple bracing

Continuous posts

Underneath the facades of these Amsterdam row houses are magnificent and enduring timber-frame structures. Many date to the 1600s and earlier.

nuded of timber resources. The settlers suddenly found themselves in the midst of virgin forests with trees long enough to run the length of almost any building. Although they did not immediately devise new techniques to take advantage of this wealth, Colonial Americans eventually developed a unique building style that featured long timbers for posts, plates, rafters, and tie beams. These buildings were strong, simpler to construct than their old-world counterparts, and, ironically, used fewer timbers (see the bottom drawing on p. 11).

The kind of building that evolved in America represents one of the most important developments in timber-frame housing. Even though framing techniques were refined over several thousand years and in all parts of the world, it appears to be here, in America, that a high-quality timber-frame house style developed specifically to accommodate the common man. In societies with a clearly defined class hierarchy, the finest efforts were invested in the reli-

gious institutions and copied at the next level down; similarities between cathedrals and castles are not coincidental, nor between castles and manor houses. How many and how fast building improvements filtered down depended on the distribution of wealth and the organization of the society, but timber-frame house construction of any consequence did not generally make it to the common levels. This is not to say that some form of timber framing was not practiced at these levels; but that since so few structures survived, clearly they were greatly inferior. The Swiss chalets (some of which are completely timber framed) and the 15th-century timber-frame townhouses common to Belgium, Germany, and the Netherlands probably come closest to being true residential styles (see the photo above).

The sad fact is that many of the wonderfully picturesque manor houses in Europe were surrounded by the hovels of the peasantry. Decent housing was to be enjoyed only by the wealthy and

only because others suffered for it. The feudal society in Japan was even more divisive. Commoners might have wanted to build houses like those built for nobility or the warrior class, but to do so was forbidden. The restriction was class, not money, although if a commoner had enough money, it was sometimes possible through bribery to obtain a desired architectural element, such as a decorative gate or sliding panels. Feudal building restrictions were not removed until 1867, and a consistent residential Japanese building style has been developed only in the last 120 years. Although Japanese timber-frame houses are quite different from Western styles, they evolved along a similar path, including the eventual casting off of the oppressive notions that brought the craft of timber framing (but not timber-frame housing) to its highest moments. When the colonists stepped onto the shores of America, and when the Tokugawa shogunate collapsed in Japan in 1867, it became possible for the commoners of these countries to attempt to live in dignity and comfort.

This newfound freedom did not immediately lead to a revolution in architecture or frame construction, for there was no real dissatisfaction with the buildings, just with their occupants. So the first timber-frame buildings in America looked an awful lot like the ones left behind in England, and the homes the free Japanese built greatly resembled the Minka buildings they had been forbidden to own. Indulging in forbidden fruit was probably one reason for this, but it's also natural to embrace familiar archetypes. It took a long time for more independent styles to develop.

In America, the colonists learned the hard way about the effects of the climate on foundation and enclosure systems. Extreme changes in temperature heaved the soil, and it was soon obvious that an exterior cladding was necessary to protect the building from the weather (see the drawing on the facing page). The first timber frames were oak, which was the wood used in England, but later frames used a great variety of species. Eventually, not only were frames redesigned to take advantage of the abundance of virgin trees, but they were also redesigned to accommodate new raising techniques. In England, small groups of professionals made the frames for most houses, using joinery and assembly methods that would allow individual pieces to be placed into a frame. But in America, a great spirit of cooperation and neighborliness brought whole communities together for raisings, and timber frames were designed in large units that could be pre-assembled and then raised in one day.

Frames also became more utilitarian. Being on free soil meant that class distinctions were dissolving; even the leaders and the wealthy would have been reluctant to act like the oppressive nobility of the old country. So in spite of the rich supply of timber, builders used their knowledge to make strong frames without wasting material or labor on embellishments and showy styles. Simplicity was the hallmark of the Early American timber frame.

American timber-frame home vernacular emerges

Early American timber-frame houses also shared a similar design, derived from generally accepted notions about function that had evolved through many centuries. In his book *Home*, Witold Rybczynski points out that these notions were vastly different from our own current requirements. The issues of comfort and privacy, for example, barely existed at certain times in history and played little part in house design. Subsistence was usually much more to the point, and the first homes often housed animals as well as people because they were critical to survival. The plan of St. Gall, shown on p. 14, reveals the way homes looked around A.D. 850. The basic ingredient was a central living area, or hall, in which all activities took place. At its center was a fire pit—no chimney, just a hole above the pit for smoke to escape. On the outside of the living area were rooms for sleeping and for animals. That's it. None of the

EARLY HOUSE SIDING

In America, climate extremes made exterior cladding necessary, and it became a vernacular element in our unique timber-frame construction system.

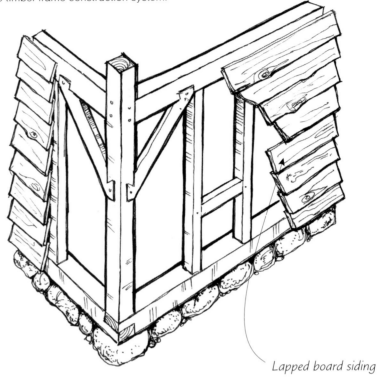

Lapped board siding

house plans shows a second-floor living area, probably because it would have been too smoky for habitation. These early plans are rather ingenious, for the central room is insulated by the animal and bedroom areas. The outer wing is terrific insulation and probably the first air-lock entry. Since structural requirements were given priority, it was also a nicely integrated plan. The living area is really the entire main timber structure, and the outer wing simply leans against it as a shedlike substructure. Every room is defined by posts and beams. Still, this was not a home that was warm or comfortable in the way we think of those concepts today: It was a place for cooking and working and sleeping—in short, surviving.

Eventually, the development of the chimney made the living space more tolerable and allowed a second floor to become common. But the central hall

stayed and simply became grander as architecture began to be used to demonstrate social position. The hall of the late Middle Ages was a soaring and much more highly embellished version of the smoke-filled hall that preceded it. The technology of the chimney and the improving craftsmanship of the carpenters refined the hall, but there was still no attempt to organize for privacy or for specific activities. When other rooms were added for living, there wasn't a hallway for passage between; you had to go through one room to get to the other. In the castles and manors, work rooms were separated from living areas, but this was done more to segregate servant from master than for convenience.

The first American homes also began as a hall and a parlor. Between them was a chimney with a fireplace facing each room. The second floor was a copy of

BUILDING FROM THE PLAN OF ST. GALL

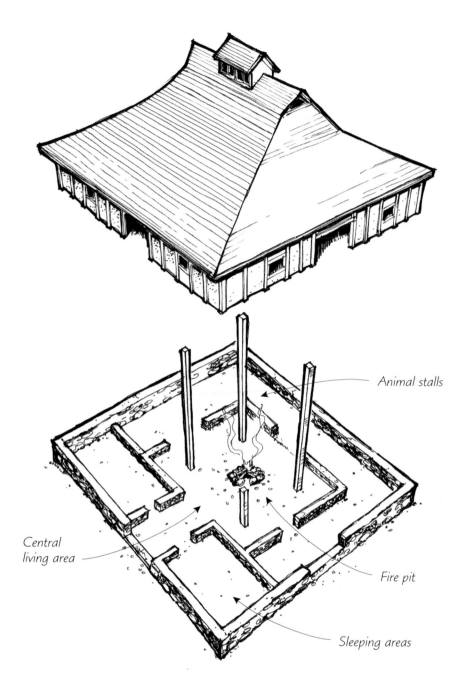

Central living area

Animal stalls

Fire pit

Sleeping areas

Animals and people shared single building. Central area with fire pit accommodated all living activities. Privacy and comfort were not among design considerations.

the first, with bedrooms on either side of the chimney. Framing was simple. The house was narrow and tall, usually four posts long and two posts wide (see the drawing on the facing page). Because people had to have shelter quickly and usually had only minimum means, the home was designed to expand as needs grew and finances allowed. The frame was easy to make and raise and provided all the living space that was immediately necessary. Later, a lean-to was added to the eave side, which often became the kitchen. This house shape is now referred to as the saltbox, and it was similar in concept to the bedrooms and animal areas in the St. Gall plans. Later houses commonly included the kitchen as a part of the original construction. The house either maintained the saltbox shape or had more room on the second floor, in which case it became a colonial style. This basic plan is so common that any other is considered an exception.

The pattern of the Early American house was still based on survival—the family gathered around the chimney for warmth and to cook; upstairs was for sleeping. Most houses used this plan because it was an easy way to fit the necessary living spaces into the frame. It was also entirely functional. Instead of grand expanses, there were low ceilings on two floors, allowing as many spaces as possible to fit within the frame and keeping those spaces warmer. It was a style that reflected the distinctly different idea of life in the new country.

Until the mid-1800s and the advent of stud framing, the timber-frame house continued to evolve and reflect the changing lifestyles of many different kinds of people from New England to the South and out to Ohio. Soon the houses had many different kinds of living areas, with hallways between major rooms for privacy. There were timber-frame farmhouses and timber-frame townhouses. There were elegant homes and simple homes, and many styles flourished in the variety and abundance of the expanding new world.

EARLY AMERICAN HOME

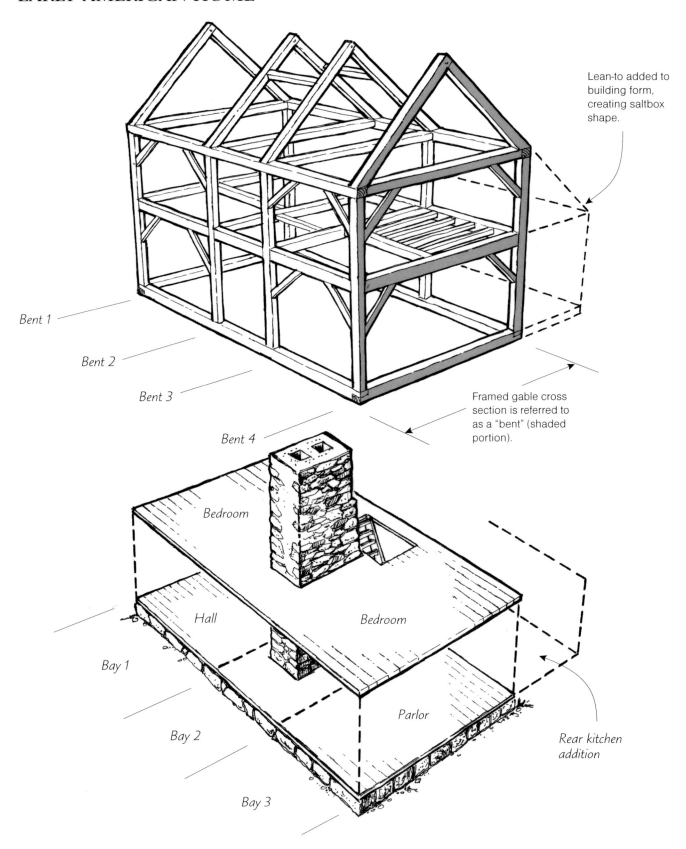

Lean-to added to building form, creating saltbox shape.

Bent 1

Bent 2

Bent 3

Bent 4

Framed gable cross section is referred to as a "bent" (shaded portion).

Bedroom

Hall

Bedroom

Bay 1

Bay 2

Parlor

Bay 3

Rear kitchen addition

Homes generally fell into design pattern based on spaces defined by timber frame. Four bents created three living zones: center bay for chimney and circulation (#2), outer two for hall, parlor, and bedrooms (#1 and #3).

Timber-frame houses have adapted well to modern living. The building method can be used to produce graceful homes that are as energy-efficient as they are beautiful.

THE MODERN TIMBER-FRAME HOUSE

As with most things, the modern timber-frame building system and the home it supports have needed to respond to our place and time. If timber framing had not lain fallow these past 150 years, it would probably have been altered radically by the great social and scientific forces of the 20th century. It is just as well, perhaps, that it was put aside before being compromised by the age of machines. What we're left with is an opportunity to bring timber framing back in its very purest form. But the revival of interest in the joiner's craft has not been enough to make the

timber-frame house thrive. For modern appeal, the whole concept of the house had to be considered. And the timber-frame house has done well, adapting nicely to the paraphernalia of our era while still providing security, pleasure, and comfort—ingredients too often lacking in the modern home.

In this section, we'll look at some of the goals in building a modern timber-frame house. As well as including practical construction objectives, such as good energy performance and practical construction methodology, these goals include the elusive ideals that allow a house to provide an extraordinary living experience, to enhance our physical, intellectual, and emotional lives.

While these intangibles are rarely on the list of requirements for a new house, they should be, for when a dwelling exudes them, it becomes a place of growth and comfort, transcending its service as shelter and becoming a home.

Homes should have soul

Homes today contain a host of modern conveniences and have become veritable cocoons of controlled weather systems. There was a time when winter was a life-threatening experience, and getting clean was too hard a task to undertake more than once a month. Today's home has freed us from worry about mere survival, and a vast majority of the population has more time

Exposing the framework reveals the "lines of strength" and "evidence of weight and stability." In this home, the timber-frame structure also becomes the mounting surface for the solarium glass.

than ever before to explore other aspects of life. Unfortunately, designers and builders spend so much time making sure a house contains all the right stuff that they expend practically no energy on its soul. Too often, houses that liberate people from harsh weather and the chores of daily living do little else. They do nothing for the senses, nothing for the spirit, and nothing to enhance or ennoble the time and energy set free. Homes should inspire.

Even something as basic as comfort is rarely considered by modern architecture, points out Rybczynski in *Home*. "During the six years of my architectural education, the subject of comfort was mentioned only once. It was by a mechanical engineer whose job it was to initiate my classmates and me into the mysteries of air conditioning and heating. He described something called the 'comfort zone,' which, as far as I can remember, was a kidney-shaped, crosshatched area on a graph that showed the relationship between tem-

perature and humidity. Comfort was inside the kidney, discomfort was everywhere else. This, apparently, was all that we needed to know about the subject. It was a curious omission from an otherwise rigorous curriculum; one would have thought that comfort was a crucial issue in preparing for the architectural profession, like justice in law, or health in medicine."

Creating a comfortable space requires more than a soft chair, and making comfortable houses is not automatic to any form of construction. Comfort comes from qualities in the building that offer a sense of security, balance, and order. Perhaps today more than ever there is a need for houses to offer these amenities, because although our lives have changed in many ways, under the surface not much is different. The anxieties today come from different sources, but they create the same needs. Our forefathers fought off freezing winters and wild animals; the future, however uncertain, was clearly in

their hands. In today's wilderness, the adversaries are not so well-defined. We struggle for security, but we are almost always at the mercy of others, and this causes instability as surely as a beast howling at the door. Much about life is disconcertingly temporal, and there is comfort in buildings that rise above the ephemeral qualities of life and conventional measures of strength.

A timber-frame home has evident strength

The timber-frame building system displays its strength quite clearly and naturally. As John Burroughs, the naturalist, writes in his essay "Rooftree": "If the eye could see more fully the necessities of the case—how the thing stands up and is held together, that it is not pasteboard, that it does not need to be anchored against the wind—it would be a relief. Hence, the lively pleasure in what are called 'timber houses,' and in every architectural device by which the anatomy, the real framework, of the structure, inside or out, is allowed to show, or made to serve as ornament. The eye craves lines of strength, evidence of weight and stability."

As Burroughs suggests, the beauty and art of architecture often lie in the form and function of the structure itself. Viewers are captivated not by the road that a bridge supports but by the splendor of the interaction of cables, trusses, beams, and ties. The wholeness of the parts performs the magic. Architects have long understood that a pleasing sense of structure can be an important ingredient in design. If the framework itself is not attractive, the architect might try to imitate structural features with finish details, for instance, by building up the exterior corner boards so that they look like supporting columns or decorating the building with imitation timbers. Designers who specialize in restaurant decor have the latter trick down to a science. By my own estimation, probably 75% of the restaurants in this country feature exposed fake timbers. Adding nonsupporting frame members after a building is complete is ridiculous, and some of the results are nothing short of ludicrous. Why would anyone feel that a plastic 4-in. by 8-in. "beam" spanning 80 ft. would lend a feeling of stability to the atmosphere? Such design error is simply not possible in a timber-frame building because the sturdiness and beauty of the structure are integral to the system.

The "threat" of overbuilding

Our forefathers reinforced this inherent strength by building, even "overbuilding," structures that would have a life beyond their own generation. Relying on hand tools and hard labor, they did things right the first time so that work would not have to be repeated. There is a vigorous sense of integrity in these unyielding buildings, which survive despite their age, and to me overbuilding seems to pose only one threat: The product might last too long. Small sin, for as a consequence the world is blessed with enduring pyramids, temples, cathedrals, bridges, houses, and barns.

As our forefathers built for the future, so should we. Beyond being ecologically important that today's houses serve later generations (which is absolutely the case), it is also psychologically up-

lifting to know that in the worst of times a house will stand and that it will have value and purpose beyond our lifetimes. It's a very uncertain feeling to have the building you live in shake in every wind. For a few years, I lived in a house that seemed to deteriorate visibly with each passing day, and I can categorically say that it caused insecurity and frustration. I began to wonder if it wasn't I who was leaning and decomposing. On the other hand, I grew up in a house that had been built at the turn of the century by a man who had made his wealth mining gold; he used the highest standards of the time, lovely woodwork and detail. When the house eventually passed to my parents, who made their wealth in children, it was given some tough tests. But when the snows and winds came, we always felt safe. When there were low spirits and little money, the house itself offered encouragement of better days to come. My feelings about good home building were born in that great, old house, and nothing less has been satisfactory since.

Durable buildings need timeless design

In design, there are many goals we may strive for to enhance and refine the essential strength and durability offered

by the timber frame. Our ancestors, in building for the future, also designed for the future, and here, too, we can follow their lead. As we have seen in the first section of this chapter, floor plans were not so much personally appropriate as they were reflections of typical living patterns and commonly held views about how houses should be arranged—houses were not designed on the basis of architectural whim or passing fancy, as are many today. The shape of buildings also followed principles that were felt to have universal appeal. For their classic, enduring architecture, Colonial Americans used simple, graceful lines that were historically familiar to them and that promised to hold strong into the future.

Modern timber-frame builders should also strive for classic lines, respecting the role the medium plays in design. Connecting large timbers with mortise-and-tenon joinery imposes limitations on the form and style of a building. You will not soon see a timber-frame dome, and if you do, stay out of it, for structurally it would be like a fish out of water. In timber-frame buildings, the walls generally should not be much higher than the posts (whose height depends on the available length of timbers). The joints are best as orthogonal

Old timber-frame structures were built for the future, not to satisfy an architectural whim. They were based on design principles with universal and enduring appeal.

Today's timber-frame buildings tend to utilize the traditional spatial layout patterns and classic architectural lines.

This Japanese-style building, designed and built by Len Brackett, combines timbers and natural form logs. The constraints on timber framing have broad boundaries.

intersections. The frame is rectilinear, and when it is assembled, the timbers gain strength through balance and symmetry. Timber frames are disinclined to perform feats for the purpose of architectural curiosity, but this is not to suggest that building with timbers means limited design opportunity. A study of Japanese architecture or a look at any of Cecil Hewett's books on English building construction will demonstrate that, within the constraints imposed by the timbers, there is challenge enough to design graceful and beautiful houses that are the essence of domestic architecture.

Using structure as an aesthetic consideration presents some interesting design opportunities, as we will explore in later chapters. Posts and beams can be used to define areas. Frame members can be placed deliberately to create a desired feeling. For instance, a large summer beam might be located over the center of a living room to create a feeling of unity, symmetry, strength, and stability. This would be a formal place in which people would group together. Another space might be left open to the roof to create a sense of expansiveness and drama. Here timbers could be arranged for a lighter, more playful effect. This might be a place for fun and informal entertaining. When

these and other techniques are used effectively, when the frame and the floor plan intertwine, then each area of the house is naturally well-decorated and feels complete, even during construction, when the house is still just a frame silhouetted against the sky.

Using traditional design patterns and available resources

Timber-frame houses are being enthusiastically accepted because they come with good credentials from the past. Their form, appearance, and spatial definition is pleasantly familiar and reassuring. The task now is to design and build modern homes that are simple but flexible, classic but in touch with

Glass and timbers have a great symbiotic fling through timber framing.

today's realities. Perhaps it is obvious by now that I think we should take our cue from the American tradition, adapting and inventing a new style while still respecting the archetypal forms. For example, to be affordable for the average person, early American houses were arranged simply, usually containing four bents and three bays. Our timber-frame houses tend to follow the same pattern, yet within this basic form we have created hundreds of different floor plans. We still rely on a central chimney, attaching a small wood stove or furnace to it to heat almost entirely any of our well-insulated houses. And we still often build with the saltbox shape (or variations of it), orienting the low wall to the wind and the high wall to the sun for good energy performance.

Although we don't have the great virgin forests Colonial American builders had, our techniques and framing styles are similar. We use the same kinds of wood, albeit in smaller and shorter pieces. Frames through history changed to suit available materials, and modern builders should be ready to adapt. For instance, a frame designed for oak timbers under 16 ft. in length should not be the same as for one using fir timbers available in 40-ft. lengths. Since we have cranes available to lift timbers, as-

sembly and raising techniques can be similar to those used in Colonial America even though we can't (or for safety don't choose to) muster a community of people for a raising. The use of a crane can and should affect the engineering and layout of a frame in the same way that the helping hands of neighbors altered frame design for the colonists. With the crane, we have the opportunity to make frames stronger by assembling more pieces together in a single unit.

Accommodating today's amenities

There are some situations, however, for which there is no historical precedent, and modern builders must invent viable 20th-century construction alternatives. A realistic route must be provided for each plumbing pipe and electrical wire. Allowance must be made for bathroom fixtures, kitchen appliances, and a heating system. It is necessary to consider the requirements of smoke and burglar alarms, stereo systems, and telephones. Rooms must accommodate king-size beds, microwave ovens, hot tubs, and computers. Some of our clients have the security system of Fort Knox; others don't even bother to lock their doors. One house has an exercise room up on the roof; another has a home theater in the basement.

Fortunately, the timber-frame building system solves more problems than it creates. Timber framing is naturally compatible with passive solar heating, for example, and with its goal of keeping areas open to one another so that heat can move through the house without fans and ducts. Since the loads of the building are directed to a few large posts instead of to many small framing members, timber-frame houses lend themselves to open floor plans. The necessary expanses of south-facing glass can be installed between posts without difficulty. Glass and timbers complement each other, and from the very beginning my company has tried to capitalize on this relationship in the houses we build. There is no prototype in history for making timber solariums, so we have invented this technology using new ideas while attempting to adhere to old standards.

A high-tech skin

The most important asset of the timber frame to modern building technology is the basis it provides for an extremely effective insulating system. With the frame bearing all the building loads, the insulation can be a completely separate system. This has the benefit of minimizing thermal breaks and simplifying construction.

The foam-core panel is basically a sandwich of interior and exterior sheathing on either side of a core of rigid-foam insulation. The panels are installed outside the frame, wrapping it in an unbroken layer of insulation.

After some experimentation, we discovered a product called a foam-core panel, which is a sandwich of interior and exterior sheathing with a core of rigid-foam insulation (see the photo above). Using this bit of high technology, we are able to wrap the timber frame in unbroken insulation, achieving the same energy performance as a super-insulated platform-framed house, but without the constant battle with moisture and air barriers (they are integrated into the panel). In fact, many people express an interest in our homes because of the buildings' remarkable energy efficiency, not because of a primary attraction to the timber frame itself. To us, developing this insulating system felt like a major breakthrough, vastly different from what we knew of European or traditional American enclosure techniques. But ironically, it was not really a new concept at all, as it resembles the primitive method of enclosing a frame with animal skins. We rarely truly invent; we just remember.

As mechanical and design innovations for the modern timber-frame house have evolved, it has become apparent that in many areas the procedures that are used in standard construction are not necessarily transferable. To keep construction efficient while maintaining traditional standards, it has been necessary to adapt materials and create new methods. Some of these developments take timber-frame house builders outside the information available in architecture and construction guides, and there are risks involved when going against the grain of conventional practice.

Code books offer challenges

National and local building codes often pose problems for the construction of timber-frame homes because they were written to govern other building techniques. When the building official is presented with an unusual situation, the tendency is to lean on the letter of the law instead of on the spirit. The result is that innovative ideas face a rocky road, even though they may be better than code requirements. For example, some building codes demand that all structural members be stamped by a lumber grader to indicate that they meet the stress grade. But most good-quality timbers come from small sawmills, for these are the places where the custom requirements of a typical timber frame are not too daunting. The problem is that small mills do not typically keep a certified lumber grader on staff, making the grade-certification requirement difficult, expensive, or even impossible. The irony is that it is usually the small mill that has the highest-quality timbers for the very reason of not having a grader to sort the best material out for another application.

Wiring is another example. Code requires wires to be in the center of the insulation cavity to prevent them from being punctured by nails entering from either side. This seems like a right-minded rule but not for every circumstance. We have a situation where the safest and easiest place to put the wire is on the inside of the foam-core panel surface and the outside of the timber. Yet the strictest interpretation of the code suggests that we have to put the wire in a more difficult and vulnerable position. In such cases, most reasonable building inspectors will use their own judgment or simply require a registered engineer's approval for the building plans.

A similar kind of problem is often caused by people in the building trades who fear the unknown. To compensate for their insecurity, they raise their prices, even though the task may not be any more difficult or complicated—just different. To prevent this sort of costly ignorance, consumers must be educated about construction procedure specific to timber-frame houses. They need to be prepared to educate potential contractors and subcontractors, and know when the price does not accurately reflect the difficulty of the job.

Dealing with codes and construction trades can make building a timber-frame house more vexing than it need be. But as this type of construction becomes more and more popular, the problems will begin to disappear. Codes will adapt regulations to govern these new situations and tradespeople will

Another factor that inhibits a quick pace is that owners tend to choose labor-intensive details. Once people see the craftsmanship of a fine timber-frame, they usually prefer high-quality finish work. High-quality materials are harder to get than cheap materials (even if they are not more expensive), and good work takes more time (and is definitely more expensive) than bad work. The moral of the story is that nothing good comes easily. A timber-frame home is built to unusually high standards and costs more time and usually more money, too.

Nature rules

A timber frame is made of wood, and wood—especially in timber dimensions—cracks, shrinks, and twists. Any timber above 4 in. thick cannot be reliably or economically dried in kilns because it takes too long. Air-drying is also impractical for the same reason. Even when it is possible to make the frame of dry timbers, seasonal shrinking and swelling results in dimensional change or surface checking.

We have made frames of timbers that were dried in a kiln and a few from timbers that were resawn from larger timbers over 100 years old. In both cases, there certainly was not as much movement as in frames built from green wood, but there was definitely visible change as the frame acclimated to its new environment. It is just the nature of wood. If you want a door that will never warp or shrink, get one of the new metal or fiberglass doors. Although a shirt made of polyester can be made never to wrinkle, there is something about cotton that is unlike any man-made fiber; if you like the feel and texture and the individual character of natural materials, it is difficult to accept substitutes. Buying quality sometimes means accepting the wrinkles, and the timbers in a frame definitely "wrinkle." This can be seen as a drawback, but it is also proof that they are the real thing.

The shrinking and checking of timbers are like wrinkles in cotton fabric—evidence of the unique character of a natural material.

become familiar with the new materials and techniques. In the meantime, it is necessary for those who wish to construct a timber-frame house to become familiar with building details and the standard solutions to various situations that may arise. In part, that is the very reason for this book.

In my experience, building a timber-frame house takes more time than building a conventional house. First of all, the plans need to be more detailed because the details and procedures are not a common part of habit and experience in the building trades. Building inspectors have a tendency to want to see more on paper so that they can satisfy themselves that code is being met. Tradespeople will need to have more explained by way of drawings so they can understand procedure and the interface of materials. Owners who are overseeing their own projects usually keep the job under control by limiting the number of subcontractors on the site at any one time, and so time is traded for quality control.

Uncompromising standards of workmanship and engineering allow timber-frame buildings to stand for centuries.

CHAPTER 2

THE STRUCTURE

Timber framing fosters excellence. Both functional requirements and aesthetic desires compel uncompromising workmanship and engineering. Weak examples of the craft are either gone or survive marginally, ravaged by forces they were not equipped to withstand. But properly designed and well-constructed timber-frame buildings stand sturdily, almost defiantly, despite centuries of use. Better than words, far better than textbooks, these many thousands of surviving timber-frame buildings silently instruct.

Building timber-frame structures to the highest standards requires a broad understanding of theory and good practice combined with some creativity and flexibility. Each frame starts out as not much more than a blank canvas, made up of the hopes and dreams of the future occupants (brought down to earth by budget limitations and site requirements). During design, there is nothing about the shape or flavor of the building that dictates more than the most general arrangement of timbers. When the shape and geometry of the structure have been determined, the wood species still has to be selected and the timbers individually sized. Information about the arrangement, species, and size of the timbers does not automatically lead to an understanding of the joints that will be used. And when the joinery is engineered and detailed, decisions still must be made about embellishments and finishes. Of course, these considerations must be juggled with the aesthetic and functional requirements for the building. Compare this decision-making process with the methodology of conventional stud framing, where once you decide where the walls go, you put them together in the usual way—16 in. on center, nailed to top and bottom plates—with usual results.

Timber framing has more in common with designing and making wooden furniture than it does with conventional building procedures. In the same way that a handcrafted chair is more than a place to sit, a timber frame is more than a structure. In both cases it is virtually impossible to separate design from construction. Be it chairmaking or timber framing, to make successful decisions about woods, finish, style, function, and construction, you must first understand the structural requirements of the craft. To get the necessary overview, examine typical engineering considerations and the physical characteristics of the timber frame. In the next chapter I'll delve into frame systems and design procedures more deeply, and in Chapter 4 I'll talk about home design. Although I'll be dis-

cussing frame design separately from house design, it is important to realize that both must evolve together when plans are being drawn.

ANATOMY OF A TIMBER FRAME

A typical timber frame can be divided into four major systems: walls, floor, roof, and bents (see the drawing below). Walls are the planes of timbers that run parallel to the ridge beam, and bents are the planes of timbers perpendicular to the walls. A simple timber

frame might contain three or four bents, two walls, a floor system on one or two levels, and a roof system inclined toward the center equally from each wall. It could be this simple, but there is no limit to how complex each of these systems might be. The systems can be further subdivided into the vertical, horizontal, or inclined timbers that make up each unit.

Historically and geographically, there is some inconsistency in nomenclature, but basically the vertical members are called posts, struts, and studs. Struts can also be inclined and are used in the

TYPICAL TIMBER FRAME

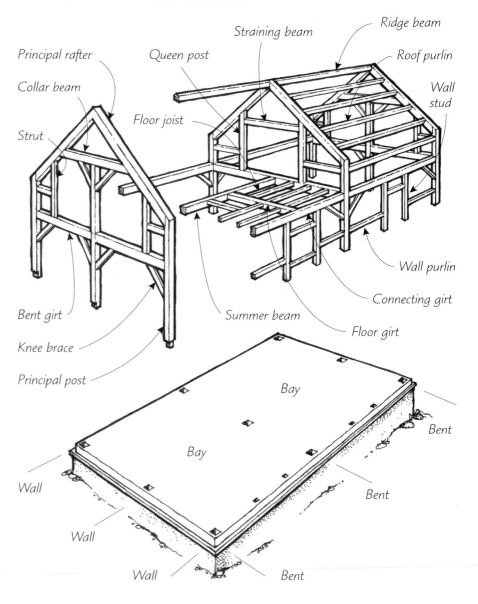

Principal rafter
Collar beam
Strut
Bent girt
Knee brace
Principal post
Floor joist
Queen post
Straining beam
Ridge beam
Roof purlin
Wall stud
Wall purlin
Connecting girt
Floor girt
Summer beam
Bay
Bay
Bent
Bent
Bent
Wall
Wall
Wall

roof system as secondary support for rafters. Studs are secondary posts, primarily used as nailers or for decoration. The horizontal members, or beams, are: girts, sills, plates, girders, joists, collar ties, tie beams, ridge beams, and purlins. Girts are the horizontal members in bents or walls that span between major posts. Sills support the post bottoms at ground level, while plates support common rafters; girders are major beams that run between sills. Inclined members are generally either rafters or braces.

The identification of most pieces in the frame is further refined by function and location. Therefore, there are bent girts and connecting girts, roof purlins and wall purlins, principal rafters and common rafters. A few other timbers have interesting names: queen posts, king posts, prick posts, crown posts, and even samson posts, as well as summer beams, hammer beams, anchor beams, and dragon beams (see the drawings below).

STRUCTURAL TIMBERS

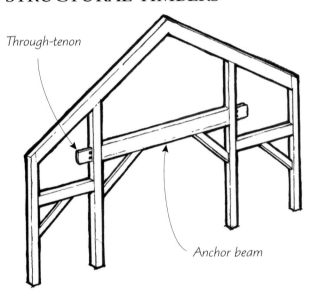

Through-tenon

Anchor beam

An anchor beam ties two posts together within bent—usually found in early American Dutch barns.

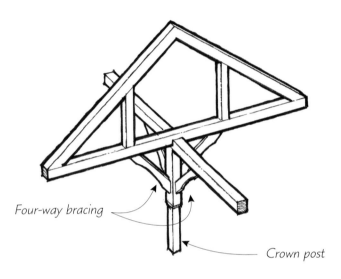

Four-way bracing

Crown post

A crown post is braced to beams in four directions.

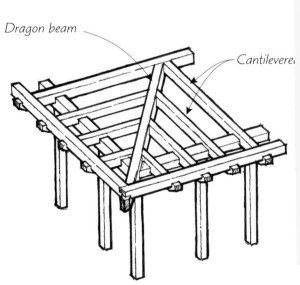

Dragon beam

Cantilevered

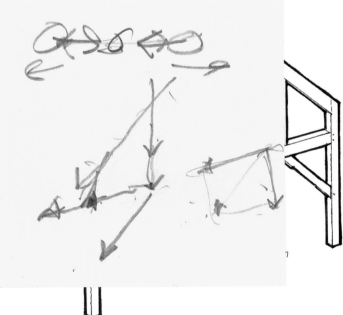

A dragon beam is oriented diagonally and typically cantilevers over lower level.

A hammer beam forms bracket to receive roof loads in an elegant but challenging roof frame.

The timbers within the walls, floor, roof and bents interact to form a self-supporting structural unit. This unit is often a complex web consisting of many hundreds of pieces, each absorbing and transferring a share of the loads in the building. The accumulating loads are collected and passed on through the frame from the minor members (which tend to fall in the center of the building) to ever larger timbers, until eventually they are received by the principal posts. These posts pass the loads to the foundation, which ultimately distributes them to the earth below. To design a frame well, each timber should be positioned to respond to specific loads and sized to resist the forces that will act upon it. Loads are directed to the posts without putting undue stress on any timber. Every joint is planned to transfer the load effectively from one timber to another and to keep the entire frame rigid and resilient, or as one of our clients said in a different context, "…flexible, but not limp."

When function comes together with form in a well-designed timber-frame building, the frame itself can become a work of art. It takes on the natural balance, symmetry, and beauty that are the essence of timber framing. The intelligent sizing, placement, and careful connection of each timber component, coupled with the athletic way loads are relayed through a frame, can result in a subtle combination of muscle and grace that is always a beautiful thing to behold.

The forces
Reading this chapter will not make you a structural engineer, but if designing timber frames required the full knowledge of one, I would not be writing this now. On the other hand, it is essential that timber-frame designers have a good understanding of the forces that will bear on a frame (see the drawings above right). Obviously, it's also important to know what to do about it: how a frame reacts to forces and how to calculate loads and to size timbers. These calculations require the use of lengthy

FORCES ON THE FRAME

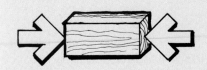

Compression
Compression occurs when forces push toward each other. For instance, loads bearing on a post are resisted by an equal reaction at the bottom of the post, resulting in a compression force in the timber.

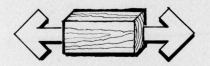

Tension
Forces pulling a timber from both ends cause tensile stress, which amounts to two forces playing tug-of-war with the timber.

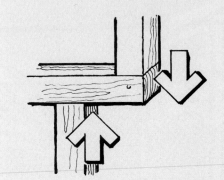

Vertical shear
Cross-grain crushing of fibers results from a huge (and unlikely) load that would actually tear the timber in half.

Bending moment
Bending subjects the upper and lower portions of a beam to conflicting tension and compression stresses. Posts can also bend when loads are applied to a building sideways. The tension side is the weak link.

Horizontal shear
Horizontal shear results from an extreme load having produced an excessive bend (or bending moment). Changes in those bending stresses along the beam cause horizontal slippage of fibers along the grain. There's a greater shear tendency at a beam's ends.

formulas or tables, which, although admittedly complicated, are not beyond the reach of the determined person. They are beyond the scope of this book, however, and so for that information, I refer interested readers to my first book, listed in the bibliography. I also must stress that it is critical to recognize the point at which the services of a licensed engineer are required. Ignorance of ignorance is the worst of traits. Pythagoras called the condition "compound ignorance" and disallowed his followers to associate with those afflicted with this "curse." Any frame worth cutting, joining, and assembling is worth an investment in proper engineering.

Still, good science should not always discredit good "horse sense." I learned this lesson the hard way, after designing and building an office for my parents' mail-order business. It was not a timber-frame building, but I used timbers for internal posts and carrying beams. I carefully calculated each timber size and demonstrated to my parents that though the beams would have to be very large to support the supplies on the second floor, the posts used to support the beams could be relatively small in cross section. We could save money on the posts, I boasted. As the building went up, my mother told me several times that the posts looked too small to her. When I started to argue the math, she stopped me and said, "Those posts are just too small." She

didn't need formulas to tell her that. The posts stayed as they were (because my mother is tolerant and I am stubborn) and the building was completed and piled high with the paper of their business.

One day, when my mother happened to be away from her usual place in the office, the elderly lady across the alley backed out of her garage, had a mild stroke with her foot on the gas pedal, and crashed into the side of the office. The car came far enough through the wall to start quite a domino effect with the loaded shelves of papers and boxes. The posts broke like matchsticks, and the forces that saved my mother (and the driver) had nothing to do with my timber sizing. While I could not have

anticipated a car coming through the wall, I have learned to pay attention to both data and opinion.

Now let's look at the four primary types of forces acting upon the frame members: compression, tension, shear, and bending moment. Although just about any exception is possible, each of these forces tends to be associated with particular timbers or framing circumstances, as you will see.

Compression

All the loads bearing on a post are resisted by an equal reaction at its bottom end, resulting in a compression force in the timber. Posts that support a girt, plate, or rafter end receive the load at their top, but a post can be loaded

TIMBER MEMBERS UNDER STRESS

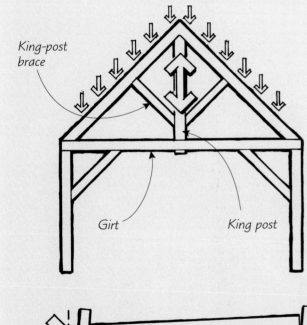

King-post brace

Girt

King post

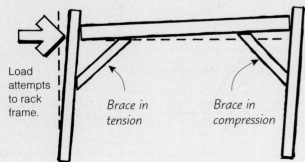

Load attempts to rack frame.

Brace in tension

Brace in compression

King-post truss
A king post is loaded downward at the bottom by the girt and the king-post braces while it is being held up at the top by the rafters. A king-post truss uses a central, single post to connect between a horizontal beam and the rafter peak. If it joined to a collar tie instead of to the rafter peak, it would be a crown post. The king post is usually connected to a bent girt or tie beam, but might only span between the peak and a collar tie instead. The classic king post has diagonal braces joining to the rafters, creating triangles that work to make the assembly function as a single roof truss. Because the lower horizontal beam of the truss (the bottom chord) is supported by the king post, there is no need for an intermediate support post.

Braces
Under load, braces keep the angles between posts and beams perpendicular and therefore prevent the building from racking out of square. To ensure that the frame is braced in every direction, braces are always used in pairs on opposite ends of a beam. When one of the pair is in compression, the opposite brace is obliged to be in tension—the brace in compression is attempting to close and the opposite one to open. The brace in compression has to crush wood to fail, but the brace in tension only needs to pull the joint apart, a relatively easier task. Therefore, while all the braces are necessary, in any given racking-load situation it's probable that the braces in compression are doing the bulk of the work.

by a horizontal beam at any point along its length. Although heavy loads are often directed into the posts, seldom is there a risk of compression failure. Wood is strongest along its grain, and posts are usually relatively large in cross section to accommodate the joinery of intersecting members. If a post failed to support its compression load, it would tend to come in the form of buckling—lean on a wooden yardstick with the weight of your body, and it will buckle sideways and break. So even though compressive failure of a timber post is unlikely, avoid using long, slender timbers or long, unsupported posts.

Where many members intersect and wood has been removed for the joints, a post might be unduly weakened in its resistance to an extreme compression load. The calculation for the maximum load in compression should be done using the smallest timber section left after the joints are cut. While the post acts alone to carry the vertical loads, the beams that join to the post can contribute strength by serving as buttresses, helping to prevent buckling.

Tension

Forces pulling a timber from both ends cause tensile stress, which amounts to two forces playing tug-of-war with a timber. It's usually a joint that fails in this circumstance, not the timber. Joints generally include the end of at least one timber, where it is difficult to generate substantial resistance to withdrawal. (Tensile capacity in a joint is achieved through the use of pegs or a locking geometry, as discussed on p. 42.) Therefore, if a timber is subjected only to tension, the net cross-sectional area needed at the joint would determine the width or depth of the timber. But there is usually more than this one force at work, which affects the choice of joinery and timber size.

A king post is a good example of a timber under tension. It's loaded downward at the bottom by the girt and the king-post braces, while it is being held up at the top by the rafters, as shown

in the top drawing on p. 27. (Collar ties between rafters must also resist the potential for opposing rafters to spread at their bases.)

Knee braces, which play the major role in keeping the frame rigid, are often subjected to significant tensile loads. Though not always the case, loads on the braces usually come from a force pushing against the side of the building; this puts the first brace to encounter the load in tension and the opposite brace in compression (see the bottom drawing on p. 27). Failure in brace connections under tension is fairly common, and frames can be made a great deal stronger if they are designed to rely on compression members (instead of a tension member) to resist the load.

Shear and bending moment

A pair of scissors perfectly demonstrates shearing action: Two forces slide by each other and sever the material in between. The shear stresses in horizontal timbers are both vertical (across the grain) and horizontal (along the grain). Unlike masonry materials, which are comparatively weak in resistance to shear forces, wood is so resilient that cross-grain failure almost never happens unless the timber is inherently defective or eventually deteriorates. It would occur if the load were so massive that the timber actually broke, with the wood fibers torn apart at the point of connection. Since the strength of the timbers at their joints is critical to frame strength, the joints must also be designed to resist vertical shearing (see the drawing below).

VERTICAL-SHEAR SITUATION

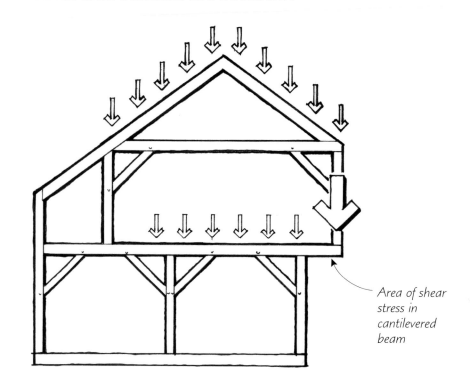

Area of shear stress in cantilevered beam

Cross-grain shear might be a problem in a garrison frame, in which beam cantilevers beyond first-story wall and carries weight of upper post and roof beyond support of lower post.

Horizontal shear (along the grain) is a much more common problem because it is easier to slide the wood fibers by each other along their grains than it is to cut across them. This kind of shear failure in a timber is the result of an extreme load having produced an excessive bend (or bending moment). Bending subjects the upper and lower portions of a timber to conflicting tension and compression stresses. Changes in those bending stresses cause horizontal shear, or a slippage of fibers along the grain. The horizontal shear stresses are maximum at the center of the beam from top to bottom and are usually largest at the ends of beams. But the great elasticity of some species allows even a timber with a long span and an excessive load to sag quite a bit, like a bow, before failing. Actually,

shear failure along the grain is more likely to happen when beams are relatively stiff but are still forced to bend. Support a yardstick on chairs 30 in. apart and it will bend a great deal under a load; put a large load on the yardstick with a 12-in. span and it is much more likely to break. So horizontal-shear analysis takes into consideration cross section, span, structural properties of the species, as well as the load.

When sizing horizontal timbers, three issues must be considered: 1) shear stress, which is the most probable cause of horizontal splitting at the beam ends; 2) deflection, which is limited by building codes to ensure that structures will be stiff enough to be serviceable; and 3) bending stress, which could cause fiber failure. Fiber failure occurs

in a timber when the tensile stresses caused by bending become too great, so the fibers simply break across the grain. Pure fiber failure is not very common and would probably be accompanied by some shearing along the grain.

Timber sizing

The transfer of loads through frame members is an essential engineering consideration in timber framing. Understanding how loads are absorbed and passed along is critical to a well-designed frame. Because loads are transferred at joint intersections, much needs to be explained about the functions of various kinds of joinery, which I'll do later. The point to note here is that all the components of the frame must work individually and collectively to gather the loads and direct them to the posts without staggering under the effort. It's a classic system: The action and reaction of every part and piece has repercussion somewhere else.

All horizontal timbers carry a load, if only the weight of the timber itself. In most cases, they also carry the weight of other materials, such as flooring, roof planking, and shingles. These materials make up the dead load on the frame, which is usually evenly distributed over the surface. In addition to dead load, there are live loads, which consist of all those things other than the building materials—snow, people, furniture, wind, and earthquakes. The numbers to plug into the equations for the live loads are determined by the local building code. Beams that bear simple live and dead loads would be floor joists, summer beams, purlins, and connecting girts.

There is a potentially large load on this cantilevered hammer beam. Both the beam and the joint must be sized and designed to resist the load. The wood is fir.

Because loads pass through the frame like streams converging on a river, many timbers must accept more than one type of load. For example, when a post bears on a beam, it could be transferring a significant load from another area of the frame to that one point. In other cases, there might be two or three points along a beam where loads are applied through vertical or diagonal members. Concentrating the load in

This frame was designed for recycled southern pine. To tone down the dark color and strong grain, the owners chose to stain the wood a lighter color.

this manner further complicates beam sizing because the load type (evenly distributed, one-point, two-point, or three-point) must be considered as well. Beams within a frame might support posts, which could, in turn, support other beams that perhaps support a floor; so that when the load is finally accumulated, the beam that must bear it all is asked to perform a formidable task. If, when designing a frame, you try to avoid such extremes (transferring heavy loads long distances sideways with beams) and instead choose simpler, more direct load paths, the frame will be stronger, will be easier to build, and will utilize smaller beams.

The darkly stained oak in this house is a dominant decorative feature. (Photo by Bob Gere.)

You can't begin to consider timber sizing without a decision about the wood for the frame, because there are dramatic differences in the strength and stiffness values of different species. A relatively weak species (red cedar, for example) can certainly be used in a timber frame, but it should be designed with short spans—it wouldn't make sense to design a frame with 16-ft. spans and then decide to use white pine or cedar. The aesthetics of the different species also have a bearing on frame design. Timbers made from light-colored wood and clear grain might be more closely spaced than those made from a wood with stronger grain characterisics, such as oak or fir. For these reasons, design the frame to fit the wood and not the other way around.

Never be afraid to oversize a timber-frame member, and never underestimate what a frame might have to withstand. If a frame could be isolated within a protective bubble, it would only have to be strong enough to hold itself together, but real life demands that frames be designed with the assumption that snow will be on the roof, wind will blow against the walls, the earth might shake and heave, and people and things will weigh heavily upon the floors. We are also asked by code and by common sense to plan for the worst: Someday the snow may be hip deep and very wet; someday the wind might be a hurricane; on any day, the inhabitants might hold a raucous party, and certainly the kids will jump from beds. When sizing timbers, err on the side of endurance, and you probably will not have erred at all.

The roof system

More than any other factor, the arrangement of timbers in the roof determines whether a frame will be built with walls or bents as the principal structural planes. Indeed, frames are often defined by the type of roof system they support. The roof is usually the most complex aspect of the frame. Figuring the angles and the lengths in the roof's geometry almost always includes demanding mathematical calculations. In addition, the roof generally contains the most challenging joinery and can require sophisticated engineering. Therefore, I'll discuss the structure of the frame from the top down.

Designing and engineering a timber roof system is serious business. Understanding the forces in play, accurately appraising their quantities, predicting their paths, and containing their de-

constructive intent are not achieved with a flight of intuition. If you don't comprehend it and can't calculate it, don't design it. That's why they make engineers. To gain more insight into the structural considerations for timber-frame roof systems, see the sidebar on p. 32, written by my company's engineer, Ben Brungraber.

There are four timber-frame roof types that I will discuss: 1) common rafters, 2) common rafters with midspan plates, 3) principal rafters with common purlins, and 4) principal rafters with principal purlins. Deciding which to use might only be a matter of personal preference, but more commonly the choice involves structural factors, including the shape and pitch of the roof, loading, wood species, available timber length, floor plan, and, of course, time and money.

The roof structure is usually the most challenging aspect of the frame, requiring difficult joinery and complex geometry. The wood of this frame is oak.

SUPPORTING RAFTERS

by Robert L. (Ben) Brungraber

Regardless of the roof system used, rafters follow the plane of the roof and collect and carry the roof loads into the posts. The designer must prevent rafters from sagging or breaking and the building eaves from spreading. Roof loads include the weight of the materials plus the locally mandated design loads for snow and wind.

Rafters supported at both top and bottom present the least challenge. A center post, or a stiff and strong enough ridge beam, allow rafters to behave as simple, but sloped, beams. These rafters exert no outward thrust at their supports, so the building has no tendency to spread, no matter how the roof pitches.

A straightforward and ancient alternative roof scheme relies on the rafters leaning against one another at the ridge. The rafters now generate outward thrust at the eave line, which the building must resist. The outward thrust increases dramatically as the roof pitch flattens. All the vertical load goes to the outer walls, doubling the compression forces there. The rafters now carry significant compression forces, along with the same bending moments as they did with a ridge support. The designer must contend with all these complications.

Propping opposing rafters against each other with a collar strut can allow designers to reduce rafter sizes. A collar strut reduces the bending stresses in the rafters by introducing even more outward thrust and compression forces in the rafter. The designer must further strengthen both the rafter foot connection and the member that supports the rafters to provide increased thrust resistance.

Some buildings cannot resist outward thrust at the eave line. The designer can put in a collar member again, but this collar holds the eaves together rather than holding the rafters apart. We call this tension member a collar tie. A collar tie in tension, unlike the compressive collar strut, increases bending stresses in the rafters. Collar ties can hold a building together, but they do it only with much larger rafters.

RAFTERS WITH CENTER POST OR RIDGE BEAM

Roof load

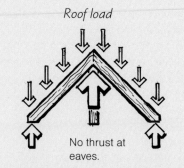

No thrust at eaves.

RAFTERS WITHOUT CENTER SUPPORT

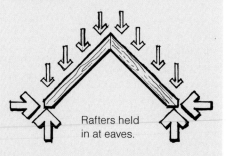

Rafters held in at eaves.

RAFTERS WITH COLLAR STRUT

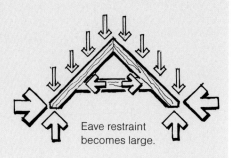

Eave restraint becomes large.

RAFTERS WITH COLLAR TIE

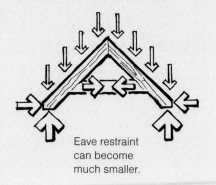

Eave restraint can become much smaller.

Common-rafter roof

A common-rafter roof is easy to install, but it has a potential structural deficiency that must be considered. Here the rafters are joined to the eave plates at their bottoms and at the top either to a ridge beam running the length of the building or simply to each other in pairs. Each rafter needs to be long enough and strong enough for the entire span. The common rafters are usually spaced 3 ft. to 4 ft. apart, with no particular regard to the location of principal posts. The problem is that there is no interconnection or opportunity for strong joinery between the roof timbers and the timbers in the rest of the frame. They are separate pieces in separate layers. With only one timber running perpendicular to the rafters above the plate level (the ridge beam), it isn't easy to stiffen the roof in that direction, and the timber frame begins to act as two units rather than one. An easy solution is shown in the top drawing on p. 34. In this design, a central post supports a ridge beam, which not only resists outward thrust but also provides the means for bracing the building in the longitudinal direction.

If a center post and/or ridge beam are not used, collar ties are usually required to limit outward thrust at the eaves. Besides the collar tie, common-rafter trusses don't usually contain additional timbers for reinforcement against spreading—which causes this system to have some difficult compromises as the building's width increases. Because of these considerations, common-rafter roofs are most suitable for small buildings.

Common-rafter roof with midspan plates

Using midspan plates to support the common rafters maintains their visual and structural simplicity while resolving most of the potential weaknesses. Obviously, this intermediate prop brings the simple benefit of breaking the rafter span in half, allowing the rafters themselves to be relatively smaller. Introducing the midspan plate also significantly reduces outward thrust on the eave plate, usually eliminating the requirement of a ridge beam or collar ties. In addition, with this supporting plate in place, it is possible for the rafter spans to be accomplished with two pieces instead of one. There are other added advantages in the two midspan-plate systems that will be reviewed here.

In its simplest form, the plate is installed on posts that pass through the bent planes to the deck. Each bent contains four posts: the outer pair supports the eave plates, the inner pair supports the midspan plates (see the bottom drawing on p. 34). Because the middle posts pass through the eave plane and the floor level(s), they are very efficient at stiffening the bent plane because they get rid of inherent hinge lines. In addition, at the point where the posts meet the plate, there is an opportunity for bracing the building perpendicular to the bent, creating a nearly perfect opportunity for the "ideal" timber frame—that point where absolute simplicity and absolute strength converge.

Another unique attribute of this frame style is that it can be constructed as either bents or walls. As bents, the four posts and the bent girts are raised first, and then the bay girts and floor system are installed between. After that, the plates are joined to the top of the posts. The rafters go in last. When constructing walls, each is prebuilt with the plate installed. They are then raised and connected to bent girts and the floor-system members. Rafters are then installed on the plates.

The second system for getting a plate at the rafter midspan is with the use of a canted strut (see the photo at right). This system has a dramatic appearance but is actually very simple. It was used a lot in early American construction for both barns and houses. When it is not possible to position posts at the mid-plate line, this roof design is a solution. Generally, the plate is oriented perpendicular to the roof plane (or close) and the load is directed through the canted strut toward a more central bent post.

Typically, this type of roof plate suggests a bent construction system. Bents are prebuilt up to the eave-plate level and then bay girts and floor systems are put into place, followed by canted struts and their supporting braces. After that, plates are joined to the eave posts and the canted struts. Note that it is possible to install significant braces in the plane of the canted plate, providing good rigidity up high in the frame.

Principal-rafter and principal-purlin roof

In this system, the principal rafters are directly in line with the principal posts so that their burden is directly transferred. Stretching between the principal rafters are principal purlins, which break the span of the smaller common rafters. The common rafters connect at the eave plates, then join to the principal purlin and from the purlin again to the peak. A typical situation would require one principal purlin for each

A midspan beam supported by a canted strut was used for the Wickwire barn project, which was featured on "This Old House." The wood of the frame is white pine; the midspan beams are fir. (Photo by Evy Blum.)

COMMON-RAFTER ROOF SYSTEMS

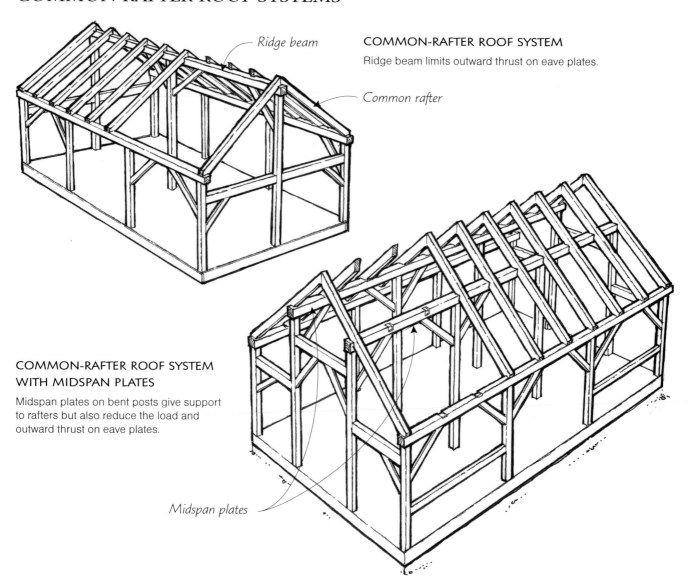

Ridge beam

COMMON-RAFTER ROOF SYSTEM

Ridge beam limits outward thrust on eave plates.

Common rafter

COMMON-RAFTER ROOF SYSTEM WITH MIDSPAN PLATES

Midspan plates on bent posts give support to rafters but also reduce the load and outward thrust on eave plates.

Midspan plates

roof slope, but there could be two or more if needed (see the top drawing on p. 36). It would not be unusual to use principal rafters that were 8x10 (or even larger), a principal purlin of about the same size, and common rafters as small as 4x6 spaced about 4 ft. apart.

Purlins make it possible to break up the span of the common rafters, so shorter and smaller (and more readily available) timbers can be used. Also, by spanning from bent to bent, the principal purlins absorb even increments of the roof load and transfer it to the principal posts. Some of the burden carried by the common rafters is also trans-

ferred by the purlins to the principal posts, with the remainder bearing on the eave plates. In this type of roof, the purlins might well be the largest timbers because they carry heavy loads and are typically unsupported in their relatively long span between rafters.

But this type of roof demands some tricky assembly, because the purlins have to be joined to the principal rafters before the common rafters can be installed. To position the purlins thus requires that individuals shin up rafters that are not stiffened by any other members. Also, the lower common rafters can be hard to install be-

cause the joints to the purlin and the plate have to be engaged simultaneously. Still, the interplay of timbers is beautiful, and the system is without structural compromise.

Principal-rafter and common-purlin roof

This last roof option has been a very popular one with my company. In this system, principal rafters join directly to the tops of principal posts and are tied together with other primary timbers in the bent plane. The bents are then connected to each other at the roof level with a series of purlins spaced about 4 ft. apart (see the bottom drawing on p. 36).

The system has many benefits, not the least of which is that it eliminates the need for top plates. It's difficult today to get timbers that are adequately long or stable for these plates, so they often have to be scarfed together. When the forests were filled with tall, virgin trees, and timbers were hewn by hand, it was almost always possible to make one-piece plates to span the full length and width of any building, and it would not be at all difficult to get any number of timbers of rafter length. With this kind of material available, and with so much handwork involved, the joiner's concern 200 years ago was not timber length but the number of timbers required. Because a common-rafter roof uses many fewer pieces than a purlin roof, I suspect this was a major reason it was favored at that time. (A 36-ft.-long frame with 20-ft.-long rafters would require 20 common rafters on 4-ft. centers, but with purlins and principal rafters, the frame would need about 33 members.)

My company stays in business because we have a measure of practicality: Our timbers are purchased from a sawmill rather than hand-hewn. Our sawyer can easily handle purlins, which are usually no longer than 16 ft. But if we asked him for two 42-ft.-long plates, four 30-ft.-long bent girts and thirty-two 26-ft.-long rafters, he'd probably try not to laugh, but he would know for certain that we had given over completely to fantasy. If he could get timbers like that, he wouldn't be able to saw them, and if he could get them and saw them, it's likely they would be of questionable quality.

So we use principal rafters and common purlins, and benefit from the other advantages of the system. Because principal rafters are part of the bents, we can raise large, complete units. (If there were a plate between posts and rafters, the bents, plates, and roof would have to be assembled separately.) By extending interior posts to the roof, we can support splices in the

Integrating the rafters into the bents allows the raising of large, complete units. The assembled bents are efficiently raised with a crane. (Photo by Bill Holtz.)

When the common-rafter roof system is used, the primary unit of assembly and raising is often the walls instead of bents. (Photo by Jim Benson.)

The Structure

principal rafters if they are needed to make up the complete length. Also, because the rafter ends join directly to the tops of the principal posts, the frame does not shrink in height as the timber dries. Remember that wood shrinks considerably across the grain but very little along the grain, so the height of the building would shrink as the top plates dried.

Other roof timbers
There are some relatively standard combinations of posts, struts, braces, girts, and ties used to solve particular design situations and to make the roof structurally stable.

Queen posts are similar to king posts, but they work in pairs. Typically, they rest on the bent girt and join either to a

PRINCIPAL-RAFTER ROOF SYSTEMS

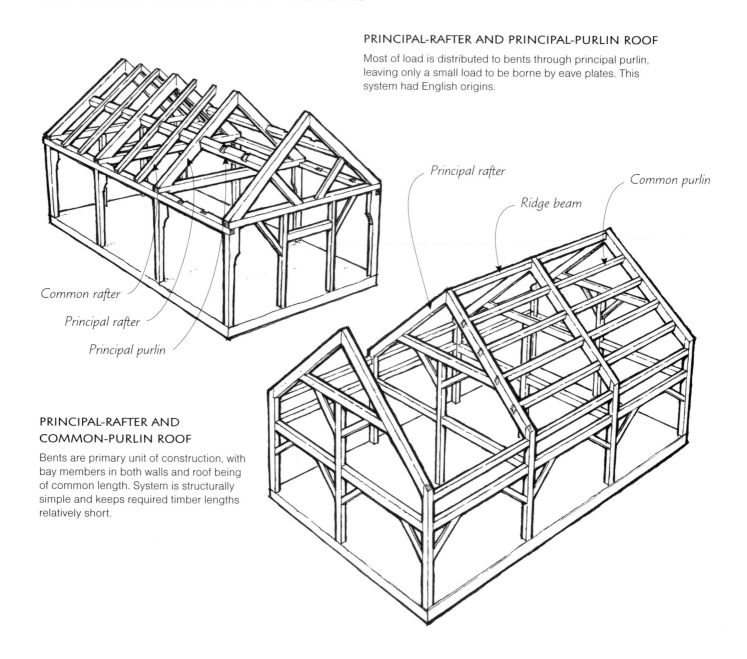

PRINCIPAL-RAFTER AND PRINCIPAL-PURLIN ROOF

Most of load is distributed to bents through principal purlin, leaving only a small load to be borne by eave plates. This system had English origins.

Principal rafter

Ridge beam

Common purlin

Common rafter

Principal rafter

Principal purlin

PRINCIPAL-RAFTER AND COMMON-PURLIN ROOF

Bents are primary unit of construction, with bay members in both walls and roof being of common length. System is structurally simple and keeps required timber lengths relatively short.

collar tie or directly to the rafters (see the top photo at right). Queen posts are commonly used when it is necessary to create upper floor living space under the central area between rafters. Because queen posts transfer the roof load directly to the bent girt, they must be placed carefully so that the point loads they impose do not overburden the girt. It's best to position them as close as possible to the supports beneath the bent girt. If the queen posts do not join to a collar tie, a straining beam between the queen posts would serve the same purpose. Knee braces are used between the queen posts and the straining beam to help support loads and stiffen the assembly.

In another type of roof assembly, elaborate bracing is used to create "trusses" that span the width of the building without interior supports or a horizontal beam connecting the walls (see the bottom photo at right). The hammerbeam frame and the scissors truss are two examples. The finest examples of these techniques were executed in the great cathedrals of Europe and demonstrate how complex structure and intricate decoration can combine to turn a common craft into art of the highest order. The most notable example of a hammer beam, in Westminster Hall in England (late 1300s), spans 65 ft., and the mechanics of it are still the subject of research, testing, and discussion. Basically, tension and compression forces are passed through a series of timbers and resolved at the base of the rafters and in the outer wall without the need for a bottom chord or collar tie.

The scissors truss was used in Europe as a way to frame a vaulted masonry ceil-

Queen posts support the principal rafters at their midspan. They are bound to each other by a straining beam, and knee braces help stiffen and strengthen the assembly. The wood of this frame is Sitka spruce.

The hammer-beam frame was developed in the Middle Ages. It creates a dramatic open-timber roof system.

The Structure

SCISSORS TRUSS

Truss is used for framing above vaults. Today, its drama and strength are used to span large, open spaces.

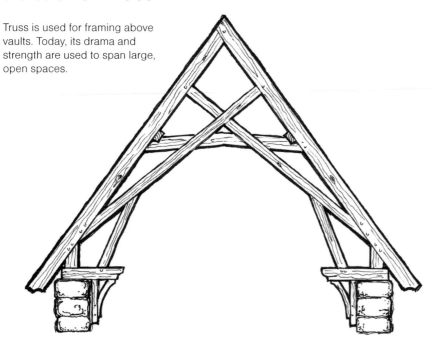

Very little space in a timber-frame house is wasted. Rooms under the roof often have interesting shapes and offer interesting decorating possibilities. (Photo by Brian E. Gulick.)

ing between timber rafters (see the drawing above). We have found this to be a simple and strong arrangement to use in a variety of situations where a clear span is required and a little structural drama is useful.

Each of the arrangements I've just discussed is designed to keep the roof from sagging or spreading, to get the load from the rafters to the principal posts efficiently. It's that simple. But when the needs of the structure are put in the pot with aesthetic considerations, an endless variety of savory combinations can be served, and often the arrangement of timbers in the roof becomes the most pleasing and dramatic part of the frame. There's something exciting about the way the forces are pulled in by one timber and passed off to another—the interplay can't help but become a focal point of the frame. In other types of construction, the roof is an unattractive assembly of gussets, steel plates, and nails that has to be hidden. Because of this, the space under the rafters is often totally unusable when filled with tightly spaced, light truss members. When this happens, you not only lose space that was figured into construction costs, but you

also lose an area of potentially high visual appeal. The interest created by the roof framing and the extra space under the eaves are two distinct attributes of a timber-frame house.

Posts and braces

Stretching up to shoulder the load from the roof are the principal exterior wall posts. These are tied to the beams of the wall and bent structures. A principle of timber-frame design is that the burden should get to these posts with the least-possible effort. When the force is passed from the rafters to an intermediate post and then through a beam to get to its destination, it might be necessary to use a beam of considerable size to prevent unacceptable bending problems at the point of transfer.

A better way to avoid overloading horizontal timbers is to design intermediate posts within the bent to reach from the deck to the rafters, as shown in the left photo on the facing page. (You see this type of bent design a lot in barn construction, because it's an easy and practical way to gain great strength.) Intermediate posts also keep the bent from hinging at the eave line, something we've learned a great deal about in raising our frames. Lifting a bent from a horizontal to a vertical position applies stresses the bent will probably never see again, but it's a fair indication of the strength of the structure. There's a tendency to design a frame in layers simply because the floor plan is usually designed that way, yet when you look at the frame as a complete unit, it's obviously much stiffer if posts pass through the levels. In addition, the natural triangulation between the sloping rafters and the long interior posts enhances the frame's resistance to loads exerted against the gable ends and the walls. If you push against a side of a triangle, the adjacent side resists your force by acting in compression, making it nearly impossible to distort the shape. As a matter of fact, a triangular structure can't distort dramatically unless one of the connections fails. Push against a rectangle, and the result is much different. The only inherent

Passing the central posts directly from the foundation to the rafters has numerous structural advantages.

In timber framing, knee braces are usually critical to the stability of the structure. They can be seen as an obstacle, but they can also be celebrated, as they are here. The wood of this frame is Douglas fir, recycled from a warehouse.

strength in a rectangle is at the corners, which have a lot of trouble staying square under a large force.

Structural triangulation is also the reason why knee braces are so important in timber framing (see the right photo above). Normally located at the upper ends of the posts, the braces connect diagonally to the joining beam and form triangles at timber intersections. Braces are usually made from 3x5s or 3x6s and are generally between 46 in. and 66 in. long. It's hard to get very scientific about brace sizing because there has been little study on the subject relative to timber framing. We follow a few general rules: The length of the brace should be a little less than half the length of the post it braces; braces are always used in pairs; a pair of braces should be used for approximately every 10 ft. in height and no more than every 16 ft. in length around the perimeter of the building. Be much more wary of under-bracing than over-bracing. These are not hard and fast rules, but we try to maintain a conservative stance. After the rigidity of a frame is ensured, the location and size of the braces can become an aesthetic decision.

If long, reversed braces can be used without interfering with the other needs of the building, a strong case can be made for joining the brace bottoms to a horizontal timber and their tops to a post. The first brace to encounter the racking load therefore responds immediately with that very effective compressive resistance. (The typical situation, shown in the drawing on p. 27, requires the first brace to receive the force to work in tension, which is not its forte.) Still, you can't just brace the bottom ends of the posts, leaving the upper 4 ft. or 5 ft. unsupported, and normally it isn't practical to have a 10-ft.-long brace consuming the wall surface. But it makes sense to look for opportunities to use reversed braces, since their effectiveness and strength can make it possible to reduce the total number of braces required.

Though diagonal braces primarily oppose lateral forces on the frame, they also help the frame bear vertical loads. The normal floor loads in a frame are first carried by the horizontal members—the joists, the girts, and the summer beams. Using figures given to us by the local building codes, we determine the dimension of these timbers by first

calculating the pounds per square foot to be borne by the timber. By calculating with sizing formulas, with an evaluation of span, spacing, and load distribution, we can assign a structural contribution to every timber in the frame once the wood species has been determined. If a beam were to fail, it would probably sag greatly first, then break. We dislike breaking, so we exercise careful control over deflection. But as the span of a timber increases and/or the imposed load becomes heavier or more centralized, to control bending we must generally either reduce the span or use a bigger timber. If knee braces help support the span, however, it should be possible to choose a timber that would otherwise be borderline. Braces help transfer the vertical load from beam to post, changing the reaction to the forces from bending to compression. And because wood is much more resistant to compression than bending, that's the good news.

The bad news is that although performance and common sense lead us to believe that we understand how diagonal braces work, when engineering the frame we are still not able to assign quantitative values to their load-bearing function. There just isn't enough data yet to put the effectiveness of a brace into the formula. And so, until more testing and analysis can be done, we calculate the size of the timbers as though the braces weren't there. The result is that timber frames have another built-in contingency to help the building survive those worst-case "100-year" natural disasters that seem ever more frequent these days.

The floor system

The timbers in the floor support the loads applied in the spaces between the bent and wall beams. You can therefore look at each space as needing an individual floor system, with the following considerations bearing upon the arrangement and size of the timbers: the distance to be spanned, the loads to be supported, the structural capacity of the joining timbers, and the design goal of laying out the floor plan with a symbiotic relationship to the timbers.

A major requirement of a floor is that it be stiff. Each timber should support its intended load with minimum acceptable deflection. A bouncy floor is an insult to the rest of the frame, comparable to putting a Geo engine in a BMW. To avoid bounciness, it is important to make sure that floors are not designed with extreme spans. A study of old barns in England shows that 16 ft. is the most common distance between bents; the study conjectures that the reason for this is to allow two yoked oxen to walk side by side in the bay (the space between bents). After a number of years in the framing business, I am convinced the real reason is that 16 ft. is the maximum practical span for a timber carrying a floor load. Beyond this, the timbers would have to become very large to limit deflection.

There are several common ways to arrange the timbers in a floor, as shown in the drawings at right. Using parallel joists spanning between bents or walls is probably the simplest approach. The joists split up the floor load evenly and,

at the same time, provide an understated look. But when the loads and spans demand that the joists be excessively large (anything above 6x8, in my view), timbers arranged this way can also seem overbearing. It is then usually more desirable to focus the loads onto a few large timbers. Large, spanning timbers such as summer beams are especially useful if they join to posts, thus directly transferring the floor loads. Like other major timbers, these beams can also be used to define living areas. For most situations, we like the interplay between large and small timbers and actually work to divide the floor with large timbers into visually manageable subdivisions. The large spanning timbers often are embellished to give the frame some formality and refinement.

In addition to their load-bearing function, the timbers of the floor help tie the frame together. If the distance from outside wall to outside wall is more than the length of a single timber (which it almost always is), there needs to be additional connection to keep the bents from spreading. When good joinery is used, floor joists or summer beams can provide continuous support.

FLOOR SYSTEMS

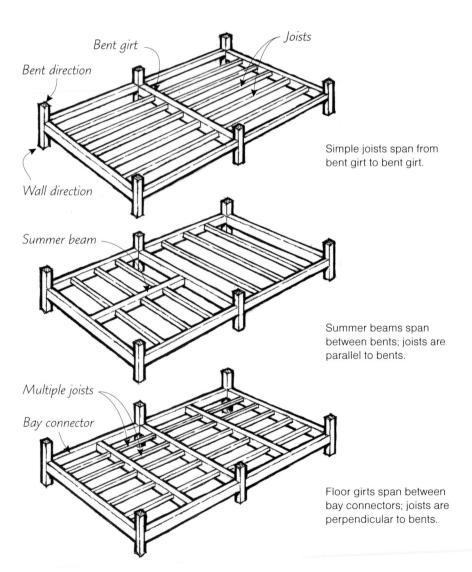

Bent girt — Joists

Bent direction

Wall direction

Simple joists span from bent girt to bent girt.

Summer beam

Summer beams span between bents; joists are parallel to bents.

Multiple joists

Bay connector

Floor girts span between bay connectors; joists are perpendicular to bents.

Depending on their sizes, parallel floor joists can be either subtle or overbearing. These joists, made from fir, affect the feeling of the room without being dominant.

JOINERY

In timber framing, joinery is practically the definition of the product. Without joinery, there is a structure made with posts and beams, but it is not a timber frame. It was the discovery of simple joinery that made the first frame possible, and it is intricately worked, complex wooden joinery that holds together some of the great architectural masterpieces of the world. Joinery is a complex subject, and here I'll just summarize a few basics.

An important guideline in timber-frame design is that the joints ought not to be more complicated than necessary. The loads in the building need to be supported by the frame, and the entire frame should be securely connected through the joinery. But beyond these rules, design concentrates on using joints that can be made efficiently and that are within the skills of the joiner. Without going out of the way to

Good joinery is the essence of timber framing. The craft of joinery in timbers can be used to enhance the beautiful effect of having the structure revealed to the living areas of the house. This frame is made from fir, recycled from demolished buildings.

FORCES AT CONNECTION DETERMINE JOINT DESIGN

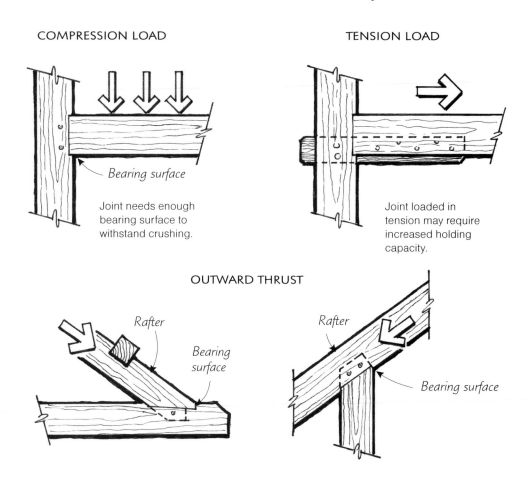

COMPRESSION LOAD

Bearing surface

Joint needs enough bearing surface to withstand crushing.

TENSION LOAD

Joint loaded in tension may require increased holding capacity.

OUTWARD THRUST

Rafter

Bearing surface

Rafter

Bearing surface

In roof joinery, large bearing surface may be required to limit outward thrust.

pursue esoteric or convoluted joints, you will invariably find enough surprises and challenges to keep the hands and mind occupied.

Most timber joints are variations on the pegged mortise and tenon—a tongue on one timber is received by a slot in the other. The simplest version of this joint is used to connect vertical timbers in the frame and for joining two beams carrying minimum loads; knee braces and collar ties generally use an angled variation. Mortise-and-tenon joints are locked with rounded pegs driven through holes drilled through both parts of the joint, although some sophisticated joints rely on wedges and geometry to lock.

The other broad category of joints used in timber frames consists of lap joints, such as dovetails and scarfs. Variations of lap joints can be used in many parts of the frame, as I will discuss later. Some of them rely entirely on their angular shapes and the weight of the timbers to lock, others are overlapped and then locked by wedging them through mating notches.

Joints are chosen on the basis of the tasks they are to fulfill, including locking the frame together, bearing weight, and transferring forces and building loads from one timber to another. A timber transferring a compression load will need a joint with enough bearing surface area to withstand crushing. A timber in tension must be firmly bound with a joint that can prevent its withdrawal. If a timber is exerting an outward thrust, as a rafter exerts on a collar tie, it needs to be restrained by

a bearing surface in corresponding orientation within the joint (see the drawing above).

The mortise and tenon
The simple mortise and tenon can be very effective in resisting both tension and compression forces. Let's look at tension first.

In tension, there are three ways a joint can fail: The pegs can break, the wood between the end of the tenon and the pegs can pull out, or the fibers can fail between the edge of the mortised timber and the pegs. Under extreme tension, all three failures would occur simultaneously—in an ideal joint. Practically, however, we lean toward making sure there is enough wood between the pegs and the end of the tenon, because this second type of failure is abrupt and gone; the others are gradual and more tenacious. For most woods, the mortise should be a minimum of 4½ in. deep, and the centers of 1-in.-dia. oak pegs should be placed about 1½ in. in from the edge of the mortised timber. Mortise and tenon widths in hardwood timbers work well at 1½ in. and should be 2 in. in softwoods (see the left drawing below).

To increase the tensile strength of the joint, increase the tenon length and thickness and use additional and/or larger pegs when the width and length of the tenon allow. For instance, in a collar tie it might be important to increase timber depth just to increase the surface area of the tenon, allowing more pegs and leaving more wood to surround the pegs. But balance this with a consideration for other joinery and a judgment about the amount of wood removed from the receiving timber. If three beams meet at the same spot on a post, enlarging the mortises

might weaken the post to an unacceptable degree. It is critical to remember that increasing the strength of one part of a joint usually decreases the strength of another part. Unless the two parts are balanced, the joint is faulty.

The ability of a joint to bear weight depends on the amount of surface area involved. Imagine for a moment the ideal situation of a load from a lightly loaded beam being transferred to the top of a midspan post through a mortise and tenon. The joint here needs only to lock the two pieces together, and the entire remaining surface area of the connection—the shoulders of the tenoned (vertical) timber—transmits the load. The joint poses little compromise to the strength of either the beam or the post, and with the full width of the beam in the middle of its span bearing on the post, the beam is in little danger of shear failure or crushing damage (see the right drawing below).

The situation changes drastically, however, when the beam bearing the load is joined to a face of a post rather than to its top. The weight borne by the beam is transmitted through the base of the tenon, and as the load increases, it becomes necessary to find a way to increase the surface area at the base of the joint or crushing of the fibers at the bearing area becomes a possibility. In a simple mortise and tenon, the load-bearing capacity of the joint is thus limited to the shear value of the tenon alone. (Wood species with lower allowable shear stresses would require larger timbers and also larger tenons to support the same load.) Of course, there is a limit to how much a tenon can be enlarged, for the larger mortise required to house it can compromise post strength drastically.

The small bearing area of the tenon not only reduces the potential strength of the beam under load, but it also gives the connection only superficial ability

SIZING MORTISES AND TENONS

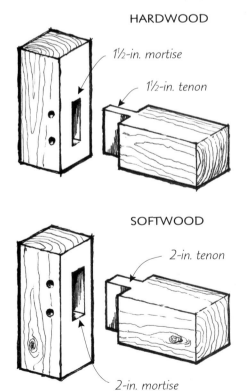

HARDWOOD

1½-in. mortise

1½-in. tenon

SOFTWOOD

2-in. tenon

2-in. mortise

DESIGNING FOR STRESS

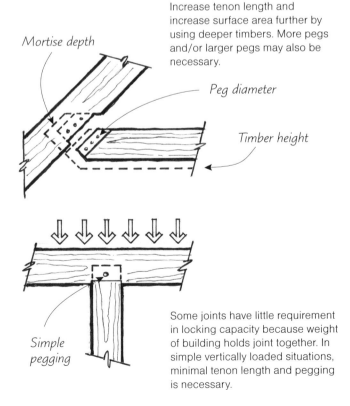

Increase tenon length and increase surface area further by using deeper timbers. More pegs and/or larger pegs may also be necessary.

Mortise depth

Peg diameter

Timber height

Simple pegging

Some joints have little requirement in locking capacity because weight of building holds joint together. In simple vertically loaded situations, minimal tenon length and pegging is necessary.

STRENGTHENING MORTISE-AND-TENON JOINTS

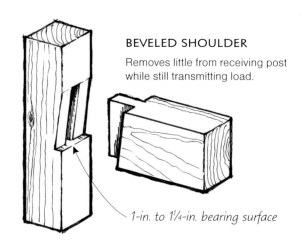

BEVELED SHOULDER

Removes little from receiving post while still transmitting load.

1-in. to 1¼-in. bearing surface

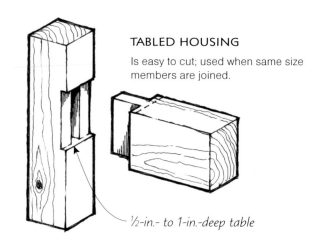

TABLED HOUSING

Is easy to cut; used when same size members are joined.

½-in.- to 1-in.-deep table

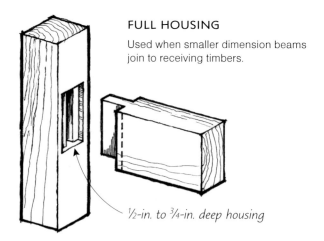

FULL HOUSING

Used when smaller dimension beams join to receiving timbers.

½-in. to ¾-in. deep housing

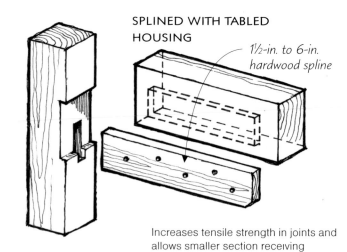

SPLINED WITH TABLED HOUSING

1½-in. to 6-in. hardwood spline

Increases tensile strength in joints and allows smaller section receiving timbers. Especially useful for softwoods and species weak in cross-grain tensile strength.

FOUR-WAY SPLINED JOINT

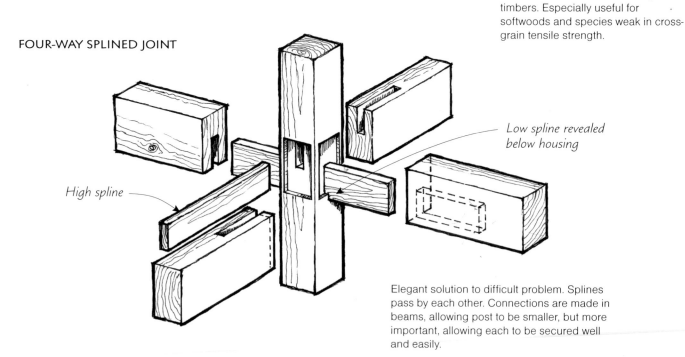

High spline

Low spline revealed below housing

Elegant solution to difficult problem. Splines pass by each other. Connections are made in beams, allowing post to be smaller, but more important, allowing each to be secured well and easily.

OPEN MORTISE-AND-TENON JOINTS

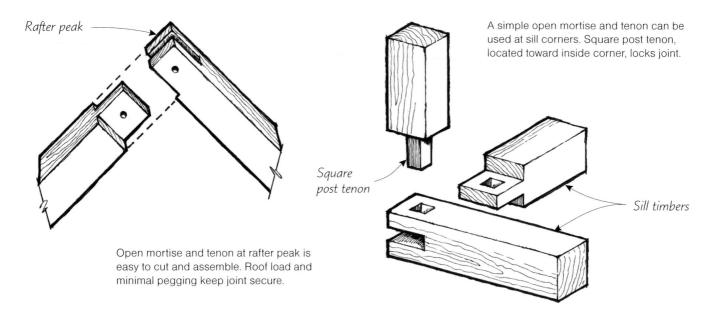

Rafter peak

Square post tenon

A simple open mortise and tenon can be used at sill corners. Square post tenon, located toward inside corner, locks joint.

Sill timbers

Open mortise and tenon at rafter peak is easy to cut and assemble. Roof load and minimal pegging keep joint secure.

An open mortise and tenon (sometimes called a tongue and fork) is often used to connect rafters at their apex and sills at the corners (see the drawings above). It's actually the mortise that is open, cut completely through the end of the timber. The tenon is cut as usual, but it's larger than in most other situations. When used for rafters, the mating members simply lean into each other and are pegged—the weight of the rafters and the roofing materials help keep the joinery secure. An open mortise and tenon at sill corners can be exactly the same joint, but placing it there is complicated by the fact that the sill usually receives a post at that location. Load support is not a problem because there is full bearing from the foundation. The best solution would be to use a square tenon from the post to lock the corner. Timbers are not often used for sills in any event because the time and expense is not usually warranted in basements where the aesthetic benefits aren't typically appreciated.

Lap joints

The other broad category of joints are those that lap one member over another. The receiving timber is notched to accept a tenon, or lap. Unlike the mortise-and-tenon joint, the tenon is not completely surrounded with wood when the joint is engaged; the joint is secured either with pegs or through the use of locking geometry.

I think lap joints evolved in response to raising techniques. Early English frames, for instance, which used a number of lap joints, were most often made by small groups of professionals and assembled one piece at a time. In this case, it would have been almost impossible to engage a mortise-and-tenon joint simultaneously at both ends, so lap joints were used instead. But as timber frames evolved in America, most raisings involved the entire community, and raising methods and joints were developed to take advantage of this manpower. Large sections of the frame, joined together on the ground to be raised at once, used primarily mortise and tenons. Lap joints, which are often inferior to their mortise-and-tenon counterparts, were kept to a minimum and were typically used only for the smaller members of the floor.

Today we use lap joints only for very minor timbers in the floor or roof (see the drawings on p. 48). The obvious problem with lap joints is that wood is removed in the compression area of the receiving beam, which can greatly reduce its bending strength. Laps should never cut entirely across the top of the beam, unless the timber was designed to have that wood removed. When a notch is made across the top of a timber, its effective capacity has been reduced to the remaining cross section. When this is done, usually a very small amount is removed and the joining timbers overlap. In most cases, at least 2 in. should be left in the center. When a dovetail is used, it need not penetrate deeply into the receiving timber for good locking—perhaps no more than 2 in. If a straight lap is used, however, the tenon has to be deep enough to hold a peg, which is usually a minimum of 3¼ in. long. The dovetail can therefore do the job with the least compromise to the supporting member. But the problem with the dovetail is that, as the wood shrinks, the joint becomes less effective in preventing withdrawal of the timber, which can be extreme when green timbers are used. To make sure the joint is securely locked and to reduce the effect of shrinkage, we use a tapered dovetail and drive dry wedges on both sides.

LAP JOINTS

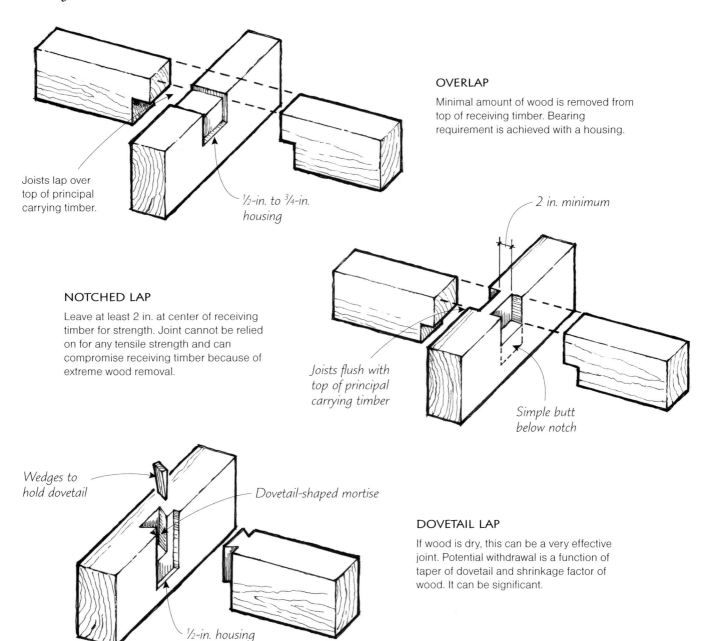

OVERLAP

Minimal amount of wood is removed from top of receiving timber. Bearing requirement is achieved with a housing.

Joists lap over top of principal carrying timber.

½-in. to ¾-in. housing

2 in. minimum

NOTCHED LAP

Leave at least 2 in. at center of receiving timber for strength. Joint cannot be relied on for any tensile strength and can compromise receiving timber because of extreme wood removal.

Joists flush with top of principal carrying timber

Simple butt below notch

Wedges to hold dovetail

Dovetail-shaped mortise

DOVETAIL LAP

If wood is dry, this can be a very effective joint. Potential withdrawal is a function of taper of dovetail and shrinkage factor of wood. It can be significant.

½-in. housing

Knee braces and collar ties are also sometimes joined with straight or dovetailed laps. The best use of a diagonal dovetail lap is for the joint between a collar tie and a rafter when the tension forces in the collar will be significant. The biggest drawback to using a lap joint for knee braces or collar ties is that it has little ability to resist torsion, which could wrest the joint apart.

Scarf joints are lap joints used to splice two or more shorter pieces into one long timber (see the left drawing on the facing page). Plates and sills most often demand scarfs because they tend to be the longest continuous members in a frame. There are hundreds of variations of scarf joints, with varying degrees of complexity and effectiveness. Because so much surface area must be cut to fit, all scarfs are relatively difficult to cut,

making them challenging and fun for the joiner. Unfortunately, no amount of precision can fasten the halves together without compromise. A scarf-jointed timber is not as strong as the solid one provided by nature. Scarfs shouldn't be used to support floor or roof loads if they fall in a span between posts. The best position for a scarf is usually directly over a post, where it can splice effectively without compromising the load-bearing capacity of the

SCARF JOINT

Opposed wedges compress and hold joint tight.

Keyed locator tenon

The scarf joint can be very strong and beautiful. This example is keyed in two directions and will be locked with wedges. Note that the brace is positioned to help support the scarf. The wood is Sitka spruce.

TYING JOINT

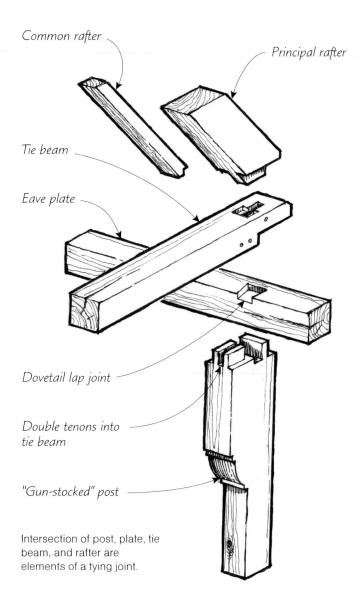

Common rafter

Principal rafter

Tie beam

Eave plate

Dovetail lap joint

Double tenons into tie beam

"Gun-stocked" post

Intersection of post, plate, tie beam, and rafter are elements of a tying joint.

beam (see the photo above). (The post tenon can be used as a key to keep the halves from slipping apart.) It is also possible to support a scarf joint with a knee brace. With various types of keys and wedges to lock the halves together, scarfs are strongest when employed to resist tension. Given their difficulty and limitations, it is sensible to minimize the number of these joints in the frame.

One of the most fascinating joints used in timber framing is actually a combination of joints used to connect several members. The intersection of a principal post, an eave plate, and a tie beam is known as a tying joint. Although there are many variations, almost every one includes at least two perpendicular tenons on the post, one to join to the plate and the other to join to the tie beam. The tie beam is then further con-

nected to the plate with a dovetail lap; it is also mortised to receive rafters. This type of connection was so prevalent through much of the development of English carpentry that not finding a tying joint in a surviving timber frame is somewhat remarkable.

A well-designed and crafted timber frame can last for centuries.

CHAPTER 3

FRAME DESIGN

Consider this: designing and making a timber frame may well be the most physically enduring act of your life. A well-designed and crafted frame can not only outlive its maker but also the skin that wraps it, the rooms that occupy it, and the generations of people who use and maintain it. In the number of centuries that can easily mark the age of a timber frame, it is safe to say the building will change. It is possible that hundreds of decorative ideas will take form and be removed, many interior walls will be built and taken down, appendages will be added, countless coats of paint will have been applied and scraped away, and a

complete chronicle of technology will pass through. In time, some of the timbers in the frame are certain to be hacked and battered, and a few might even be amputated, but like a silent and loyal sentinel, the basic form of the timber structure will remain, along with the intimate spaces enveloped by its brawny edges. Gaining respect for these implications is proper preparation for a task that will commit both human labor and forest resource in fair quantity.

In the preceding chapter, I reviewed the taxonomy of frame parts and styles, outlined the elements of timber-frame engineering, and covered the basics of joints and their uses. Now, I will delve a little deeper into the structural and architectural issues affecting frame design, with an intent to build an understanding of the timber frame as a complete building system. Like any construction methodology, timber framing has its subtle limitations and rules, along with those that are governed by building codes and common sense. It also has a full palette of options and techniques to achieve a wide-ranging possibility of form, function, and appearance. Between the constraints and the potentials, there are myriad elegant and timeless timber-frame possibilities for the homes of our new millennium.

Frame design arises from many issues, including: site, climate, spatial requirements, budget, architectural style, timber availability, aesthetic preference, and the skills of the maker. Usually, the requirements of the architecture and the building program are the primary influences on frame design. Form, floor plan, and frame configuration grow on paper together, not as distinctly separate elements. It makes no sense to design the frame according to some arbitrary criteria and then attempt to squeeze the floor plan into it. Likewise, the timber frame should not be forced to perform the awkward dance of a floor plan designed with no consideration for the frame. To bring the magic of the frame to the living space, there

must be a symbiotic relationship between them; to design this way, there needs to be full knowledge of both. This chapter is about the frame.

A STANDARD OF DURABILITY

Timber framing's heritage does not come from romantic legend nor from a misty, nostalgic memory. It's an active and living legacy: millions of timber-framed buildings are in use around the world. Indeed, there are many places where timber framing is still the dominant form of wood-frame construction. Contemporary timber-frame craftspeople in North America have become another link in the tradition, and as such, we have a responsibility to honor those practitioners who preceded us by not diminishing our inheritance, but instead by making some deposits into that consecrated account. We need to bring to this work the best of ourselves, our culture, and our technology while adhering to the visible and tangible standards we have been left.

Most important, timber-frame structures should be designed and built to reflect their strength and durability. Evidence suggests that 150 to 300 years is a practical standard of longevity for a timber frame and that 500 years is certainly possible. Perhaps the most appropriate objective is to build the frame to last as long as it took for the trees to grow that provided its timbers. Achieving this demands not only a quality of structure and enclosure to support and protect the building but also a quality of architecture and craftsmanship so that people will want to maintain and preserve it. No doubt, the second quality may be as important as the first, because if people don't like the house, it is doomed, no matter how well built.

One of the more straightforward requirements in considering the frame is that compromising the integrity of the structure is not one of the options. Though there is some built-in redundancy, each timber and each connection generally plays a significant role in the completed frame. Therefore, the imperatives of the structure simply

To withstand the heavy snow at 10,000 ft., the frame for a mountain chalet has big plates, deep rafters, and a big overhang. The timber ends are painted to protect them from the dry weather and the harsh sun.

can't be traded against. In the hierarchy of elements in the building, the frame that holds the whole thing up ought to hold dominion and be considered sacrosanct. What it needs should be satisfied in design and construction, and what it is should not be violated after construction.

Timbers and their connections are always designed specifically to meet expectations of loads and forces (see Chapter 2). There are no generic frames because there are no generic places. A frame on the windy coast of North Carolina is different from a frame in a Missouri hollow. When we design for an extreme snow load on a mountain chalet at 10,000 ft., we want to hold the frame up (see the photo on p. 51); when we design for a potential hurricane to hit a Caribbean bungalow, we want to hold the frame down. The structural requirements for a frame perched on an exposed hill are different from the requirements for a frame nestled into a protected hillside. Tucked away in the joints and the geometry of the frame, there should always be an intelligent response to the climate, the geology, and the site itself. Timber frames are not just tough brutes; done properly, they are also very smart.

In the design process, the shape, the size, and the organization of the frame is determined by the needs, the desires, and the budget of the owners. Once these decisions are made, however, the requirements of the structure should dominate over the fussy details of design. Major posts, for instance, should not be moved for temporary furniture arrangements. So, although timber frames and floor plans are usually designed together (as we will demonstrate in Chapter 4), it is also true that the frame submits to the floor plan and then the floor plan must in turn submit to the frame. This dance switches leaders. Another factor in the design of a frame is the choice of timbers to be used (see the sidebar at right).

COMMONLY USED TIMBER SPECIES

Northern red oak.

Eastern white pine. (Photo by Linda Cohen.)

The criteria for selecting the best timber species for a project usually involves an analysis of cost, aesthetics, strength, and availability. Where these issues rank in importance is a personal decision, but it isn't certain that cost and quality are directly related. In general, species that are regionally prevalent are also usually the least expensive. Therefore, it is almost always best to use local timbers when possible.

Oak
In the East, oak is used extensively for timber frames. In general, oak is strong, with a distinctive and lovely grain. It is appreciated by framers because it cuts well in its green state, but it also shrinks more than the softwoods because of its thicker cell walls. There are many types of oak, falling into two general groups: red and white. Structurally, there are four classifications—red oak, northern red oak, white oak, and mixed oak—with each allowing a number of subspecies. White oak tends toward a brown color and is appreciably more rot-resistant because of its closed-cell structure. Red oak tends to have a reddish overtone. Of these, northern red oak has the highest-allowable bending stress. The oaks are faring well in the recent growth generations, yielding timbers with few knots or structural defects from relatively young trees. Oak timbers have a practical maximum length of about 24 ft.

Eastern white pine
This is the only eastern softwood in wide use for timber framing. Good pine is quite beautiful, works nicely, and takes a finish well. It also does not shrink nearly as much as oak. The white-pine timbers we use are gleaned from trees that grew in third- and fourth-growth forests, so the wood is not nearly as clear and strong as its virgin-growth ancestor. (Eastern white pine was once of such impressive strength, size, and quality that it was claimed by the King of England for use as ship masts.) Therefore, when buying white pine today, it is very important to try to obtain the highest-quality timber available. Because of its lower-strength structural properties, white-pine beams will typically be larger in cross section than other species.

Shortleaf and longleaf pine
High strength and stiffness make this wood one of the most popular in the country. Shortleaf and longleaf pine grow in the Southeast. Because they grow straight, tall, and without a lot of lower branches, timbers are available in remarkable sizes and qualities. The grain is pronounced and pleasing, and the color is strong, with yellow overtones. These species also have a high rate of shrinkage, which ought to be moderated (with patient storage or a kiln) before use. Timbers from these trees can easily come in lengths up to 40 ft.

Shortleaf southern pine.

Douglas fir.

Sitka spruce.

Douglas fir

This western softwood is one of the premier structural woods in the world. Its strength is comparable to oak, and it is very stiff. Douglas-fir timbers typically have grain that is very tight and uniform. Even in smaller logs, the wood quality is very good, and the grain has fine character. Timbers in very long lengths are available. As with all of our timbers, we like to purchase from mills that buy from well-managed forests.

Sitka spruce

In color and character, Sitka spruce has the tones of white pine but the texture of oak. It is also strong, stiff, and light in weight. In fact, its strength-to-weight ratio made it the wood of choice for early airplane builders. Sitka spruce grows along the northwestern coast, from Oregon up to Alaska. Though this is clearly one of the premier wood product species in the world, being used for everything from musical instruments to highest-grade millwork, it is sold out of our national forests for use as paper pulp, which is disheartening.

White spruce

White spruce is primarily an Alaskan and Canadian wood. It tends to grow straight and tall and yields a very desirable structural product. It is primarily harvested for use in conventional construction 2x sizes but also makes a good-quality timber. White spruce is light in color and rather bland. Large sizes and long lengths are available.

Recycled timbers

The dominant structural materials in the heyday of the American Industrial Revolution were longleaf pine and Douglas fir. These woods were harvested with reckless abandon to build the mills, warehouses, and factories that sprouted throughout the country from the late 1800s to the late 1940s. Much of the material used in these construction projects was magnificent, having been harvested from the old-growth forests of both the Southeast and the Northwest. The timbers from these old buildings are sometimes so good that their qualities are essentially extinct. If the buildings must come down, all of the material should be reused if at all possible. Getting this wood and working with it is a labor of love, but the resulting timbers are beautiful, stable, and have stories to tell.

Laminated timbers

By cutting wood into smaller dimensions, drying it in that state, and then laminating it with glue to timber dimensions, a dry and very strong timber can be created. Laminations are also used where special shapes are desired. Timber frames can be entirely made with laminated material, or certain timbers can be laminated to create an arch or other unusual shape. The technology for making laminated timbers is advancing, with both quality and appearance improving. We often mix special laminated shapes with solid, sawn material to good effect.

Recycled Douglas fir.

Laminated timbers (from a project for Norm Abram and his wife, Laura).

TIMBER AVAILABILITY

Frame design should be greatly influenced by the available timbers. Simply put, the proposed design should call for timbers of a cross section and length that can be readily acquired. It would be frustrating to find that you had designed a frame around timbers you couldn't get. I've found that it's best to check with sawmills while designing.

Most mills have definite limitations; for instance, small outfits often can't cut anything longer than 16 ft. In addition, the trees themselves have their own natural limitations. Northeastern species, such as red oak and white pine, grow much shorter (and generally smaller in diameter) than Douglas fir and southern pine, for instance. Loggers also play a role in the availability of long timbers. If they are used to cutting for veneer or furniture stock, they habitually cut long, beautiful logs into short sections. We once gave 25-ft.-long measuring tapes as Christmas presents to a few loggers, feeling certain theirs must have stopped at 12 ft.

In a timber frame, the longest timbers tend to be plates, rafters, central posts, and tie beams. If you can't get timbers of appropriate length, it is probably wise to design a frame style that employs fewer long pieces. The common-rafter systems, because of their requirement for longitudinal plates and numerous rafters to spring from the eave to the ridge beam, usually demand many more long timbers in comparison to a common-purlin system, in which most of the timbers in the frame are not longer than the width of a bay. For example, if the frame had dimensions of 28 ft. by 36 ft. with a 10-in. pitch roof, a common-rafter system with midspan plates would need four 36-ft.-long timbers for the plates and about 20 timbers to be approximately 20 ft. long for the rafters. In the same frame, using the principal-rafter and common-purlin system, only eight 20-ft. timbers for the principal rafters would be necessary; the rest of the frame's timbers would not need to exceed the width of a bay, typically not more than 16 ft. (see the top photo at left).

In the principal-rafter and common-purlin system, the frame is segmented into distinct bays, which reduces the need for excessively long timbers and the making of scarf joints. This frame has three 16-ft. bays.

In this frame, of recycled fir, we were fortunate to have very long timbers available for the plates. Had that not been the case, scarf joints would have been required.

Long timbers can be created by scarfing shorter timbers together (see p. 49), but it is important to consider the time and skill necessary to make good scarf joints. Also, scarf joints must be well supported because they are intrinsically weaker than a solid timber. Due to their sometimes extreme length, plates often require at least one scarf connection, but there is good opportunity along the plate's length to locate the joint in relation to supporting posts and braces so that the strength of the frame is not jeopardized. On the other hand, to require a scarf joint for every common rafter would rarely be considered cost-effective or sound engineering. Frame design is best when it uses available resources and when it is kept simple.

SIMPLICITY, PRACTICALITY, AND ECONOMY

Frame design is best when it favors simplicity over complexity. One benefit of using timber-frame construction is the implicit dynamic spatial definition and organization in uncomplicated building forms. Part of the trick is the wood itself. Each timber has an individual identity and character. Spaces created by timbers don't have to turn geometric cartwheels to be interesting and unique. Within the natural shapes and shadows created by the wooden timbers, there is both a multifaceted mystery and a constantly unfolding character. Timbers and their spaces are never static. They are altered constantly by changes in daylight and illumination, and they wear their increasing age in a patina that is both unmistakable and ever more beautiful (see the top photo at right). In this context, artful design is oriented toward that which efficiently fulfills the many design functions and is most easily created.

Without leaving the boundaries of the established timber-frame construction systems, there is tremendous variety and flexibility. The permutations of timber arrangements and spatial possibility within the basic forms have not been exhausted in several thousand years and won't be in a thousand years to come. In timber frames, that which is sensible, practical, and honest is not also boring or stultifying. Each frame and each space has its own character and individuality. And even if the frame for the house was built using ideas and systems from many years ago, there is nothing old about how the resulting architecture and living spaces can look, feel, and function. In fact, there are many ways in which a timber-framed house is one of the most forward-looking building systems available, as you will see in the following chapters.

The craft of timber framing is practiced primarily at the timber intersections. How timbers are joined one to the

Timbers and the spaces they define have a dynamic and character that are both unique and constantly changing with light and time.

other greatly determines the frame's strength, and the skill with which it is accomplished greatly determines the frame's quality. Because there is complexity and challenge enough in basic frame shapes, frame design should simplify and reduce whenever possible. The best frames are those with the most economical use of timbers and the least-complicated joinery (see the photo at right). Engineering demands and architectural considerations will bring enough challenge to the timber framer and enough vitality to the frame without adding unnecessary timbers or creating unnecessary difficulties. Today, timber-frame design is aided by engineers, who can help in material selection and use.

Engineers play a role

Part of the value an engineer brings to timber-frame design is the calculated use of timbers. By bringing a complete structural-systems analysis to the project, including the values of the sheathing and planking materials, an engineer can reduce the board footage and piece count to only that which is essential. Because the spacing and sizing of timbers is done with a full

The best frames are often those with the most economical use of timbers and the least-complicated joinery. Recycled Douglas fir was used for this frame. (Photo by Paul Irwin.)

Common-rafter systems usually require significantly fewer pieces for the roof than other framing patterns. This frame, on the Columbia River, was built using a mix of species. (Photo by Jim Benson.)

awareness of the capacities of all related materials, the science of engineering is a great enhancement to this traditional and vernacular building system. A typical roof system, for instance, would have common rafters or common purlins on 4-ft. centers to receive planking or insulated panels, but it may be possible to increase the spacing to 6 ft. or even 8 ft. when appropriate materials are used for planking.

Also, keep in mind that the framing systems themselves have varying degrees of difficulty and timber economy. One advantage of a common-rafter system is that it can dramatically reduce the piece count in the roof system. In the 28-ft. by 36-ft. frame shown in the photo above, the number of pieces in the roof system, not including the eave plates, might only be 22 to 24 timbers, whereas the common-purlin system would need about 40 timbers between the purlins and the principal rafters.

The principal-rafter and principal-purlin system uses a great many timbers also and is additionally more difficult to cut and erect, as described in the last chapter. Each of the frame styles has its own attributes, which gives the designer more options to solve aesthetic and structural situations. But when all other things are equal, and the budget holds sway, opt for the easiest system with the fewest number of pieces. Simplifying the timber frame is a win-win situation. The frame is made more affordable, is more easily accomplished by the maker, and requires less resource from the forest.

Another factor in the design equation is wood shrinkage. The timber framer must take into account wood's natural tendency to shrink and expand with changes in humidity.

THE SHRINKAGE FACTOR

Timbers shrink as they dry. That's a reality. The questions are when, where, and to what effect (see the sidebar on the facing page). For the most part, air-drying and kiln-drying are not terribly practical. Air-drying requires too much patience (two to five years) and kiln-drying too much money (two to four months in the kiln). Therefore, most frames are built with timbers that will eventually shrink to a somewhat smaller dimension and different shape. Even when the timbers are essentially dry, in most cases there is still likely to be some shrinkage as they move from the ambient relative humidity of the exterior conditions to the warm and protected environment of a house. Good timber frames can be built from green timbers or dry timbers, but it is important to design the frame accordingly.

Timbers recycled from dismantled buildings are one of the primary sources of dry timbers. Reusing timbers comes naturally to timber framing and seems to be a part of its tradition. I have inspected many Early American timber frames only to discover that some of the timbers clearly had been used in other frames prior to becoming a part of the one I was studying. One of the frames I inspected was built in the early 1700s. Just how old were the previously used timbers that were a part of its frame? This kind of recycling and reuse does not often happen with 2x4 studs. Each piece is too small and insignificant to survive the blunt and brutal intent of the typical wrecking crew. Timbers survive the demolition process because someone will pay for them. My company pays for them because they are worth buying. Even when the timbers are significantly damaged on their outer surfaces, there is almost always usable (and usually beautiful) timber available underneath. All it takes to find the beauty is careful and minimal resawing.

Scattered throughout the country are small mills providing timbers with low

MOISTURE AND SHRINKAGE IN TIMBERS by Robert L. (Ben) Brungraber

Wood is just a bundle of long, strong straws (or cells made of cellulose) oriented along the tree trunk and bound to one another with a semi-strong glue (lignin). Living wood is loaded with water, most of which dries away after the tree is felled.

Wood behaves in two very distinct ways as its moisture content decreases. The first water to leave is the "free water," found within the cells and used as a living medium. Although the free water is the majority of the water that eventually leaves, the only effect its departure has on the wood is to lighten it—much as a soaked sponge is lightened, but not reshaped, by squeezing. After the free water is gone, the "bound water" starts to go. This water is located

within the cell walls, is bound to the cellulose molecules, and is part of the very structure of the material. As this water leaves, the wood changes; continuing to lighten, but increasing in strength and stiffness, while shrinking the cellulose. As the cellulose shrinks, so do the cell walls, and therefore the wood itself shrinks and distorts—just as the squeezed sponge would shrink and distort if you left it on a windowsill for a week.

Luckily, as the cells' walls shrink, only their diameter decreases and not their length. This means that a full-sawn, wet, 8-ft. long 6-in. by 8-in. timber turns into a stable 5½-in. by 7⅝-in. piece—but one virtually 8 ft. long.

Saying that wood only shrinks "across the grain" will not adequately predict the expected shape changes. Because of the way a tree grows and lays up new cells, wood will shrink about twice as much in girth (circumferentially) as it does in diameter (radially). The difference in these two shrinkage rates means the cross-sectional shape of a rectangular timber cut from green wood will be distorted, as well as reduced, when the timber dries. Timbers with heart centers respond to this shrinkage differently than timbers free of heart centers (see the drawings below).

Timber shrinkage is very like the phenomenon of how steel hoops for wood barrels are tensioned by preheating them and letting them shrink over

dry and stable wooden staves. This is fine for steel hoops; in fact their tension holds the barrel together, but it does not pass unnoticed in a timber. This tension tends to separate the straws, resisted only by that semistrong lignin. Tension perpendicular to the grain ("tension perp," in the trade) is probably wood's weakest property. In fact, the shrinkage-induced tension stresses are usually higher than the lignin's fracture capacity, and the stresses are relieved only by opening a "check."

It is important to note that this check only separates one cell from another—it doesn't break any of the cells. Therefore checks, shrinkage, and distortion have no affect on the overall strength of a timber.

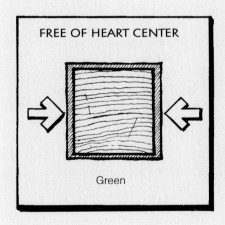

FREE OF HEART CENTER

Green

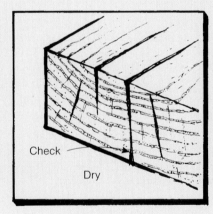

Check

Dry

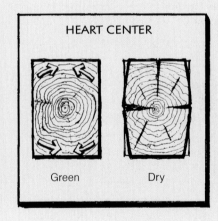

HEART CENTER

Green   Dry

moisture content without air- or kiln-drying. Some are cutting standing dead trees in areas that have been burned or have suffered a blight; some are going after "buckskins" and "deadfalls," which are barkless and fallen logs lying on the forest floors. A few mills are even willing to air-dry timbers for a season or so as a service to the timber framers. There are also attempts being made to find the appropriate technology to kiln-dry large-section timbers economically.

In the meantime, though, most timber frames must be built with timbers that are bound to shrink after construction. Timber frames are affected by the cross-grain shrinkage in two ways: one is primarily aesthetic, an issue about which we have only moderate influence; the other is potential dimensional changes in the structure, a problem we can substantially control in frame design.

Aesthetical considerations
Shrinkage opens gaps at the connections and will cause checks on the tim-

ber surfaces. There is little affect on the structure, so the topic of discussion is appearance, which is a matter of opinion. One opinion (mine) is that good-quality timbers look great, before and after they have dried. Mainly, I like my timbers from the trees of our natural forests, and I like their gnarly, independent response to being captured into a human conception. Some do not go gently—I like them too, sometimes especially. I don't like photographs of wood grain that are forgeries of wood paneling, and I don't want my timbers

Salvaged hand-hewn white oak was used to make the frame for this home. The timbers had been in service for about 250 years before they were used here; they can last for centuries more.

to be "perfect" laminates or extrusions. Give me the checks, the twists, the knots, and the wane that remind me of the beautiful—and unruly—forests that serve up the wood.

Good timber framers can minimize the visual "defects" by orienting the timbers in the frame in a manner that will not reveal the faces where the greatest amount of checking is likely to occur. They also house the joinery to hide some of the shrinkage at the connections. These kinds of tricks (and many others) can help, but not nearly as much as learning to appreciate wood's natural qualities.

How shrinkage affects structure

The wood shrinkage in timber frames that affects the dimensions of the structure is most important. Remembering that wood shrinkage occurs almost entirely across the grain and is negligible along the grain, the most important consideration in frame design is the ex-

tent to which the structure will be reduced in height as the horizontal members dry. In the building's length and width, the affect of shrinkage does not tend to be significant because minor separations are revealed at each connection rather than the accumulated affect showing up at the edges.

Vertically, though, the matter is different. The compression load of the building presses downward, so any shrinkage will reduce the building's height accordingly. The problem lies primarily with beams that interrupt the posts in the frame. When they shrink, so does the building. For this reason, timber frames should not be built like platform frames, with one building layer built upon another, for this would introduce too many horizontal beams and allow excessive shrinking in the frame. Frames are designed with posts that pass through the layers, which fundamentally reduces or eliminates cross-grain shrinkage. Whenever possi-

ble, beams for floor levels and connecting beams should connect to the post faces rather than being positioned on top. In this way, a floor level may shrink a little (and uniformly), but the building's height is not altered by the intermediate beam changes.

Any frame system with plates should be carefully analyzed to anticipate the probable accumulated shrinkage. A large beam can shrink by ⅜ in. or more if the timber is completely green. With the rafters sitting on top of the plate, the two members' total shrinkage could be more than easily absorbed by the finishes. Another example of a situation with potentially unacceptable shrinkage is the tie-beam connection. Beautiful and clever as it is, the connection piles the cross grains of a plate, a tie beam, and a rafter on top of one another, which, when the wood is green, is simply too much inevitable shrinkage for most of our buildings to absorb. There are several solutions: 1) Don't pile beams on top of one another. 2) Use plates that are dry or dimensionally stable (pretty dry). 3) Use a principal-rafter system in which the posts pass from the foundation to the rafter and all the beams fall between. My company uses all three of these strategies on a regular basis. With recycled timbers, we will design for common-rafter systems and even tie-beam joinery, but with purely green material, we tend to choose principal rafters and through posts.

RAISING METHOD

Because of the size and weight of the timbers used, another important issue to consider during the design phase is how the raising will be accomplished.

While designing the frame, plan the raising. Will you be lifting bents or walls? With a crane or by hand? Will there be separate roof trusses? It's necessary to know something about the site to determine what is possible. We once arrived on a much ballyhooed "beautiful" site only to discover that, yes, it was just a few hundred feet from the road, but it was practically straight up. We had a difficult enough time getting tools on the site, never mind the timbers. We seriously considered a helicopter but finally wound up transporting the timbers one at a time with a bulldozer. The raising proceeded slowly as we hung from trees and invented lifting mechanisms.

Most timber frames today are raised with a crane. It's less expensive than hiring a lot of people and very much safer. The only reasons to raise a frame by hand is because there are a lot of people available at no cost and the frame is small enough to do the task safely. I never recommend a hand-raising unless it is approved and directed by a master timber framer. It's a great deal of fun and a terrific event for a community, but it is hard to imagine anything quite as dangerous. If you thought to write to me about the advisability of proceeding with a hand-

Assembled bents can be extremely heavy. Their weight, the conditions of the site, and the capacities of available cranes for lifting should be known in the early stages of design. This frame is oak.

raising on your own: forget it, the answer is already written—please don't.

As the frame is being designed, it is important to know about the conditions on the site and the lifting capacity and cost of the available cranes. For instance, if the site does not allow the crane to get close to the heavy frame sections being lifted, it could require a large-capacity crane with a long boom, which, if you can find one to hire, could cost significantly more money than a smaller crane. The raising possibilities are determined by the design of the frame. When complete bents are assembled, including its principal rafters, the whole section might easily weigh 2,000 lb. to 4,000 lb., or more (see the photo above). That's a lot. If those bents needed to be built a long way from where the crane can reasonably park, there might be some unpleasant surprises. (I once received a bill from a crane company for "trying to lift timber frame." It was a hard check to write.) Therefore, as the frame is being planned, think about the sections that will be assembled, their weight, and their distance from the crane as they are being placed in the frame.

Principal-rafter systems tend to require larger preassembled sections than common-rafter systems. In common-rafter systems, typically the sections are lifted up to plate level and then the rafters are put on separately. Of course, preassembled wall sections might also be very heavy, but it is much easier to separate wall assemblies (than bent assemblies) into smaller units for lifting, if that becomes necessary.

Lifting complete frame units, be they walls or bents, allows the raising to be accomplished quickly and can make for stronger frames than those that have been designed to be lifted in smaller units. For example, the frame on p. 62 has central posts that spring from the deck to the collar beam. This bent section (as with most principal-rafter bents) is designed to be assembled and raised as a unit; it would be difficult to piece it together in the air. Due to this organization, there are no obvious hinge points; the frame design imparts great stiffness to the structure. On the other hand, the frame on p. 63 would be assembled in wall sections up to the eave plate. After the walls were in place, the angled rafter struts would be set into place separately. Essentially, the bents of this example were assembled when the walls and rafters were connected. One of the disadvantages of this particular frame type is the clear separation between the roof assembly and the wall assembly as structural elements, leaving a hinge line at the eaves. To stiffen the frame, it would be important to have roof braces parallel to the ridge and wall sheathing with sufficient strength to keep the end walls rigid.

With these technical details in mind, the timber-frame home can now begin to take shape on paper, based on the needs and desires of the owners.

BUILDING FORM

Site conditions, building program, and architectural considerations are the primary influences on the shape of the building. Whether the building is linear or boxy, tall or low, has many appendages or none, conforms to a sloped site or sits on a flat spot are all determinants to which the frame must be adjusted.

Timber frames adapt well to most needs but not all desires. Low-profile buildings work as well as steeply pitched, tall buildings (see the bottom photo below), and we don't have difficulty conforming to hillside sites (see the top photo below). Adding forms or extensions to a core volume is easy also because the links are readily available in the large openings between posts. The

roof systems are also able to accept intersecting gables and dormers when necessary. What timber frames resist is the dancing geometric roof forms that seem to have become popular in the 80s and 90s. America's suburban "development" architecture in conventional stud construction is apparently striving to add value by adding roof facets. Most often the convoluted

This house was built into a hillside. Appropriate to its context, the architecture is vertical, and the spaces in it soar. Its frame is Sitka spruce. Note the mix of common rafters and common purlins in different parts of the building.

This building was designed horizontally to fit the site. The intention was toward simplicity and a low profile. Douglas fir was used for the frame.

shapes don't even create livable spaces; they're just complex roofs as ornament. Timber frames can do what is necessary, but this razzle-dazzle without purpose is too wasteful of timbers, craftspeople, and money. Building with timbers keeps the architecture honest.

Honest but not boring, limiting but not stultifying, timber framing charges its architecture to justify the complexities by making use of the spaces it defines. But it is within the language of the craft to create a large variety of shapes and countless arrangements. My company has built some roof systems with plenty of dormers, some with arrays of hips and valleys, and some with both. Many of our buildings make unusual twists and turns to fit sites and other design requirements, and some are unusual shapes. Octagons, for instance, are not terribly difficult (see the top photo below).

Designing buildings with multiple additive elements, or extensions, is easy to achieve either as a part of the original conception or as future additions. Natural openings between columns are

An octagon frame is flanked by two gabled buildings to form the basis for this dramatic house in its sylvan setting.

Gable extensions attach most easily to principal-rafter and common-purlin buildings when they are designed to fit the dimensions of the bays. In this oak frame, the extensions and the central dormer all are aligned with principal posts.

CONNECTING TO A BENT-FRAMED BUILDING

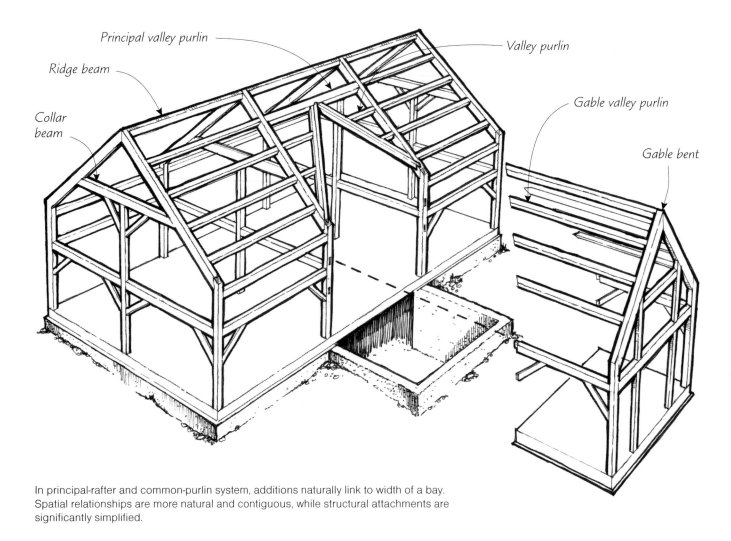

Ridge beam

Principal valley purlin

Valley purlin

Collar beam

Gable valley purlin

Gable bent

In principal-rafter and common-purlin system, additions naturally link to width of a bay. Spatial relationships are more natural and contiguous, while structural attachments are significantly simplified.

the most logical places to make the spatial and structural attachments. Because of this, the bay widths and the spaces between posts in the bent planes become the logical dimensions of many types of additions (see the bottom photo on p. 61). This allows the additive forms to have spaces that are visually and structurally contiguous with the spaces defined by the core timber frame, while the principal posts, beams, rafters, and purlins help to bear the loads and receive the necessary attachments (see the drawing above). This is especially evident on the eave sides when intersecting roof members are involved. Compound-angle connections are difficult enough, without

also passing through principal rafters for an addition that is wider than the bay's width.

When intersecting building forms are contemplated in widths greater than a typical bay (not usually more than 16 ft.), a common-rafter system, in which walls are the primary building element, can be the solution (see the drawing on the facing page). When walls are built, the arrangement requires that the posts be aligned parallel to the building's ridge beam, but not in the other direction. This factor makes it relatively easy to adjust the post locations to accommodate the width and location of the intersecting building.

SPATIAL DEVELOPMENT

Within a given building form, there are a vast number of possibilities for how the timbers could be arranged to create the building's shape (see the drawings on pp. 64 and 65). Not only are there a variety of framing systems, but there are also nearly limitless arrangements of posts and beams within the typical framing configurations. The organization of the spaces and the look and feel of the individual rooms, as well as their articulation with each other, are hugely influenced by the location, pattern, density, size, species, finish, and orientation of the individual timbers. Because there are so many options and

CONNECTING TO A WALL-FRAMED BUILDING

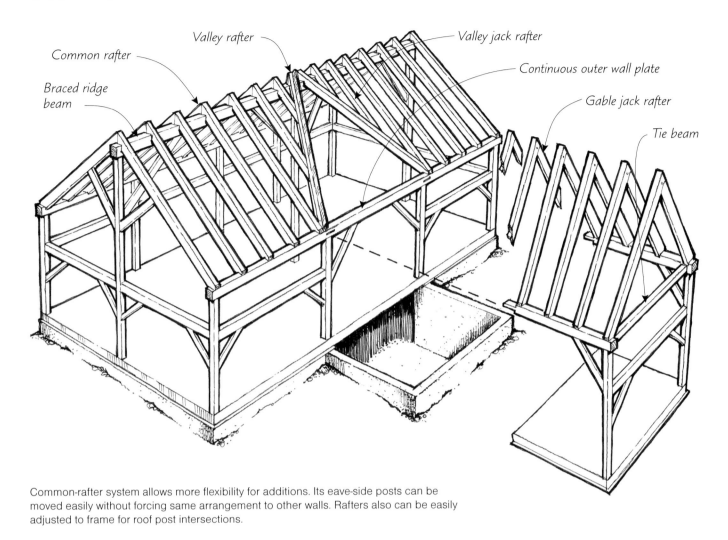

Common rafter

Valley rafter

Valley jack rafter

Braced ridge beam

Continuous outer wall plate

Gable jack rafter

Tie beam

Common-rafter system allows more flexibility for additions. Its eave-side posts can be moved easily without forcing same arrangement to other walls. Rafters also can be easily adjusted to frame for roof post intersections.

so much potential between a pile of timbers and the completed timber frame, this construction system demands more creativity, sensitivity, and knowledge than most building techniques. A major objective of timber-frame design is to use the timbers for more than structure, to integrate the living areas with the timbers in a balanced and harmonious way.

The natural spaces in timber-frame houses are bays and aisles. Bays are the areas between bents and are often the dominant spaces because of the strong influence of the large section timbers typical in the posts and beams of a bent. These spaces run from the front to the rear of the house on each level. Most timber-frame houses have from

two to four bays, the common width of which ranges from 8 ft. to 16 ft. Typically there are three bays, with the outer two being wider and containing the primary living areas. This arrangement dominated home design in early America. They were known as "double-pile" houses. Spatial delineation was the common element, but the finishes and material choices were left to the builder and the owner.

Running perpendicular to the bays are the aisles, which, like bays, are usually not much wider than about 16 ft. If a frame is designed as a series of walls instead of bents, aisles are often more natural spaces. The posts in the walls must be parallel to one another, but in

the bent direction interior posts do not have to align, which offers some design flexibility. If defining the spaces with aisles is more beneficial to room layout, this is one of the best reasons of all for designing a frame with plates.

Barns are often arranged in aisles, having a central entrance for vehicles at the gable end, which allows the unloading of equipment and animal feed into the outer aisles. Most timber-frame churches and halls are also built like this, but in houses the proportion of common living areas is usually more conducive to the use of bays. To emphasize this point, imagine a building about 30 ft. wide by 36 ft. long with equally spaced posts, creating three

ONE BUILDING SHAPE: MANY FRAMING OPTIONS

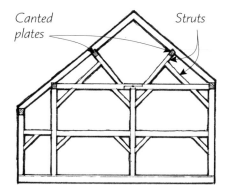

Canted plates

Struts

This system features canted plates, supported by struts. Primary pre-assembled units would be two tall walls, lower wall, and two canted assemblies. Shrinkage is likely to occur at five plates and tie beam. Scarf joint in tie beam is supported by a post.

FRAMING SPACES WITH COMMON RAFTERS AND PLATES

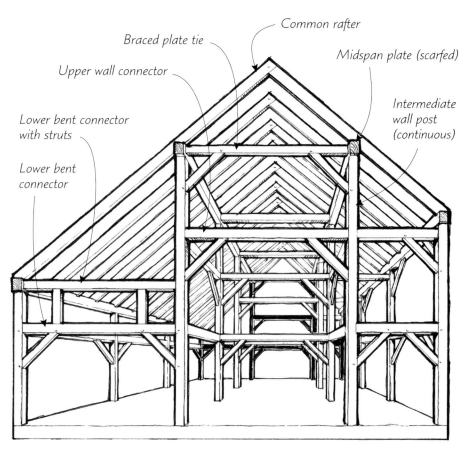

Braced plate tie

Common rafter

Upper wall connector

Midspan plate (scarfed)

Lower bent connector with struts

Intermediate wall post (continuous)

Lower bent connector

When walls are primary structural unit, aisles become natural spatial configuration. Strong lines of plates and perpendicular soaring rafters influence dynamics of space as well as efficiency of structure.

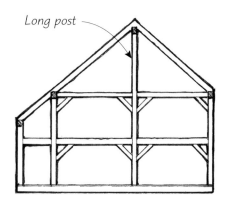

Long post

Long post, stretching from foundation to ridge beam, passes through building layers, stiffening eave line and giving support to ridge beam. Bracing between central post and ridge beam further strengthens structure. Primary raising units are the four walls.

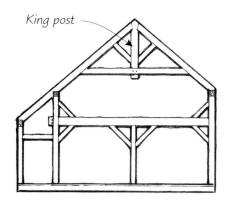

King post

King-post truss creates clear span in second-floor area. Open areas would be dramatic, but connection between lower frame and trusses is feeble and would require further stiffening with sheathing. Three walls and trusses would be pre-assembled for raising.

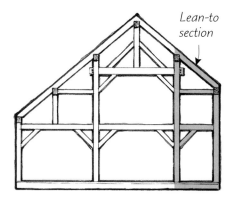

Lean-to section

Lean-to section of frame integrated into bent section, rather than being additive element. For raising, six wall units would have to be built, making this configuration complicated. One-point load on middle of beams should be avoided, if possible.

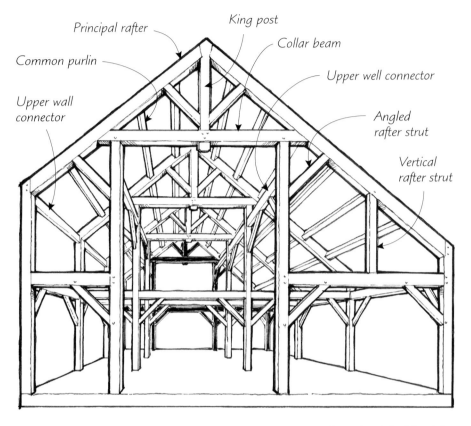

Principal rafter

King post

Common purlin

Collar beam

Upper wall connector

Upper well connector

Angled rafter strut

Vertical rafter strut

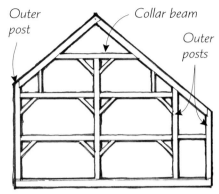

Outer post

Collar beam

Outer posts

This logical and simple bent arrangement allows extended rafters to create additional space on one side, while rest of bent is symmetrical. Outer posts rise to rafters, and middle one rises to collar beam. Shrinkage of individual members will have very little effect on building's height.

With bents as primary structural unit, bays are dominant spaces. Bents break building into logical segments, interrupting longitudinal timber arrangement. Common purlins segment rising roof, which can be an important design influence. In all of these examples, the entire bent would be raised as a unit.

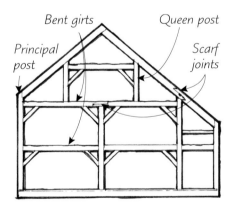

Bent girts

Queen post

Principal post

Scarf joints

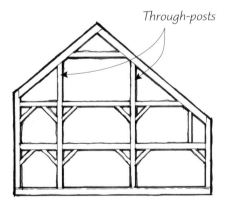

Through-posts

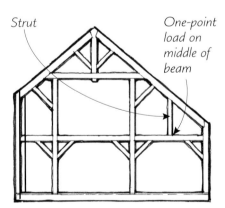

Strut

One-point load on middle of beam

Short timbers and scarf joints make up bent. Queen posts are classic, but their point load on upper bent girt should be carefully analyzed. For raising, bents could be assembled and raised entirely, or broken into three sections: 1) three principal posts and bent girts, 2) lean-to section, and 3) upper roof assembly.

Structurally, this is probably best of bent assemblies. All posts connect directly to rafters, which reduces settling to rafters themselves. Through-posts also make bent stiff and strong.

Location of posts creates unique spatial sizes and qualities. This configuration has large central aisle and narrow aisle on building's tall wall. Strut on lower side transfers one-point load to middle of beam, which should be avoided.

Frame Design

With a clear-span king-post truss, the space in the structure is entirely open. The living room is on one side, and the kitchen-dining areas are on the other. The primary frame is northern red oak, but recycled southern pine was used for the glass wall.

bays and three aisles. The bays would be 12 ft. on center, and the aisles would be 10 ft. on center. It is easier to think of a potential living space as half a bay (12 ft. by 15 ft.) than half an aisle (10 ft. by 18 ft.). While a large room might well use an entire bay, for it to use an entire aisle (10 ft. by 36 ft.) would be very difficult and awkward. Most of the rooms thus fit within bays, with one or two spaces being defined with aisles.

The most efficient way to use space within a house is to stack living areas from outside wall to outside wall in each bay and aisle. But what is most efficient is not always most desirable. Often it is advantageous to leave areas open through several levels or to change floor and ceiling levels in certain areas to improve proportions or to create visual distinctions between spaces. We often leave a portion of a central bay open to allow heat to travel into the other living levels, but (thinly disguised) this is also an excuse to create a view of more of the frame and to introduce a feeling of spaciousness and drama to the home. It's also possible to leave a bay completely open, front to back and floor to peak. This is especially effective in an otherwise small and tightly organized house. Taken to extremes, efficiently used space sometimes feels miserly and cramped, but just a small touch of "spatial generosity" can mitigate that entirely.

Level changes in a floor plan can be used effectively to follow the slope of the site or to alter the feeling of a room. Because in timber framing we are not confined to common stud lengths, within a given timber bay or aisle it is possible to have floors (and ceilings) on several levels. This also can solve the structural problem of several joints intersecting a post at the same spot, thereby weakening the post. The builders of old barns almost always put floors and haylofts on several different levels, as joinery dictated. There is no reason why this framing consideration can't be used as a design feature in houses as well. Public spaces and places for entertaining, such as living rooms, family areas, and dining rooms, should have higher ceilings than places for contemplation or intimacy.

The living area in this house is arranged in an aisle space instead of in a bay. A portion of the middle bay is left open for dramatic effect and air circulation. A small open area can make otherwise cramped areas feel expansive.

When bays and aisles are not large enough in themselves to serve a design purpose adequately, it's possible to enclose an area with its own frame. Using a clear-span trussed-roof system, not only is it possible to create a large, unobstructed area (usually with a cathedral ceiling), but such a space also allows the decorative effect of the timber frame to blossom. In most situations, the truss would have beams spanning the width of the space—a king-post truss is a good example (see the photo on the facing page). The drama of the open roof is best suited to living and family rooms, but we have used it for bedrooms, entries, kitchens, porches, and even baths; the extra volume in the open roof might be an inefficient use of space (depending on whether there is enough volume to be considered usable), but it is surprising

how easy it is to trade a little economic folly for a fine feeling. Remember that just because this option calls for a whole frame, there's no reason why the frame has to be large. The idea works just as well with small spaces.

Timber frames define and exalt space for living. The posts and beams make the restraints and potentials both visible and natural, increasing the freedom to arrange and rearrange as desire and need suggest. With both structural integrity and spatial flexibility, in time the space plan is certain to be modified or altered completely, with the changing patterns constantly anchored to the immutable timbers.

Developing the floor plan with the frame is not a leap of faith—it's a heap of planning. At this stage, the frame recedes and begins to play its role as the definition of space.

CHAPTER 4

HOME DESIGN

A timber-frame home is so influenced by the integrity of its structure and the beauty of its timbers that one might infer that a good frame automatically makes a good house. It can be tempting to design the frame first, to make it strong and theoretically good-looking, and to superimpose the floor plan upon it later. There's a comforting linearity to this way of thinking—you take care of the more objective structural issues, such as timber size, joinery, and beam spans first, before turning to the subjective design issues, such as spatial orientation, stylistic expression, proportion, and so on. Indeed, if you work this way, you will probably be rewarded with a very nice frame. You also run the risk of creating a pretty miserable home. For it is the conscientious and deliberate melding of all the elements into an integrated and seamless whole that draws out the full potential of timber framing as an architectural medium. To underestimate the importance of the abstract considerations is to risk making a house that sits awkwardly on its site, that has an irresolvable poor traffic pattern, or that simply fails to be attuned to people and the environment. Timber frames define spaces, but not before the purpose of, and aspirations for, the spaces have been understood and configured. Remember that the purpose of a building is to define and enclose spaces. The content is the spaces; the context is the form and substance of the spatial definition—in this case, the timber frame and the skin that wraps it.

Good house design is hard work, made more so by the fact that the path to it is not clearly mapped. You can enter any library and find volume after volume about construction procedure, with endless detail on how to make a house strong and safe. But how to make it look and feel good? How to make it work well with the needs of the people who live in it? This is much more illusory stuff, rife with theories and opinions. Perhaps the only generalization you can make about timber-frame house design is that timbers are not inherently a design or spatial benefit; if they enhance and simplify instead of cluttering and complicating, you can bet it was planned to be that way. It didn't just happen.

In this chapter, I'll share some ideas about designing timber-frame houses, beginning with the all-important preliminary work. Although much of this material does not contain the word timber, I do not digress, for good timber-frame house design is based on principles and practices of design that are good for any house. After covering these initial design concepts, including the building program and site study, I'll look at generating floor and frame plans. Finally, I'll backtrack a little to explore some ways to use the natural spaces created by timbers and to discuss some of the design options that various arrangements of timbers provide both for the whole house and for each room. Of course it's impossible to learn to design a house from reading one chapter in a book, but there's much to be gained from developing an understanding of each element in the design process.

RULING NOTIONS AND THE BUILDING PROGRAM

It may seem obvious, but nothing is quite as important in design as understanding and addressing the reasons why a building needs to be built. Every house is born as a notion, and this original motivating idea is the seed from which the plan of the house grows and is ultimately defined. The first step is therefore to open that conceptual notion to scrutiny. It may be lofty or mundane; it may concern stylishness or a desire to conserve energy. It may express how a family wants to live or focus on a relationship with the outdoors, with artwork, or with furniture. Most often there are several notions at work simultaneously, but too often there is one that rules all the others and paints its colors into every corner of the house.

A few examples illustrate how diverse and powerful ruling notions can be. One of the most common notions I see establishes a particular architectural style as a design prerequisite. In other words, the house is already a cape (or a ranch or an underground house) before there is any understanding of the site, regional influences, or the living requirements of the occupants. This may seem innocent enough, but it's not. For while the strongly vertical lines of alpine architecture look great in the mountains, they look out of place on the plains. And while sprawling horizontal architecture may fit a family's image of expansive living, it might not fit their craggy hillside site. People will probably always have a preferred architectural style, but this should be considered an ambition of the design and not a ruling notion.

Another ruling notion I frequently see concerns the timber frame itself. People often approach my company for a frame of a particular size and shape but don't have any idea of how the frame will relate to the living areas—this will be worked out later, we're told. We try to point out that "a 24x36 saltbox frame" is not the right starting point for a home. Under these conditions, the features of the frame can turn into obstacles, and the building process can turn into a remodeling project as the floor plan is forced to submit entirely to structural parameters.

A recent ruling notion I encountered focused on a very fine, very large Oriental rug, inherited by our clients. They had never been able to enjoy the rug because their living quarters were too small, so when they approached us about a house, they wanted to make sure there was plenty of room for the rug. A second notion was that the master bedroom should be on the first floor—no more going up and down stairs for them. These people were not wealthy and could not afford a large house, so you can imagine the difficulty of designing a small house with room for a 24x30 rug and a downstairs master bedroom. All early renditions of the plans had small, elongated spaces (kitchen, dining, entry, master bedroom, and bath) gathered around the rug. It finally became essential to spend some time talking about these ruling notions. The rug stayed, ruling as ever, but the master bedroom went upstairs.

Good house design attempts to balance function, economy, form, and energy performance into a unified package. But unless the ruling notions of a project are diagnosed and their consequences projected, the design will probably be thrown off center. Plans can still be drawn, and the house can

Good house design balances needs and desires with budget and site requirements.

certainly be built, but strong forces will be at work, and they will elbow their way into the design time and time again. Obviously, overlooking economic realities could mean that the ceremonial first meal is cooked on a hibachi in a drafty shell. A house built to satisfy an artistic compulsion might well be better to look at than to live in. Energy conservation is important, but there is a big difference between living on the inside of a solar collector and being comfortable. After defining the ruling notion, put it on the back shelf, address the many other design issues, and come back to it later. If it survives as the dominating force, it deserves to be.

The next step is to create a building program. A building program is nothing more than a list of requirements for the house, the landscape, and exterior activities. It should include not only physical requirements but also personal ideas about lifestyle. It might be important, for instance, that the living room be large enough for two settings of furniture, receive direct sunlight, and have easy access to an exterior terrace. If it is important that the master bedroom be separate from other bedrooms and that it have enough room for morning exercise, this should be noted on the building program. After the program is completed, it's much easier to look at practical construction issues—how the house will be sited, how the rooms will be arranged—and the many decisions relating to materials.

Potential home builders should use the sample building program in the appendix on p. 228 and think carefully about each answer. Be sure that when you've finished you have described the home you aspire to build. This does not mean that the final design will satisfy every whim. It simply means you determine the trade-offs while the plans are being drawn, instead of discovering them later as faults. So be prepared for the compromises that you will inevitably have to make.

Molding a house to its site is one of the most important aspects of house design. This house nestles into the steep contours overlooking a river.

THE SITE STUDY

When the building program is complete, it's time to study the site and roughly describe the house that will sit upon it. Understanding the site is an essential part of design, and having a complete house design prior to a knowledge of where it will be built is like buying the pants before you know who will be wearing them. Placement of the house should be sensitive to land contours, trees, flora, views, and sunlight. At the same time, seek summer shade, protection from the wind, and isolation from noise. Economics suggest careful consideration of the location and expense of the driveway, the septic system, and the water supply.

Laying out a building on a site is mysterious work. Whether the site brims with potential or is featureless, there is always one place for the house that is better than any other. You wander about the property like a lost divining rod in search of that precious spot. It will help, during this part of the work, to take an analytical approach. Begin by drawing a site plan that shows all the major features of the land (see the drawing below). The easiest way to start the site plan is to photocopy or trace the site survey map. (If a site survey does not exist, consider having one made.) At the very least, use a description from the deed and draw the site and its contours from your own measurements and observations. On the plan, show all positive and negative features, such as the trees that should be saved, lowland or swamps, creeks, views, roads, potential access directions, and neighboring houses.

Solar-gain considerations

Of paramount importance in siting is access to the sun; therefore, also include on the plan the direction of solar south. Achieving a good relationship with solar south is probably the simplest part of siting because it can be done scientifically and reaps measurable rewards. Using only good orientation and proper proportions of glass and insulation, passive-solar houses are no longer considered difficult or awkward. Their design begins with the two basic siting rules that follow.

The first rule is that the house should face as closely as possible toward solar south to receive the maximum amount of solar heat. Solar south is not the same as magnetic south, because of longitudinal differences and variations in the earth's magnetic field. There is a simple method for determining solar

SAMPLE SITE PLAN AND SAMPLE BUBBLE DIAGRAM

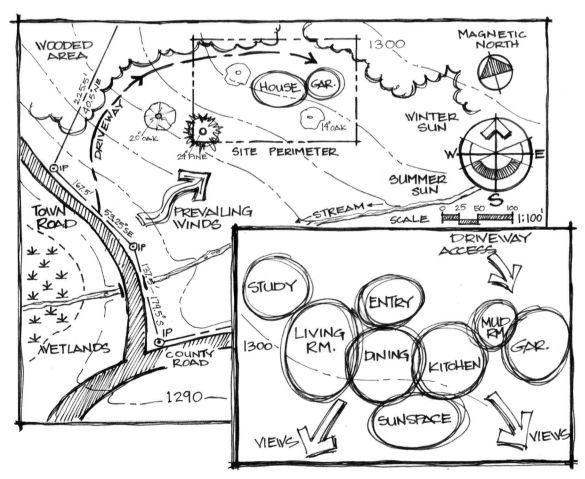

south. Go to the site at solar noon (exactly halfway between sunrise and sunset, usually listed in a local newspaper). Hang a string with a weight to make a plumb line, and mark the direction of the shadow, which will be cast toward solar north; the opposite is solar south. Determine the compass heading of solar south, so you can locate it in the future. It may not be possible to orient the building directly toward solar south, but a rule of thumb is to stay within 25.5°, because within this range you lose less than 10% of the potential solar gain through vertical glazing.

The second rule is to try to eliminate winter shading. The angle of the sun's arc changes throughout the year, being highest in June and lowest in December. Placing yourself in the position of the house, try to follow the path of the sun from sunrise to sunset as if it were a December day. The arc you would follow depends on your latitude. (For instance, at my house the sun follows an angle of about 24.5° to the horizon on December 21 at solar noon.) Better yet, get out there on a December day and watch what happens. You are looking for anything that obstructs the sun, such as hills or trees. Depending on what you find, the house may have to be moved, or trees may have to be thinned and pruned.

While trying to eliminate December shading, in the summer you will be grateful to have some. If there are deciduous trees, the house might be positioned so it is shaded by the crown of a tree in June, but less obstructed after the leaves have dropped off in the fall. But remember that even bare branches can cause heavy shading. These may have to be pruned to allow sunlight to pass through.

BUBBLE DIAGRAM HELPS SHAPE BUILDING PROGRAM

A thorough understanding of the site is then blended with the building program to create the basis for the house plan. Try to fit all the important elements of the home onto the site with a bubble diagram, as shown on p. 71. In addition to living areas within the house, also locate the driveway, parking area, garage, woodshed, septic system, terraces, gardens, barn, pasture, and any other required feature. The process of completing this diagram will naturally spur some decisions about the floor plan. For example, if the driveway needs to be located toward the east of the house to complement features of the land and to reduce expense, it would not make sense to put the garage on the west. If a parking area were positioned on the north side of the house, it would not make sense to put the main entry on the south. And if it were possible to site the house to capture a view, you would probably rather see it from the living room than the laundry room. Likewise, it is not usually prudent to waste solar-heating potential on a little-used bedroom when it could be better used in a major living area.

With the position of a few essential ingredients, many other parts of the house follow. For instance, because you would be going from the car to the house on the east side, it makes sense to put the kitchen to the east so that groceries would not have to be carried across the house. For convenience, the dining area should be close to the kitchen. The kitchen is roughly located toward the southeast, and the living room is toward the southwest, with the dining room in the middle. Laundry, bath, and other utility areas are shifted toward the northeast, opposite the kitchen, to keep plumbing areas together and to separate them from the living room. The rather extravagant formal entry falls adjacent to the living area. If you use this plan as an example, a meaningful design will begin to emerge, combining the wistful desires of the building program with the attributes and constraints of the site.

Also arising out of this process should be insight into the general shape of the house. Once again, it is important to be sensitive to the land rather than to rely on preconceived notions. Obviously, the shape of the house must accommodate the living areas and their relationship to the outdoors. It should be open

Classic building forms, such as this story-and-a-half Colonial, are natural in timber-frame construction and are seldom design failures. (Photo by Brian Gulick.)

to the sun, buffer winds, and make the views available. Perhaps most important, when making decisions about the building's shape and volume, consider economics and energy conservation. These two concepts fit together because they have a similar goal: to pack as much as possible into a structure with a small total surface area. As a building is stretched out and convoluted, its foundation area is increased along with the surface area of the walls and the roof, creating a need for more labor and materials. The additional surface area also allows more heat to move from the inside to the outside. Still, good architecture demands that we try to find a balance. The shape and form of the house should have a harmonious dynamic with its place and intrinsic aesthetic value.

INFLUENCES ON SHAPE AND STYLE

For timber-frame houses, intrinsic aesthetic value means that the shape of the building should be true to the language of the material. Remarkable symmetry and beauty are almost inevitable when timber framing is practiced well in its simplest form, and there can be no doubt that it begs to create rectilinear buildings that directly reflect the shape of the timbers (see the photos on the facing page and below). To shape a curvilinear building, for instance, risks that the timber frame will become awkward and clumsy, and perhaps that the joinery will be stretched beyond its limits. Very complex buildings having numerous corners, layers, jogs, angles, turrets, and dormers (as in highly decorative Victorian-style buildings) are best

constructed with frames that have their fudge factors well hidden behind plaster walls. Timber-frame buildings of such complexity need difficult joinery, require the best efforts of the finest timber craftsmen, and cost like the dickens.

Let the dictates of the site and the building program be the greatest influences on house shape and style. At every turn, choose simplicity over complexity—there is no shame in simple, classic building forms, which seldom disappoint and almost never fail. Most of the traditional styles that dominate architecture were born as timber-frame structures; they were refined through the centuries as the skills and aspirations of the builders evolved, but it was an evolution with no radical leaps. Instead, the master builders were

Here's an interior view through a bay of the house on the opposite page. (Photo by Brian Gulick.)

A STANDARD SET OF PLANS

LANDSCAPE — "L"

SITE DIAGRAM	L-1
LANDSCAPE PLAN	L-2
PLANTING SCHEDULE	L-3

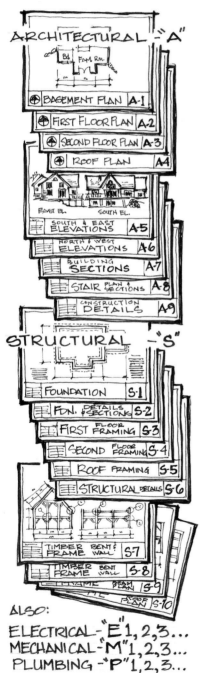

ARCHITECTURAL —"A"

BASEMENT PLAN	A-1
FIRST FLOOR PLAN	A-2
SECOND FLOOR PLAN	A-3
ROOF PLAN	A-4
SOUTH & EAST ELEVATIONS	A-5
NORTH & WEST ELEVATIONS	A-6
BUILDING SECTIONS	A-7
STAIR PLAN & SECTIONS	A-8
CONSTRUCTION DETAILS	A-9

STRUCTURAL —"S"

FOUNDATION	S-1
FDN. DETAILS & SECTIONS	S-2
FIRST FLOOR FRAMING	S-3
SECOND FLOOR FRAMING	S-4
ROOF FRAMING	S-5
STRUCTURAL DETAILS	S-6
TIMBER BENT & FRAME WALL	S-7
TIMBER BENT & FRAME WALL	S-8
FRAME BENT PLAN	S-9
	S-10

ALSO:

ELECTRICAL—"E" 1, 2, 3...
MECHANICAL—"M" 1, 2, 3...
PLUMBING —"P" 1, 2, 3...

confident enough in the design formula, or vernacular patterns, that they used the same styles to construct a full range of architecture, from peasant cottages to the palatial manor halls in Europe and from the working-class Cape Cods to the grand Colonial estates in America. In our time, the only real problem with the classic architectural forms is that their essence has been diminished, even violated, in the vapid interpretations in our sprawling suburban tract developments. The patterns are rich, the potential permutations of form and detail without end. It's not the building system or its design possibilities that fall short. Only we, with our limited understanding or vision, do that.

NOTES ON DESIGN

Once the site plan is established, and the building shape and style have been decided upon, it's time to generate floor and frame plans. But before embarking on this step, consider a few other points.

Be prepared to do (or have done) the most meticulous, complete set of final plans possible. Houses are simply too expensive and too complicated for decisions to be left to a carpenter on a coffee break. The bitter reality of housebuilding is that it is like getting mugged by a thief; the house will demand the entire bankroll and frisk you again before the job is finished. The route from the bank to the completed house must therefore be carefully mapped, and only with a full set of plans can you know that the house will meet your expectations and do so within budget.

A full set of plans means that every item in the house has been accounted for and every detail in the assembly has been precisely explained—from the depth of the foundation hole, to the configuration of each joint in the frame, to the mounting of the last closet pole. This detailing defines the material and labor necessary before the

project commences and is the only way to control costs. Detailed planning does not mean there can't be modifications during the process; it just means those modifications and site adjustments are educated improvements, not last-minute decisions.

At left is the standard set of plans the people in my company use. The plans cover everything: landscape, structural, electrical, plumbing, mechanical. Creating such a personalized, custom set of plans is likely to cost between 5% and 10% of the total building cost (which is real money), but it is almost always an excellent investment. I have worked with a few home builders who have done a fine job with their own design and planning, but most people do not have the skills or time necessary to do a good job with blueprints. Home builders choosing this course should be wise enough to know what they don't know and, at the very least, retain professionals who will act as consultants.

If you choose to work with a professional architect or designer, select this person carefully. The ability to create good architecture out of the simmering pot of information collected on the site and from the building program is a talent that does not come to every person. A good designer can stir it all together and bring to the house those tasteful lines that go down easily with the ecology of the site and the geography of the area. Enduring designs are born in humility, of the understanding that very few buildings are an aesthetic improvement over no building at all. Unfortunately, this is not a concept always stressed by schools of architecture. Too often, architects emerge from their educational dens and immediately attempt to capture the world with the latest artistic snares. At the very least, make sure the designer you choose is familiar with the timber-frame system—suggest this book and others in the bibliography. Also make sure the designer has a copy of your building program and refers to it often. At interim meetings, you might even want to go over the list together to analyze decisions that have been made. And remember, working with a professional does not mean noninvolvement. A designer should not be expected to put together a house design without a great deal of input from the clients.

Of course, an alternative to designing your own home or hiring a professional designer is to use a stock design as offered by some timber-frame companies. This could be the ultimate design crapshoot, but if you start by going through the preliminary design steps discussed earlier and then work with a company that can make the necessary adjustments on your behalf, the process can work quite well. Just don't compromise. It's your house and your money. It is always amazing to me that people are quite willing to make the largest investment of their lives on the basis of the least-expensive plans, usually with the consequence that the building has no response to the site and little connection to the requirements of the owners.

GENERATING FLOOR AND FRAME PLANS

This stage of design is a little more complicated than the previous steps, because the designer must decide about dimensions, building forms, and precise spatial relationships and then address how the house is expected to work. The birth of the floor and frame plans out of the notations in the building program, the wanderings on the site, and the musings about the bubble diagram are rather magical events. Out of the chaos comes order, and sometimes no one person involved is quite sure what made it happen. But if the groundwork has been accurately laid, even the first efforts to design a floor plan can be quite successful.

Begin with a block diagram, (which ought to be a reflection of the ideas and information from the bubble diagram), as shown at top right. Modifying the blocks as necessary, develop

EVOLUTION OF A FLOOR PLAN

1. Develop block diagram from bubble diagram.

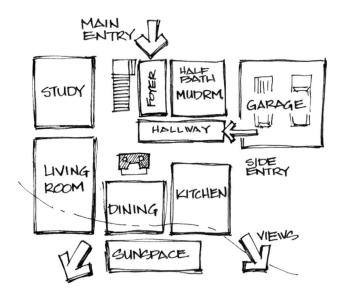

2. Draw simple floor plan with a logical arrangement of posts and beams.

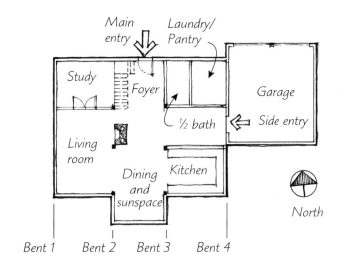

3. Develop floor plan further, with partitions, exterior walls, stairs, and major fixtures.

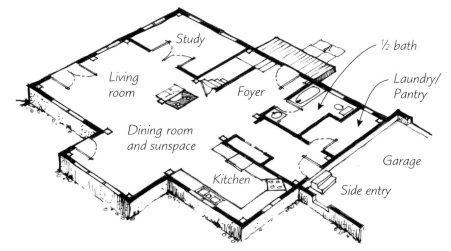

FINAL FLOOR PLAN

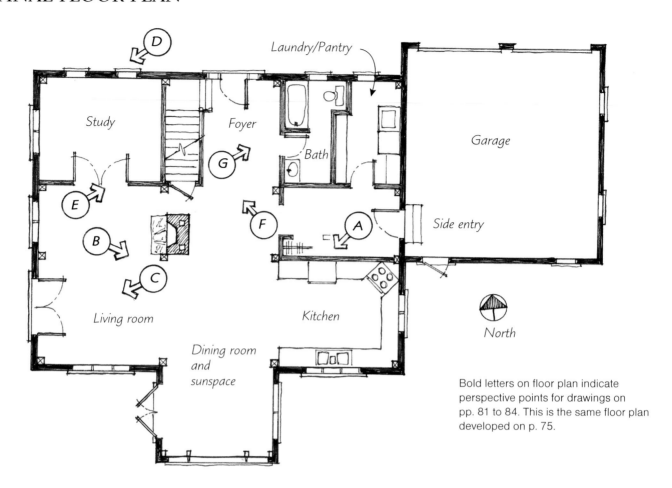

Bold letters on floor plan indicate perspective points for drawings on pp. 81 to 84. This is the same floor plan developed on p. 75.

their arrangement into a floor plan, locating major posts and beams. In these first attempts, the goal is to find an acceptable configuration of rooms and timbers, to see if the sizes of the spaces seem adequate, to study their relationship to each other and to the circulation of traffic. The early floor plans should quickly evolve to include some basic plan elements, although there is no need for exhaustive detail at this stage. Stairs, chimney, partitions, major appliances, cabinets, plumbing fixtures, and door and window locations should be shown because the plans can't be properly analyzed otherwise. The bathroom space won't make much sense unless it is seen in relation to potential fixtures. The kitchen must be seen with cabinets, and bedrooms should have their storage furniture and closets.

Locating posts and beams in the earliest renditions of the floor plan makes

sense both structurally and aesthetically. Posts can't be located without anticipating the relationship they will have with intersecting beams and studying the affect of these timbers on the overall plan. But while it's necessary to consider the floor plan, the frame plan, and indeed the shape of the building as a unit, it's also important to realize that all these components should be able to stand on their own merits. This means that if it is helpful to change the building's shape to suit the floor plan, this should not be done at the risk of creating a house that is awkward or ugly. And while beams and posts can be moved to accommodate design goals, these decisions should neither cause the frame to become structurally deficient nor make it overly difficult to assemble. This may seem obvious, but it is the most common pitfall in timber-frame house design. It's all too easy to

remove a critical timber or brace, to stretch a beam beyond its normal capacity, or to contort the frame into an uncomfortable position.

To avoid these failings, it's necessary to keep redrawing floor and frame plans as you continue to refine and alter the design. Creating initial frame plans requires a concept of the shape of the house, an idea born from aesthetic judgment and an understanding of the site and the potential living spaces. The skills and intuition of a good designer are essential here. In its crudest form, the initial frame plan can be a stick representation of potential bent plans as posts and major beams are positioned on the floor plan. As the design progresses, show the relationship of bent girts, summer beams, and connecting girts to the floor plan with dashed lines. It is not necessary to go into further detail on beam arrangement until the plan is more finalized, but it is useful to shade the posts on the floor plan to show they consume space.

As illustrated in the previous chapter, the development of the bents is critical. Bents are usually the dominant structural element in the frame, and they also determine the shape of the building. The way timbers are placed in the bents affects ceiling height as well as the feel of the spaces in the house. So not only should each bent be structurally sound, but as you juggle post length, beam heights, and rafter intersections, you also need to think about the use of floor space and volume. As the floor plan becomes more defined, the frame plans should likewise develop into a complete set of plans. Eventually the bent plans must show all members, with accurate dimensions on timber locations and lengths.

As the design develops, also sketch onto the bent plans the locations of windows and doors. Most people strive to center these on a wall for symmetry, using the floor plan to determine their positions. But in fact, windows and doors are best centered between braces, which aren't even visible on the floor plan. Sketching them on the bent plans makes it easier to remember that, when viewed from the inside, windows and doors are actually seen in relation to the timbers in the frame.

Designing a floor plan is filled with uncertainty because dreams finally meet hard reality. It's a time for listening to common sense and practicality. Do not design beyond the budget. Pay attention to the movement of the sun and the direction of the wind. Conserve energy. Consolidate pipes. Give people a place for privacy as well as places to congregate. Above all, even if the decisions seem complex, the floor plan should not be; you will never go wrong if you simplify. The house can be intriguing without being mystifying.

USING BAYS AND AISLES

Simplification is natural when the spatial arrangements are as strongly delineated and rationally organized as they are in the typical timber frame. Commonly, timber-frame buildings have three bays and four bents. The usual outcome in this setup is for the outer bays to contain the primary rooms, while the central bay is reserved for passage, one or two entry points, and possible living areas. Each outer bay usually accommodates compatible rooms. For instance, the more formal and private areas would be placed together in one bay, while the work and utility areas would be grouped together at the opposite end of the house. Rooms on the other levels are organized to be compatible with the

This aisle solarium was created by extending the roofline in two of three bays.

In this central bay, the dining area is connected to the solarium but is also open to the living area in the adjacent bay.

Here's a look through a central bay that leads from the entry to a dining area with a tall, south-facing roundtop window overlooking a lake.

rooms on the first level. Rooms with plumbing would be stacked, for instance, and second- and third-floor rooms requiring privacy would be placed over the more private rooms of the first floor. This common-sense approach is the reason why traditional timber-frame homes are a model for many modern designs, even for non-timber-frame houses.

A bay may contain one room, such as a living room or large bedroom, or several rooms. In the latter case, intermediate posts and summer beams or joists are used to define the areas and to pro-

vide attachment for partitions, although very often several rooms function in a single bay without partitions; here timbers suggest the transition from one space to another, as detailed in the next section. Kitchens and dining spaces work well this way, as do living rooms, studies, and TV areas. It's also common for areas to be open to each other among several bays—my company has built a number of houses that have almost no partitions on the first floor. A single living level might contain the kitchen, dining area, living room, study, several entry halls, and a bathroom. The bathroom would be en-

closed, but all the other areas would be defined only by timbers. A benefit to an arrangement as open as this is that heat can move freely throughout the house, but the obvious drawback is the lack of private space.

Especially in open floor plans, aisle spaces might be used in combination with bay-defined areas, allowing living areas to orient in the other direction, if desirable. Because the post positioning is often in alignment in both directions, it is often possible to change the spatial relationship to the frame simply by moving furniture.

An aisle is just a space formed by structural elements perpendicular to bay spaces (see the top photo at right). A building's gable side being wider than the length of the eave side, or of similar dimension, is one reason why aisles could well be the dominant orientation. We are most familiar with the aisled arrangement common to churches and cathedrals. These monumental buildings are designed to uplift and inspire. The central aisle forms the primary aspect of the sanctuary, with aligned columns and rising rafters, the shape itself has taken on religious connotations. In residential design, the same orientation can dominate, but it is usually appropriate to bring a more human scale to the volumes.

Clear-span open-roofed areas can be either completely separate, attached to the rest of the house from just about any angle, or integrated into the other bents—same shape, different arrangement of timbers. (See Chapter 9 for more details.) It's typically easier to keep the frame separate, because you can then fit it to the house without having to align it with the other bents. When all living areas will be on the same level, several living areas might use the same space, with boundaries defined more by furniture or function than by walls (see the bottom photo at right). Since no living space would be needed under the roofline, the pitch of the roof could be decreased to reduce wasted space, and the trusses could be designed primarily for beauty. Living areas can be arranged any number of ways, but more variety is possible if smaller wings are appended to a larger central core. If bedrooms, baths, and utility rooms can be moved into attached, appropriately sized frames, they will not have to find definition inside the main structure. Obviously, consolidation of the floor plan is indicated when the desire for heat efficiency is strong or the state of the owners' finances is weak.

Aisle spaces, such as this one, run perpendicular to the bays. In this case, the central bay is open to a second-floor loft area and a large window.

A clear-span roof with exposed timbers creates a large unobstructed space. A feature of this room is the hammer-beam frame.

TIMBERS INFLUENCE ROOM DESIGN

Although the arrangement of bays and aisles is important in the design, the timbers in each wall and ceiling of a house exert enormous influence on the feel and use of the rooms. The way timbers are arranged within a room is therefore affected as much by the occupants' planned usage and ambition for the overall mood of the house as it is by structural requirements. As you've already seen, timbers can make a space feel expansive or cozy, public or private. They can also enhance impressions of massiveness or airiness, formality or playfulness, even brightness or darkness. The wood species and general finish treatment of the timbers further heighten the effects created by their arrangement—rough-sawn pine timbers left natural will add rusticity, whereas high-quality fir timbers stained and oiled to a glossy finish will give the house elegance.

Some insight will inevitably be gained and ideas will probably be refined while you work through the building program. Narrow the choices by thinking of the rooms and their potential contents as a three-dimensional still life, with the timber frame serving the role as the picture frame. You probably would not want to imprison a Frederic Remington in a heavily embossed gilt frame, nor would weathered barn boards suit a Renoir. If the desired ambience of the house is formal and the furniture will be ornate, give the frame that quality, too.

My company has a guideline that we follow to achieve the ultimate integration of a timber frame with the living area. We apply this guideline to large rooms and small, important and secondary. We use it on rooms with partitions and those that will never have walls. It is a straightforward criterion, stating simply that to give a space boundaries, each room should be defined with timbers. This means that rooms should be designed with posts in

The character of the wood, the plain lines of the frame, and the unadorned treatment of the timbers create a casual atmosphere for this dining area.

Under the roof, spaces are usually defined by the rafter pairs of the principal bents.

the corners and beams around the perimeter, as illustrated by most of the interior photos in this book. Under the roofline, this might mean having a pair of rafters at each end of the room. As well as offering visual advantages, this rule also makes sense from the standpoint of construction. A carpenter can easily attach plates and studs for partitions to timbers in simple, rectangular wall sections. If timbers are not arranged this way, partitions often must weave around them, causing both studding and finish work to become unnecessarily complex. Of course there will be cases where it's not possible to design a post in each room corner, but these should be exceptions.

Defining spatial divisions with timbers

To further understand available options in timber arrangement, let's explore several ways to manipulate some of the framing members in the floor plan shown on pp. 75 and 76. (This is the same house that was generated from the bubble diagram on p. 71.) Notice that the bents start out exactly the same, with bents 2 and 3 receiving the sunspace and dining-room gable extension. The alternatives I'll illustrate here don't alter the basic floor plan, but they do affect the timber-frame details and the use of space. You can gain a perspective on the views using the floor plan shown on p. 76.

Let's look first at the passage between the kitchen and dining room on the south side of bent 3 (see the drawings at right). The posts, the braces, and the beam form a clear and elegant division between the two spaces, a doorway without a door, a partition without a wall. Curving the braces softens the angles and makes the arch more formal. For an even more distinct separation, eliminate the braces, frame the passageway with two posts, and then add built-ins for storage between the door frame and the outside posts. Integrating finish details in this manner helps keep the house uncluttered. I chose this option for the final floor plan. While doing so for the sake of this sam-

THREE WAYS TO FRAME A PARTITION

Straight braces are simple but show strength.

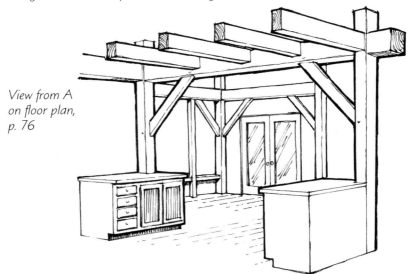

View from A on floor plan, p. 76

Larger, curved braces soften angles and make arch more formal.

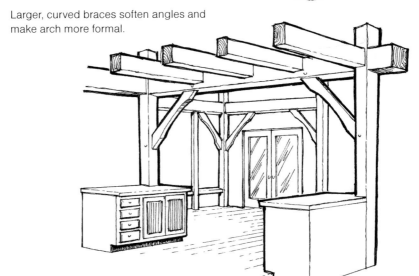

Two posts, an arched header, and built-in shelves provide distinct separation.

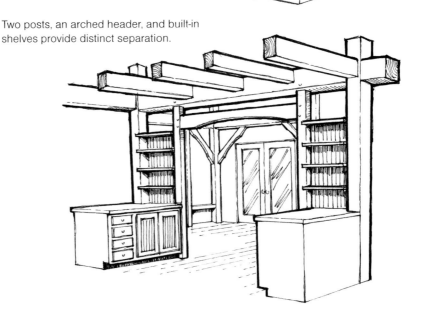

DEFINING AN OPENING

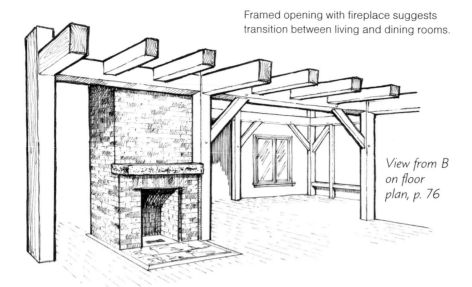

Framed opening with fireplace suggests transition between living and dining rooms.

View from B on floor plan, p. 76

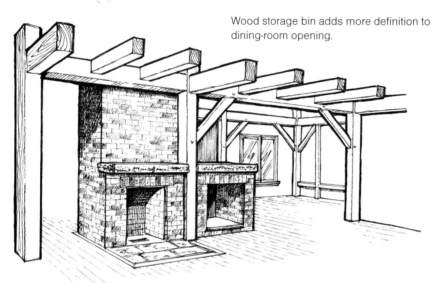

Wood storage bin adds more definition to dining-room opening.

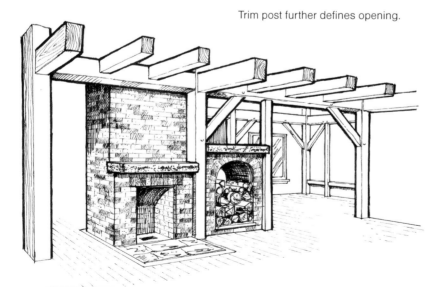

Trim post further defines opening.

ple design effort, I want to point out that it is just this sort of individual treatment of the frame as a design tool that can make future flexibility more difficult. Such decisions should be made sparingly.

When changing members of the frame, pay attention to structural require-ments. In this case it's okay to remove the knee braces, because the reversed braces above the bent girt add rigidity. Knee braces are occasionally used for appearance where they're not needed for strength, but it is important to know for a fact when they're necessary and when they're not.

In bent 3, there are several framing options. The original design (shown in the top drawing at left) suggests the transition between living room and dining room, but to further define it (and for convenience), I added a wood storage bin next to the chimney (see the middle drawing). For the visual at-tribute of having only subtle divisions between defined spaces, I would keep the bin shy of the ceiling, and if I felt that the masonry didn't integrate well with the frame, I might add a trim post to the bin edge, creating a narrower passageway (see the bottom drawing). Should this trim post be balanced with a post on the opposite edge of the chimney? I think not, because the frame is too much locked into the ex-isting conditions. Rather, I will choose to trim the edge of the masonry on the south side with non-structural post and leave the north side of the masonry to fend for itself. The frame needn't punc-tuate everything.

The drawback to this series of changes is that the dining room now has hard boundaries, which will make it smaller. Without the extra posts and wood bin, the east and west sides of the dining room had more space for traffic and to accommodate an extended dining table for large groups. But given the new boundaries, the extended dining table will probably have to be arranged in the north-south orientation. With the open area of the gable extension, the dining area will feel large enough.

On the south end of bent 1, there is a French door leading out to a deck. There are two choices here. The door can be framed with timbers or simply centered between knee braces (see the top two drawings at right). I favor the latter approach, because timbers around the door add a feeling of weight, which contradicts the intent of the door. By contrast, the arch formed by the braces suggests an opening. Simplicity wins out on this one. I would keep the door trim as soft as possible, either opting for no trim at all or painting a simple wood trim the same color as the walls.

The north end of bent 1 is identical to the south, except there is a window instead of a door. But before making any decisions, consider the other ingredients in the study. Are there bookshelves and built-ins? Is there wainscoting around the perimeter of the room? Should this room have subdued light? Assuming the answer to all these questions is yes, I might consider framing this wall differently from the one having the French door. To stick with the theme of integrating finish elements within the frame, the wainscoting will be capped with a small timber made from a compatible wood. Timbers will frame the sides of the window, and bookshelves will be built in between the window trim timbers and the outside posts. The warming effect of the extra timbers will also benefit the room by absorbing enough light to keep the room cozy. For symmetry, the window is centered (see the bottom drawing at right).

On the opposite wall of the study is the first interior partition. When interior partitions align with timbers (as they should), you must determine the side on which the knee braces will be visible. Splitting a timber with a partition requires that partition framing be individually fitted around the braces—a time-consuming task. Usually I expose the braces to the central areas to give

FRAMING DOORS AND WINDOWS

Trim posts frame door.

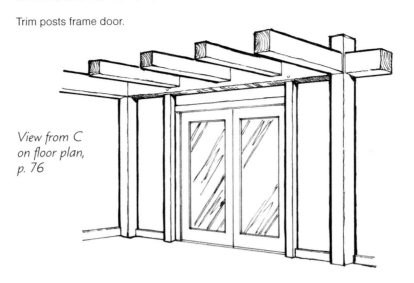

View from C on floor plan, p. 76

Knee braces and simple trim frame door.

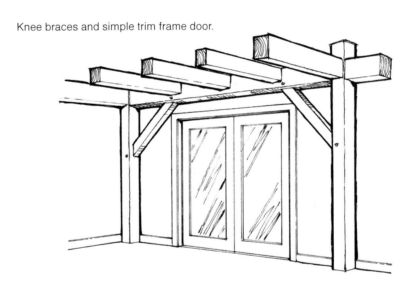

Timbers, bookshelves, and wainscoting work together to frame window.

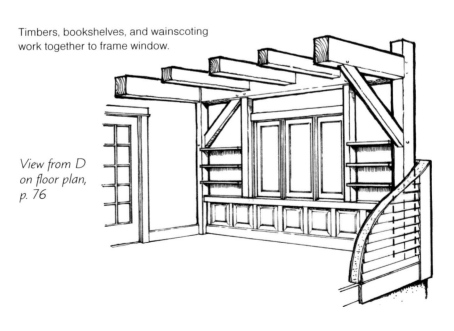

View from D on floor plan, p. 76

INTERIOR PARTITIONS

Built-ins cover partition wall in study.

View from E on floor plan, p. 76

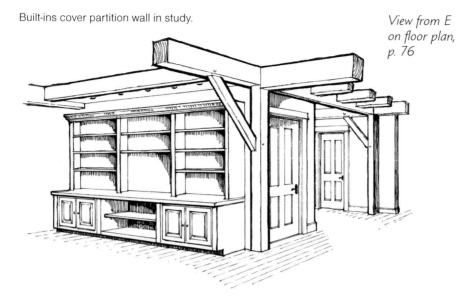

Frame is exposed on stair side of partition.

View from F on floor plan, p. 76

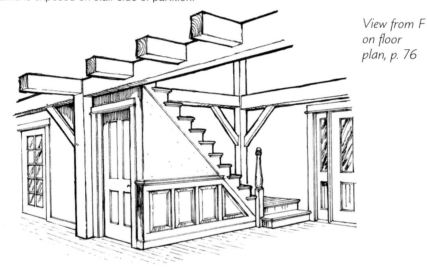

Frame exposed around entry and on west wall of bathroom.

View from G on floor plan, p. 76

the house more continuity. This particular wall is a toss-up because one side faces the privacy of the study and the other is somewhat hidden by the stair. What clinches the decision in favor of the stair wall is the floor-to-ceiling cabinet in the study that would cover the braces anyway. So the best thing to do is to build the partition on the study-side of the braces, leaving their full thickness exposed to the stair. Still, the brace that falls on the upper part of the stair and the posts will cause some difficult finish work, because the stair parts will have to be scribed around them (see the drawings at left).

The wall of the main entry opposite the stair is a plain partition wall with a door for entry to the bath. For plumbing reasons (see Chapter 8), and because so little of the frame would be visible anyway, it makes sense to move this wall toward the bath and expose the frame to the same degree as the opposite wall. When finished, this would be just a wall with a door and exposed timbers. The spaces between would be useful for art display.

The downstairs bathroom in this house is neither large nor luxurious, and I don't care if the effect of timbers is lost there. In the laundry room, throw aesthetics out the window and allow the needs of the room to dictate timber and window arrangement. The only inhibiting factor is the symmetry of the exterior wall—if possible, the window should be centered between the braces to be in alignment with other windows.

This brings us back around to the east wall of the kitchen. Here the ingredients that need to interact with the frame are a window and the base cabinets. You'll want as much morning light as possible, so make the window large. To keep the arrangement simple and consistent with the other changes, I might choose simply to center the window between braces with simple trim.

Frame and stairs often have a tight interrelationship. Oak newels and rails meet the oak frame in this house. (Photo by Bob Gere.)

CEILING FRAMING

Another strong influence on the home design is the arrangement of ceiling joists. Posts in the walls can be as much as 16 ft. apart, but ceiling joists can rarely have spacing of more than 4 ft. apart because they generally support loads from the floor above or from the roof. The affect of such closely spaced timbers (and not insignificantly, over your head) is strong; the way a room feels is greatly influenced by the ceiling beams. If they lack symmetry, the room will feel disjointed, and if the ceiling is low, the beams will make it feel lower. The structural requirements are defined by the loads that must be carried, but there is almost always a variety of ways to satisfy the requirement. In the kitchen, for instance, you could simply span between the two east-west timbers with joists. The span would be less than 10 ft., so the joists would not be large. By using a simple, repetitious pattern and increasing the span between joists as much as possible, the least expressive treatment is created.

On the other hand, if the kitchen would benefit from a focal point, particularly if there were a working island in the center, a large summer beam would be a great addition (see the top photo at right). It would further subdivide the space, bring the effective ceiling height down, allow the joists to be smaller, and might even prove handy for hanging kitchen utensils.

The ceiling for the living room also deserves examination. The first impulse is to raise it. It could be beneficial to have more volume for this space, partly to create a different feeling from the other living areas and partly because different ceiling heights are just more interesting. Of course this could cause some finishing difficulties on the second floor, but it might be worth it. The first step in changing the height is easy—simply move a series of bent girts and connecting girts up another level. Were I to do that, bent 2 would have the greatest change because it would need girts on the common level for the study

while also receiving the timbers for the raised living-room ceiling. But this is not difficult or complicated. However, for the purposes of this exercise, let's keep the ceiling heights consistent.

Because timber framers are not constrained by stock lumber lengths, we tend to choose higher-than-normal ceiling heights for two reasons. First, because we easily can. It is simply a matter of where the floor beam's joinery is located along the length of a post. Second, in a timber-frame building, the bottom of the joists is the effective height of the ceiling because it

Summer beams were used in this kitchen space. The large timbers bring the effective height of the ceiling down.

A summer beam is a central element in this living area, but the ceiling joists create the room's canopy.

COMPLETE FLOOR PLAN WITH FRAME

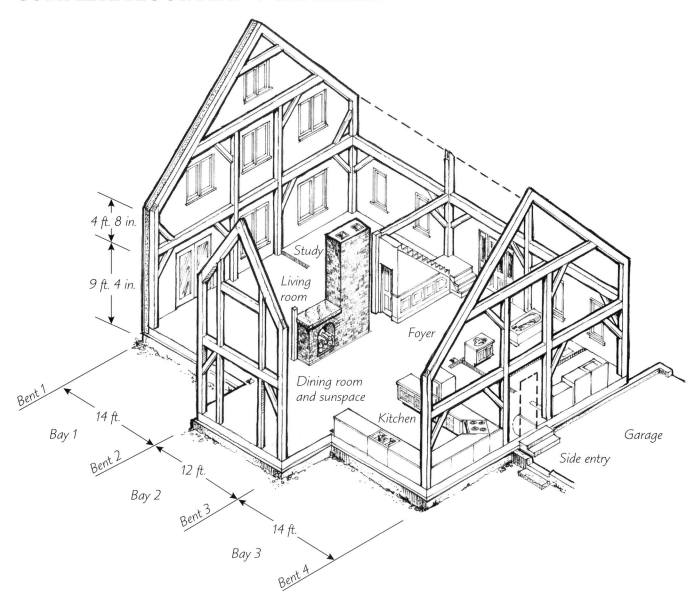

4 ft. 8 in.

9 ft. 4 in.

Study

Living room

Foyer

Dining room and sunspace

Kitchen

Garage

Side entry

Bent 1

Bay 1

14 ft.

Bent 2

Bay 2

12 ft.

Bent 3

14 ft.

Bay 3

Bent 4

is the perceived bottom of the room's canopy (see the bottom photo on the facing page). For these two reasons, the top of the joists (the second canopy layer) should be at least 8½ ft. to 9½ ft. The sample plan will have a first-floor ceiling height of 9 ft. 4 in.

With that decision made, let's look at a few different ways of framing the living-room ceiling. The first is a series of equally spaced joists, spanning from bent to bent, a simple and practical approach. Also, because each joist would probably have to be fairly large (approximately 5x7 in oak and 6x8 in fir) to make the span, this option

could actually be too overbearing for some tastes.

The next arrangement uses one large summer-beam timber in the middle of the room. The ceiling is now much more interesting, and the joists can be smaller. The problem is that this solution ignores the fact that there are two other posts that could also carry beams. So I think this option would look odd, especially since the reason for the extra post is to define the fireplace—a major ingredient in the room. The next logical step would therefore be to locate a summer beam on each fireplace post (see the photo on p. 90). This strong,

asymmetrical arrangement would influence potential furniture settings, but it could work, especially since the room seems to be aligned in this direction anyway. If this system were chosen, I'd want to keep all the joists the same size, even though the shorter spans could use smaller timbers, because varying joist sizes would be visually disruptive. Though there are other options, I think I would choose this straightforward arrangement. It focuses the room on the hearth and emphasizes a hierarchy in the frame, with the large summer beams framing into the central bent posts.

FLOOR PLAN FOR TYPICAL THREE-BAY HOME

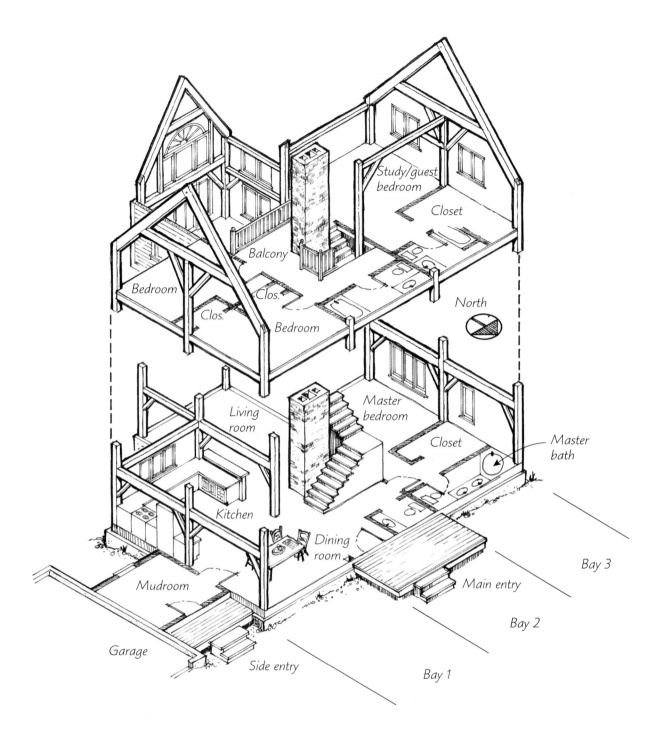

The completed floor plan of the example house is shown on p. 87. It is only one of an endless variety of options for how a frame and floor plan would be developed together. Though some manipulation of the frame is clearly possible, usually the simplest route is best. The points I wish to emphasize are that it's worthwhile to work hard to make the design right, and that the construction system need not be an obstacle to that pursuit. Consider function and resources in every corner of the house, for every surface, in every room; aspire to make art. There's no shame in falling short, but it's silly not to try.

FLOOR-PLAN OPTIONS

Now I want to present two additional house plans to illustrate other ways frames and space plans might evolve. I'm using these only to demonstrate how floor and frame plans can work together, not to represent a design ideal.

FLOOR PLAN FOR HOME ON SLOPED SITE

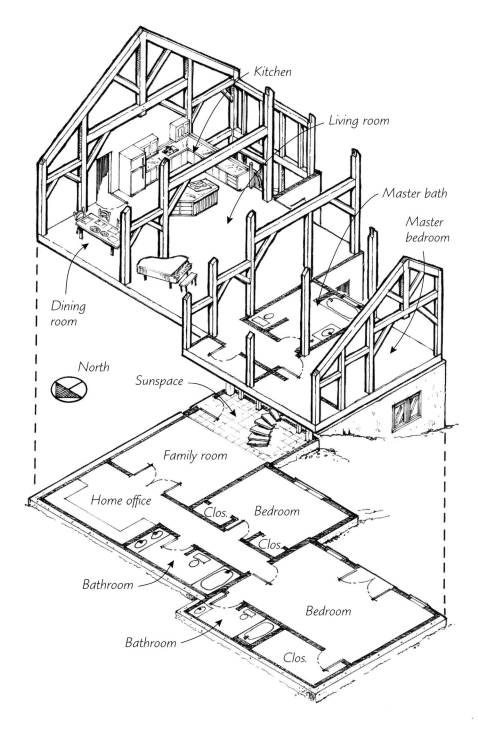

Kitchen

Living room

Master bath

Master bedroom

Dining room

North

Sunspace

Family room

Home office

Clos.

Bedroom

Clos.

Bathroom

Bathroom

Bedroom

Clos.

access to the outer bays on both floors. The first floor is essentially open through two bays, with the third bay containing the master bedroom and master bath. The kitchen and dining areas take up the first bay, forming a generous country-kitchen arrangement. They are naturally divided by the central post and summer beam. In the middle bay, the chimney and stairway help isolate the living room from the entry. Walls aren't necessary.

With the living room's open roof, there will be a dramatic effect for that space, and the other adjacent spaces will benefit as well; light will spill through, and the added volume will make the whole house feel larger.

The second floor follows the first, with plumbing stacked and bedrooms falling over the major areas of the first floor. Two bedrooms use the first bay, naturally separated by the central post. In the third bay, a larger room and full bath are positioned in a direct reflection of the master bedroom below. Because the second-floor spaces are open to the roof, the volumes will be large and interesting, even in the smaller bedrooms. Such bedroom spaces are ripe for making sleeping lofts with nifty ladders and other fun things. Having the living room open to the second floor adds some real appeal to the central space. With planning and luck, there might even be a great view through the living room end wall.

This house packs a great deal into a very basic configuration. It falls into place without a struggle, partly because the spatial requirements are not extravagant (no spa or exercise rooms), but mostly because it is based on a "pattern language" that has been used for timber-frame houses for centuries.

The heart of the second house plan (above) is formed by a light and open-roofed space that includes kitchen, dining, and living areas. It has a generous entrance foyer, a laundry room and the master bedroom on the same level. Designed for a sloping site, the ground

Design properly begins on the site and includes many personal considerations, including budget. Different people with different sites and budgets would come up with different but equally serviceable plans.

The floor plan shown on the facing page follows the design logic described

in this chapter, depicting a classic three-bay house oriented toward solar south. The house is 24 ft. wide and uses a very simple three-posted bent for the center bay. A fifth bent describes the gable of a vaulted living room and extends to the south. The central bay houses the stair, entry, half-bath, chimney, and living room. It also provides

In this living room, a pair of summer beams and posts frame the fireplace and accentuate the organization of space.

floor is also open to sufficient light and ventilation to encourage its use for additional bedrooms, a family room, and a home office.

In this design, there are two basic bent styles, five bents used, and four bays. The larger bent forms the basis for the living room and a smaller one, based on the same king-post arrangement, is used for the master-bedroom area. The south-facing sunspace, which also houses the stairway to the ground floor, is a continuation of the roofline. The kitchen, dining, and living areas are completely open, both to the roof and to adjacent spaces, but are defined by the bents and post arrangements. There are no hard lines.

In the master-bedroom wing, on the other hand, partitions separate all the spaces. Still, the timbers define and form the basis for the boundaries. Though the master bedroom itself is not large in plan, it has a very generous volume and a couple of wonderful tall windows for seeing the views and receiving light.

In the ground floor, the only timbers are on the south wall. The rest of the space is framed by conventional means. By using the enclosed foundation space in this manner, the square footage available to the building is used well. Even with the extravagance of the open space to the first floor, relatively little volume is wasted.

Though these plans are quite different in their use of enclosed space (and potential cost), they have in common a consistency in the way the frame makes potential visible and flexible. Either of these houses could have completely different spatial plans in the same frame-defined volume. Then again, different space plans might have inspired frame plans unlike these. Designing timber-frame homes is like that: appearance is simple and uncomplicated, but it is also constantly revealing intriguing mysteries and pleasant surprises.

The development of insulation systems in this century has changed people's expectations of interior comfort. Higher R-values make it possible for passive solar heat to be retained for long periods. (Photo by Brian E. Gulick.)

CHAPTER 5

SKINS AND FRAMES

Through most of human history, people expected temperatures in their homes to rise and fall with the temperatures outside, to be only moderations of exterior extremes. But the development of insulation systems over the first two-thirds of this century changed that, and homeowners today expect to have full control over the weather in their rooms. Both ends of the country have been made more habitable because of machines that heat, cool, humidify, dehumidify, and even purify the air; it is now possible to live in both cold and hot climates without suffering. The problem, however, is that the control is both expensive and ephemeral, achieved through the consumption of wood, coal, oil, gas, and electricity. The temperature in the house is transformed temporarily, but it soon passes through the walls, roof, and floors into the outside atmosphere. The machines in the house deliver newly tempered air before we discover the escape of the old, but while this may keep us comfortable, the energy sources consumed are almost always not renewable; once used, they are forever gone.

For many crazy years (most notably between 1925 and 1975), the actual cost and true value of fuel were far apart, and our precious energy resources went up in flames. During this time the average American home was a poorly designed energy guzzler, lacking only a funnel on top to make the pouring in of fuel easier. In his book *The Natural House* (Horizon Press, 1954), Frank Lloyd Wright himself contended that insulating the walls of a house was hardly necessary. He felt that it would be worthwhile to insulate the roof, "...whereas the insulation of the walls and the airspace within the walls become less and less important. With modern systems of air conditioning and heating, you can manage almost any condition." Indeed. Why worry about conserving energy when fuel is cheap and when you can get a heating unit that "can manage almost any condition"? Unfortunately, there are homes everywhere that still use the large and thirsty monsters Wright was talking about.

When the energy crunch hit in the mid-1970s, it was natural to turn to the sun and wind to replace oil and gas. It wasn't immediately clear that the basic precepts of house design might need to be reevaluated, so liquids were pumped, air was pushed, and heat was stored in every conceivable medium. That's when folks discovered how wasteful the average American house is. We found that solar collectors and wind generators—no matter how tech-

nologically sophisticated—are woefully overmatched when heat is passing through the house at a full gallop.

Engineers and architects generally agree that the way to reduce energy consumption is to design houses that naturally collect heat during cold seasons and reject it during hot seasons. This done, you install the best possible insulation so that desired temperatures can be retained without assistance for long periods of time. It's a concept that works in both warm and cold climates—reducing cooling and heating requirements—and that is so theoretically simple that you really have to wonder how we managed to stray from it in the first place.

Perhaps we have been lulled into a blind reliance on the technical wizardry of our times. Or perhaps we just went to sleep as we submitted to a homogenized national architecture, forgetting the reasons behind historic regional differences. In any case, we have grown to rely on machines and cheap fuel sources rather than on materials and forms to keep us comfortable.

Ironically, solutions are often too simple to see. A friend of mine told me a story about he and a colleague (both Ph.D.s, which is germane) moving one of them and his family to a different city. They drove together in a rental truck, which was towing a car on a special trailer that holds the front wheels. Leaving Princeton, the two were turned away at the New Jersey Turnpike because the three parts constituted an illegal tow. To get around the problem, they found an alternate route through backroads and lesser highways. After many extra hours of traveling, they finally made their way to good, and less-restricted, highways of Connecticut. Finally sailing along, they both simultaneously realized that one of them could simply have driven the car separately. The truck and single-axle trailer would have been legal on their own.

THE STUD-FRAME DILEMMA

Perhaps the largest barrier to reducing fuel consumption in our homes is that conventional stud-framing methods are inherently contrary to good insulating practice. They were simply not invented with insulation in mind. In the mid- to late-1800s, when stud framing was being developed, people achieved thermal comfort primarily by drawing closer to the hearth: No thought was given to the system's compatibility with insulating materials because there were no insulating materials. So stud framing evolved with the single purpose of making construction easier.

But because the framing, insulation, and sheathing in stud construction are all installed separately, each component compromises the other (see the drawing on the facing page). Studs suffer a reduced life because moisture from air trapped in the fiberglass may cause them to rot. The fiberglass insulation would be much more effective if it weren't interrupted every 16 in. to 24 in. by a stud and if it didn't absorb moisture. The whole unit would be a better air seal if it weren't composed of hundreds of individual pieces. To prevent air infiltration through the gaps, the studs and insulation are covered with a thin, vulnerable sheet of plastic to act as a vapor barrier. Unfortunately, the vapor barrier is immediately punctured with thousands of screw or nail holes made while workers attach the sheathing.

In addition, the fiberglass itself is not the best insulating material. It's relatively inexpensive and easy to stuff into the spaces between framing members, but it doesn't trap air very well. Insulation value is provided by pockets of dry, still air, and the fact is that air moves through fiberglass quite easily, which is why it is used in other applications where the goal is not to trap air but to filter it. By today's energy-conserving standards, the typical batt of fiberglass amounts to being a pretty good sweater but not much of a coat.

TYPICAL STUD WALL

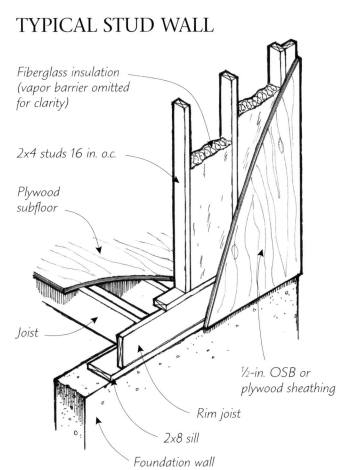

Fiberglass insulation (vapor barrier omitted for clarity)

2x4 studs 16 in. o.c.

Plywood subfloor

Joist

½-in. OSB or plywood sheathing

Rim joist

2x8 sill

Foundation wall

Foam-core panels are applied to the outside of the frame, surrounding the walls and covering the roof.

Builders and architects are working hard to circumvent the inherent insulative deficiencies of stud framing, but most of the new solutions demonstrate that we really ought to try thinking in new ways. For example, one popular system uses two parallel stud walls with batts of insulation in both walls and more in the space between—three layers of insulation, two walls, and a highway for mice. Another method is to build a conventional stud frame and then attach a light plywood truss to the outside to carry additional insulation. When completed, the composite is a fortress wall 12 in. to 16 in. thick. Stud framing is dominant throughout the world, and it won't soon be replaced. But outside of the housing industry, people have developed effective insulation systems precisely because they haven't had the constraints imposed by this construction method. Walk-in freezers, coolers, thermos bottles, energy-efficient water heaters, and

liquid gas tanks are all examples. Each one of these devices uses a continuous, uninterrupted membrane of rigid-foam insulation, a simple and sensible alternative, but one that was impractical for housing until the recent development of rigid foams.

Foam core meets timber frame

In 1976, after building a few timber-frame houses and feeling limited by conventional building materials, I began to search for a better insulation system. At the time, my company was using a built-up enclosure of horizontal 2x4 nailers and rigid-foam insulation (see p. 99), and while this is still a viable technique for some projects, I was convinced that we needed something wholly different if timber-frame homes were truly to make a comeback. Our built-up method was no improvement over conventional insulation because it was labor-intensive and suffered from thermal breaks. In addition, it was

wasteful, because a properly built timber frame can withstand all building loads without relying on sheathing for rigidity or infilling for support. In fact, what we were doing was building a frame around a frame. I knew that if we could take full advantage of the self-supporting nature of the timber frame, our buildings would be more economical to construct, and the insulation values would be greatly improved.

Endless phone calls, some library research and several trips over quite a few months led me to query people who specialized in making walk-in freezers. These were people with no particular ties to any kind of product, whose businesses depended on using the finest insulation. Two companies were receptive to my questions; one was especially helpful and invited me to visit its research laboratory. The technicians there gave me a short course on insulation, demonstrating why interrupting it with framing members is not good practice and why fiberglass is really second-rate stuff. By using a dyed vapor and changing the atmospheric conditions on either side of a test wall, they were able to create convection currents inside the wall cavity, which caused air to filter through the fiberglass.

For its insulating walls, this company preferred a composite of materials called a foam-core panel. These panels are also called stress-skin panels, stressed-skin panels, and structural insulated panels (SIPs). I have chosen to refer to them here as foam-core panels because it implies less structural capacity, which is appropriate to our use of the panel as a stiff skin, not as an independent structure. The panel is nothing more than a sandwich of a thick core material bonded to two thin outer skins. According to the U.S. Department of Agriculture's *Wood Handbook*, "The facings resist nearly all the applied edgewise loads and flatwise bending moments. The thin, spaced facings provide nearly all the bending rigidity to the construction. The core spaces the facings and transmits shear between them so they are effective about a common neutral axis. The core also pro-

vides most of the shear rigidity of the sandwich construction." What this means is that the structural principle behind a foam-core panel is similar to that of an I-beam (see the drawing below). The outer skins perform the same role as the beam flanges, while the foam core functions like the I-beam web. As in an I-beam, the skins resist tension and compression while the core carries the shearing forces and supports the skins against lateral wrinkling. Even if the core of the panel were not insulative, foam cores use materials economically, gaining strength without heaviness or great expense.

Panels used in refrigerated warehouses and freezers utilize rigid foam for the core and typically use galvanized sheet metal for the skins. For these applications, the panel was designed primarily to insulate effectively, while having sufficient structure to remain stiff and to transmit loads. Conceptually, it was perfect: a proven product with features well suited to the needs of timber-frame construction. However, a panel with metal skins is not exactly appropriate for residential construction. The challenge my company faced was to find a way to make a panel with skins that could serve as interior finish and

exterior sheathing surfaces. (For reasons of economy, we immediately dismissed the idea of screwing drywall and nail-based sheathing to the metal skins.) There were also a number of construction details to work out before foam-core panel technology could be successfully integrated into timber-frame homes. For instance, we would have to find a way to run wires, install windows and doors, and attach trim and finish materials. We were even uncertain about the best method for attaching panels to the frame and to each other. It was alternately exhilarating to see the potential and overwhelming to be confronted with so many obstacles.

Luckily, I wasn't alone with the thought that foam-core panels might be suitable for residential construction. Several companies became interested in developing the panel for the burgeoning timber-frame industry. It was because of their intense efforts at the beginning of our experimentation—and continuous improvements in the performance and quality of the product—that we are now able to use foam-core panels with confidence.

The typical panel we now use has oriented-strand board (OSB) for the exterior skin and plaster-based drywall for the interior skin (finish surface), although we often use panels having OSB on both sides. (I'll talk more about the materials in foam-core panels later in this chapter.) Like a human skin over a skeleton, panels are almost always applied completely to the outside of the frame, surrounding the walls and covering the roof. The timber frame and the insulating membrane are therefore separate, resulting in big benefits. Because the interior finish, insulation, and exterior sheathing are all installed simultaneously, on-site labor is saved, and the building is closed in quickly. Another benefit is the protection given to the frame. Since no part needs to be buried in a wall cavity or exposed to the elements, the frame is not subject to deterioration from weather or moisture. Using this system, the panels take

HOW A FOAM-CORE PANEL WORKS

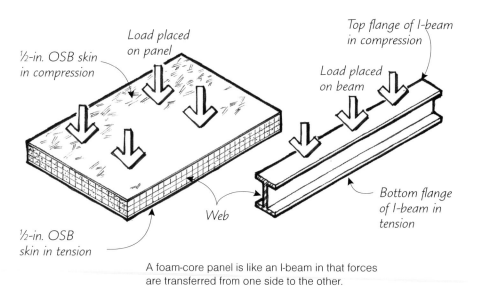

½-in. OSB skin in compression

Load placed on panel

½-in. OSB skin in tension

Web

Top flange of I-beam in compression

Load placed on beam

Bottom flange of I-beam in tension

A foam-core panel is like an I-beam in that forces are transferred from one side to the other.

the beating; in time, they could be replaced if necessary, but the frame should survive the ages unscathed.

Urethane and expanded polystyrene (EPS) are the two foam types currently used for the panel core (for more information on these materials, see pp. 113-115). Urethane cores can be laminated to the skins with an adhesive or injected in liquid form between separated skins. EPS cores must be laminated to the skins. A typical core thickness for a urethane panel is 3½ in., yielding an R-value somewhere between 24 and 28, while an EPS core has to be 5½ in. thick to achieve a similar R-value.

Insulation levels in walls and roof

Conventional wisdom suggests there should be more insulation in the roof than in the walls, so at first it might not seem to make much sense to have such high R-values in the wall panels. Theoretically, because warm air rises, air in the upper regions of the house will be substantially warmer than that at the lowest level. When heat is lost through the roof, convection currents draw up more warm air, resulting in a high temperature differential between the upper and lower areas of the building—witness the uninsulated attic on a hot summer day. We are discovering, however, that as we slow heat loss through the roof, the temperature differential from the peak to the floor narrows to within a few degrees. What makes this especially remarkable is that most of the houses we build are open to the peak, so the distance from the top of the ceiling to the floor might be over 25 ft. In a house insulated with foam-core panels, heat is lost only through conduction, not convection, and at a very slow rate because the rigid foam in the panels is a poor conductor. It makes sense to us to keep the entire thermal envelope at approximately the same insulative level, because if the temperature of the air next to roof and wall surfaces tends to be about the same, R-value should be at least proportionately equal.

When insulated well, rooms with high ceilings have little temperature differential between the roof and the floor.

Out of curiosity, one of our Massachusetts clients monitored the winter temperature in his home for one week. He hung a series of thermometers between the 25-ft.-high peak and the floor and found that the maximum temperature difference was 5°F and that the average for the period was 2°F. With the introduction of a small fan, he was able to reduce the temperature differential to 0.5°F—quite an achievement and an excellent testimony to a good insulation system.

But as effective and successful as foam-core panels are, they are not correct for every circumstance. Three factors should influence the choice of enclosure system for any timber-frame project: structural integrity, energy performance, and cost. The system must be strong and durable, able to resist wind loads on the walls, snow loads on the roof, and the awesome load of time. Energy needs should be reduced to the lowest practical level, keeping in mind that it doesn't make much sense to spend $10 to save $1. Relative to its value as a fuel miser and as a tough shell for the house, the system must warrant the cost of construction.

The most difficult of these criteria to determine is energy performance. Too often, there is R-value myopia, and judgments are made entirely on the basis of what the manufacturer's wrapping says you have stuffed in the cavities. Unfortunately, the wrapping goes without the warning that your actual performance may vary. An R-value of 50 would be a poor joke if it were used on a north wall that was 60% glass, and all the insulation in the world won't save a house that is riddled with air leaks. I recently went to examine one of our houses that wasn't performing up to expectations, although everything seemed to be in place and done according to usual procedure. But because the windows seemed colder than normal, I decided to remove the side casing. Sure enough, not one window, door, or skylight had any insulation or caulking between the jamb and rough opening. Added up, the uninsulated area amounted to a 4-ft. by 4-ft. hole in the house. Good insulation, bad workmanship; the system tilts.

The energy audit

There are really quite a few factors that need to be in proper balance to achieve good energy performance. Because it is so important to analyze all issues in relation to each other and because the calculations are so complex, a local engineering firm often does a computerized audit of our homes early in design. Such audits are available throughout the country (they are required by the building departments in some states), through utilities, heating suppliers, or private engineers. I personally like to work with a firm that expects to make money doing the audit, not afterward.

The energy audit considers wall- and roof-surface area and orientation, window- and door-surface area and orientation, volume, available degree days, infiltration values, below-grade treatment and insulation, and heat generat-

ed by occupants and fixtures. Estimated auxiliary energy requirements are estimated on a yearly, monthly, daily, or even hourly basis. Both gains and losses are estimated. Once all data about the house are entered into the program, it is simple to manipulate values to see the effect on the bottom line. For example, we might model a house with triple glazing or low-E (emissivity) glass and find that the added cost doesn't warrant the slightly improved performance. When the most desirable option is determined, the energy audit can also predict what the fuel cost will be on a yearly basis for each type of available fuel. Even if the audit does not perfectly reflect actual fuel consumption, I have found that it is usually quite accurate, if conservative. I agree with those states that have made an energy audit a requirement. If building departments are going to insist that electric outlets be no lower than 14 in. (my pet peeve), then they ought to be equally concerned about the measure of fuel consumption.

An energy audit is also the best method to weigh the cost of the enclosure system against the cost of the heating system and the fuel to run it for the next 10 or 20 years. If the long-range numbers are anywhere near close, it makes sense to choose better insulation, not only to save money over the long haul but also to help husband our resources and protect our environment. We strive to identify the point of diminishing returns, the very top of the proverbial efficiency curve, so that we'll feel confident when additional insulation or better windows cannot be justified in light of the small gain.

Following the energy audit, and after a careful analysis of each component of the building's envelope and another look at the bank account, the optimum enclosure system is chosen. I'll discuss the selection, installation, and manufacture of foam-core panels later in this chapter, but first let's look at a few alternate types of enclosures.

ALTERNATIVES TO FOAM-CORE PANELS

I can think of several reasons why a person might choose not to use foam-core panels and instead choose an alternative system.

• First, small buildings under 1,200 sq. ft., having little volume and surface area, are likely to reach the top of the efficiency curve with a less-expensive enclosure than panels. For some buildings, panels would be useful and cost-effective on the roof where there is little waste, but the walls should be treated differently. There are usually many penetrations in the walls for windows and doors, which generate a great deal of scrap and cause installation to be more difficult. I am not suggesting that insulation values be compromised, only that depending on the situation, it may be possible to achieve optimum performance with an alternate system.

• High-quality panels are not readily available in all regions, and trucking them from one end of the country to the other isn't very practical. If the project is in an isolated backwater, it may be necessary to do some low-tech manufacturing or use an alternate system.

• Panels might be too costly for the budget. We have found the installed cost of panels less expensive than the installed cost of any system with a competitive performance value. Although the cost of panels is relatively high per square foot, the installation labor is usually reasonable because the panels go on so rapidly. For most of the alternate systems the materials are less, but installation is labor intensive. Builders who don't place a high value on their labor might therefore find other systems attractive. We've raised frames for several clients who decided to use an enclosure system they could manage with their own resources.

• Some people simply have an aversion to the inorganic nature of panels. Or they can't believe panels can offer the permanence and security provided by using wooden materials for sheathing attachment. For these people, no words are persuasive. I offer only my empathy with the sentiment and suggest alternatives to follow.

• A building not occupied all the time, such as an office, shop, or vacation home, might not justify the insulating value typical of panels. By using one of the alternatives (and lowering performance standards greatly), a lot of money can be saved. Still, it makes sense to err on the side of energy conservation.

• Timber framing is an ancient method of construction, and people often want to use it to create a historical reproduction. Panels are inappropriate in this situation because the added thickness outside the structure does not reproduce the look of early timber-frame homes.

With all the alternatives that follow, keep in mind that with a timber frame, you already have a building that structurally supports itself. The insulating system needs to be stiff and offer good thermal value, but its structural requirements are modest. Also remember that with these systems, the roof and walls will probably be treated differently. Foam-core panels allow them to be treated identically because the same premanufactured components satisfy the requirements of both. But when built-up systems are used, it makes sense to customize the materials and treatment to the specific situation— timber frames typically have widely spaced timbers on the wall and only a wind-load consideration, while roof timbers tend to be more closely spaced, and the loads are more significant, depending on the area. Refer to the energy audit to determine if the chosen insulation values suggest using a greater R-value on the roof.

The infill stud system

The infill stud system is the most-difficult, least-effective way to enclose a timber frame (see the drawing above). It's also the way that most old timber frames were enclosed, so it's the method normally used when an owner wants to replicate the appearance of an old house. Basically, infilling is the process of building stud walls between

INFILL STUD SYSTEM

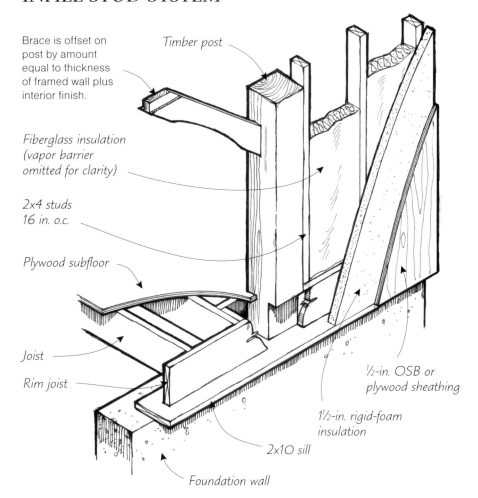

Brace is offset on post by amount equal to thickness of framed wall plus interior finish.

Timber post

Fiberglass insulation (vapor barrier omitted for clarity)

2x4 studs 16 in. o.c.

Plywood subfloor

Joist

Rim joist

½-in. OSB or plywood sheathing

1½-in. rigid-foam insulation

2x10 sill

Foundation wall

For the infill stud system to work easily, the braces are pushed toward the inside of the building so that they won't be obstacles to studs and finish work.

the timbers and packing them with fiberglass insulation. The walls are then wrapped on the outside with a layer of 1½-in.-thick rigid-foam insulation. Because the walls are attached between timbers and not to the outside of the frame, the entire thickness of the timbers is not revealed to the living space. In addition, the timbers wind up fitting poorly to the adjacent studs after movement and shrinkage, allowing a great amount of air infiltration. It stands to reason that there is also a potential for condensation to occur in the cavities where this air infiltration is taking place. A building publication recently reported that many of the posts and beams in a four-year-old timber-frame house enclosed with this method already had significant moisture damage. The infill stud system should only be used if the timbers are dry or if the occupants are prepared to be vigilant about caulking the gaps that develop.

Probably the one advantage of this method is that it requires only conventional materials and simple carpentry. Because the walls don't support any compression loads, single top plates are fine; headers and sills need only be a single stud. All framing can be 24 in. on center. Infilling is made much easier if the timber framer joins all minor members, such as knee braces, toward the inside of the building by the thickness of the framed wall, including the drywall. If the frame is built this way, each stud wall can then be assembled and nailed on the deck and raised as a unit. The infill stud system can be greatly improved by extending 1½ in. of each 2x4 outside the frame, allowing 1½ in. of rigid foam to be placed over the timbers and then another 1½ in. of rigid foam over the entire assembly before the exterior sheathing is applied.

The exterior stud system for walls

By simply moving the stud walls fully to the outside of the frame, the problems created by infilling can be avoided. The timbers can now shrink or move without causing infiltration or compromising insulation quality; fin-

EXTERIOR STUD SYSTEM

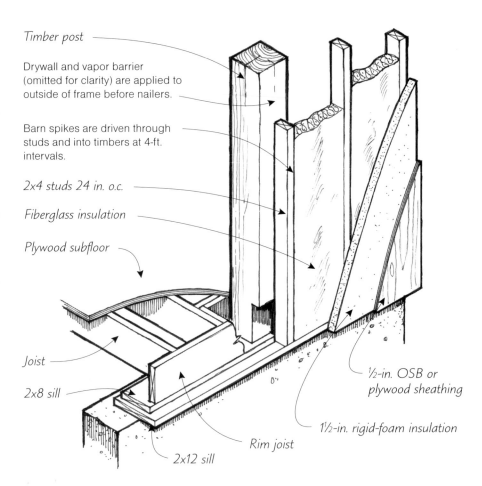

Timber post

Drywall and vapor barrier (omitted for clarity) are applied to outside of frame before nailers.

Barn spikes are driven through studs and into timbers at 4-ft. intervals.

2x4 studs 24 in. o.c.

Fiberglass insulation

Plywood subfloor

Joist

2x8 sill

2x12 sill

Rim joist

½-in. OSB or plywood sheathing

1½-in. rigid-foam insulation

ish work no longer has to fight the frame. Walls can still be conventionally framed, although as in the infill stud system, many structural members can be reduced or eliminated because the timber frame is self-supporting (see the drawing above). Installation is somewhat backward, because the drywall and vapor barrier are attached to the outside of the frame first to avoid infilling between timbers. (Choosing to install the drywall after the studs means that each post will need a stud adjacent to it for drywall attachment.) At this point the drywall will be attached only to the sills and girts of the timber frame and will be quite flimsy. If the studs will be 24 in. on center, choose ⅝-in.-thick drywall (instead of ½ in. thick) to maintain stiffness. Before the stud frame goes up, tack the vapor barrier to the drywall.

There are some inherent problems with this system. First, the drywall must be protected from the weather, which means you must work quickly and take fastidious precautions. The best protection is to have the roof on first, but if the eaves project well beyond the walls, it will be hard to make a good connection to the top plate. Until the roof is on, it's a good idea to keep a tarp rolled up at the peak of the building to pull down over the drywall when necessary.

The second problem is that the stud walls can't be pushed up into position as units, because the drywall blocks the path. So whether the walls are fabricated on the deck or another level surface, they'll have to be carried to the outside of the frame and hoisted into position. It's thus best to keep the walls to a manageable size—that is, not much longer than 16 ft. or taller than 8 ft. to

HORIZONTAL NAILER SYSTEM

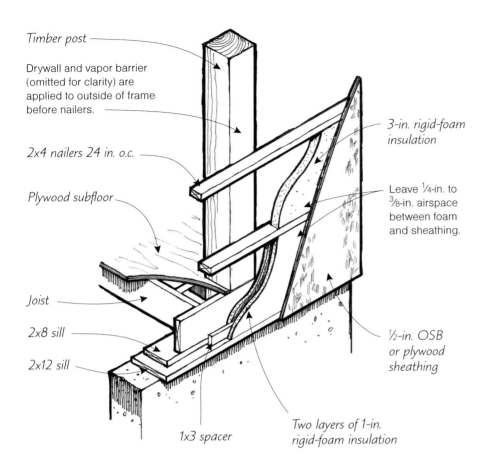

Timber post

Drywall and vapor barrier (omitted for clarity) are applied to outside of frame before nailers.

2x4 nailers 24 in. o.c.

Plywood subfloor

Joist

2x8 sill

2x12 sill

1x3 spacer

3-in. rigid-foam insulation

Leave ¼-in. to ⅜-in. airspace between foam and sheathing.

½-in. OSB or plywood sheathing

Two layers of 1-in. rigid-foam insulation

10 ft. Achieve this by planning for walls to meet at the centerline of posts and girts. When the walls are positioned on the frame, toenail them with 20d galvanized nails wherever there is sufficient nailing surface. Also, spike the studs to the timbers with barn spikes at 4-ft. intervals, penetrating softwood timbers by 2 in. and hardwood timbers by 1½ in. To keep the studs from splitting, predrill a ¼-in. hole before spiking.

After the stud walls are in place, install the wiring and electrical boxes. Then pack in the fiberglass. For improved performance, nail sheets of rigid foam over the stud frame. If rigid foam is not used, horizontal siding can be attached directly to the studs. If the studs are 24 in. on center, the siding has to be at least ¾ in.; overlap shiplapped boards

to create a conventional clapboard appearance. Vertical siding would require that horizontal furring strips be attached to the studs first.

The horizontal nailer system for walls

This system consists of 2x4 nailers attached horizontally to the timbers with rigid-foam insulation in between (see the drawing above). It takes full advantage of the nonstructural nature of the enclosure wall; the light-duty nailers exist only to stiffen the wall and to provide attachment for the interior and exterior sheathing. For good support, a 2x12 sill is absolutely essential. Because the sill is also the bottom nailer, it must extend beyond the frame by the same width as the other nailers.

As in the exterior stud system, the drywall and vapor barrier are applied to

the outside of the frame first. Then rough window and door bucks are premade and toenailed to the 2x12 sill and to timber girts on the outside with 20d galvanized nails. Rigid-foam insulation is ripped to a width that allows the nailers to be 24 in. on center—if the nailers were 1½ in. thick (typically the actual thickness of a 2x4), this dimension would be 22½ in. If you're using plywood for exterior sheathing, make sure the top edge of each 4x8 panel falls on the centerline of a nailer. For a higher R-value per inch and a better perm rate (the rate of moisture absorption), I would choose rigid-foam insulation made of either extruded polystyrene or urethane. It should be ¼ in. to ⅜ in. less in thickness than the width of the nailer to allow the exterior sheathing an air film behind it to prevent warping.

Begin application of the foam by laying a bead of caulking on the 2x12 sill. To create a wire chase between the sill and the next nailer, use two 1-in.-thick rigid-foam boards separated by a 1x3 spacer (if you used a solid foam block here, the chase would have to be routed in the block). Then lay a bead of caulking on top of each layer of foam and put on a nailer, forcing it down against the foam and toenailing it to the timber frame or to window and door bucks. Repeat the procedure all the way to the top of the wall. At the end of each wall, use a vertical stud to cover the ends of the spacers. Applying additional sheets of rigid foam over the whole system, when all nailers and insulation are in place, is a good way to compensate for thermal breaks. Then screw or nail the drywall to the nailers. Wiring and electrical outlets should be run while the insulation is being installed so that cuts in the foam can be made easily. Check your building code. Some will require the wiring to be in a conduit because it will be exposed to the weather for a while, or there may be a requirement for inspection before sheathing is installed. Vertical siding can be nailed directly to the nailers, but horizontal siding will require vertical furring strips to be installed first.

An advantage of this method is that installation is easy and can be done one piece at a time. A crew of two can manage the entire process. In addition, layering horizontally takes advantage of gravity and makes it significantly easier to get a good seal between materials—this is difficult to do with vertical studs because you have to run up and down the ladder so much, constantly trying to push the stuff together. High-quality foam performs better than fiberglass, and caulking improves the seal. Still, there are a number of breaks because of the nailers.

This is a good alternate enclosure method, and you can vary the thickness of the insulation to keep costs in line. Our shop was built with a variation of this system, using furring strips for nailers with 1-in.-thick EPS between them. The interior and exterior finishes are vertical boards. The system gave us a decent finish, minimal insulation, and minimal cost.

The Larsen-truss system for walls and roof

The Larsen truss was developed by John Larsen specifically to address the difficulty of retrofitting older buildings with better insulation. Acknowledging that the buildings did not need additional support, just more insulation, he set out to create a nonstructural framework to contain insulation and hold sheathing. Larsen designed a light truss that uses 2x2s as flanges and plywood for the web. These trusses can be made by anyone with a table saw, glue, clamps, and a little patience. They can be made to span the height of the walls or the length of the rafters and are lifted and managed easily by one or two people. Because the width of the plywood web is variable, you can use as much insulation as necessary without a great deal more expense for wood. The web is usually only ⅜ in. thick and does not need to be continuous, so there isn't high conduction through the material. For a new timber-frame structure, this option would make sense only where rigid foams were either totally unavailable or totally unpalatable to the client.

Installing a Larsen truss is similar to installing exterior stud walls, except that the truss is always attached a section at a time (see the drawing at left). Drywall goes on the frame first, along with the vapor barrier. A truss is then secured to the timber posts by nailing the exposed edges of the inside flanges with galvanized nails that penetrate the posts by at least 1½ in. Wiring is run, and electrical boxes are installed, then the fiberglass insulation is applied as tightly as possible to the plywood. It's not necessary to use additional rigid foam on the outside. Exterior sheathing is nailed directly to the outside flanges.

The Larsen truss makes a cavity for a great thickness of insulation at a low price—from 12 in. to 15 in. of fiberglass is not unusual. But most of the difficulties with the system stem from this thickness, for the distance between the inside edge of the frame and the outside edge of the truss is so great that they bear almost no relationship to each other. The trusses will therefore appear as unnatural appendages to the building if they overhang the foundation, or the foundation will have to be reconsidered to accommodate the trusses. I endorse the latter option. A simple solution is to design pilasters into the foundation wall to support the posts and to use the wall itself as a base for the trusses. (See pp. 122 and 124 for a discussion of pilasters.) Besides the aesthetic problem of the exterior walls overhanging the foundation by 12 in.

LARSEN-TRUSS SYSTEM

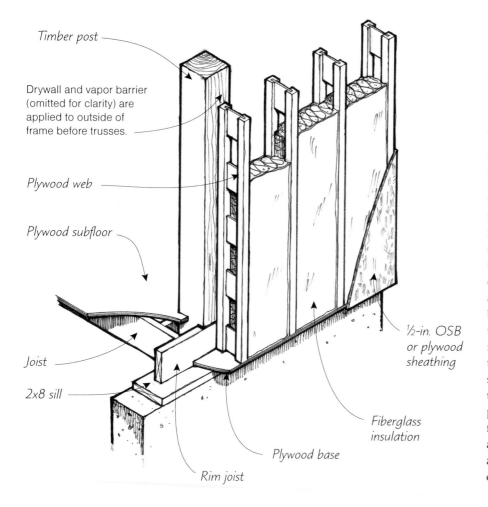

Timber post

Drywall and vapor barrier (omitted for clarity) are applied to outside of frame before trusses.

Plywood web

Plywood subfloor

Joist

2x8 sill

Rim joist

Plywood base

Fiberglass insulation

½-in. OSB or plywood sheathing

or more, it's also hard to seal the bottom of the insulation cavity.

Extreme wall thickness also creates some difficulties at exterior windows and doors. Jambs need to be as wide as the wall is thick, causing extra expense for materials and labor. Extreme depth at the jambs might also restrict light from spreading well as it enters the house. The condition can be eased by beveling the jamb sides back at an angle, a nice but expensive touch.

Larsen trusses can also be used effectively on the roof (see the drawings below). But because fiberglass roof insulation must be ventilated to avoid potential moisture buildup, the thickness of the truss and insulation must be planned to allow an airspace of at least 2 in. between the insulation and the exterior sheathing. The airflow must pass from the eave to the peak; holes will have to be drilled for each cavity at the eaves, and a ridge vent will be necessary at the peak. (Commercial materials for eave and ridge vents are available through most lumberyards.) Begin by attaching the drywall and the vapor barrier to the outside of the roof timbers. To install the trusses, snap a chalkline along each eave and lay the trusses 2 ft. on center, their bottom edges aligned with the chalkline. Trusses can be fixed to each other at the peak, and the inside flanges should be attached to the timbers in the same manner as on the walls. Cut the bottoms of the trusses perpendicular to the

USING LARSEN TRUSSES ON THE ROOF

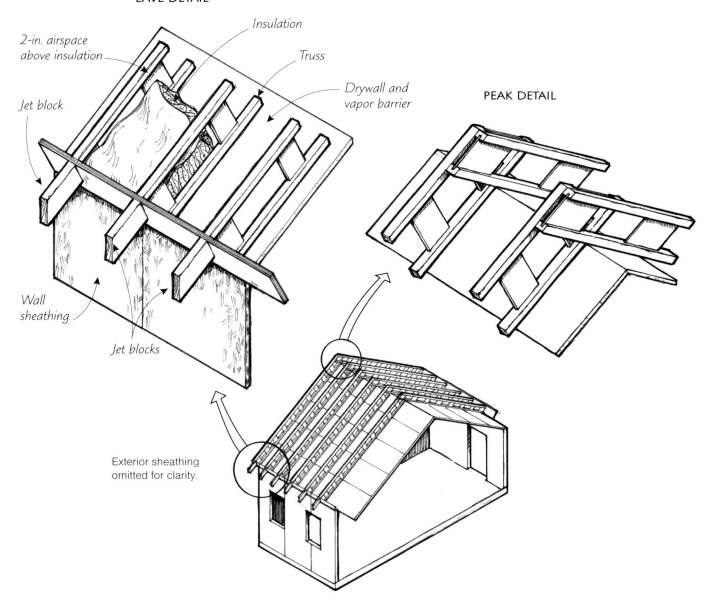

EAVE DETAIL

2-in. airspace above insulation

Insulation

Truss

Jet block

Drywall and vapor barrier

PEAK DETAIL

Wall sheathing

Jet blocks

Exterior sheathing omitted for clarity.

RIGID-FOAM ROOF INSULATION

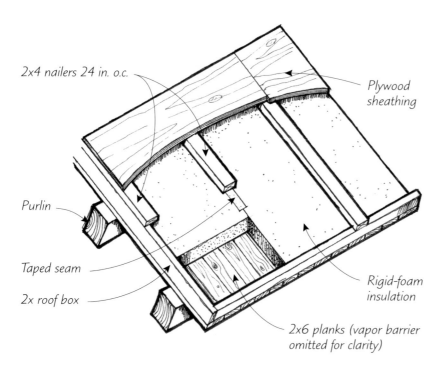

- 2x4 nailers 24 in. o.c.
- Plywood sheathing
- Purlin
- Taped seam
- 2x roof box
- Rigid-foam insulation
- 2x6 planks (vapor barrier omitted for clarity)

FOAM-AND-NAILER ROOF INSULATION

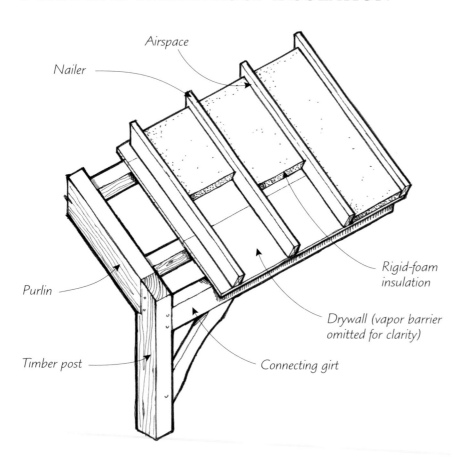

- Airspace
- Nailer
- Purlin
- Timber post
- Connecting girt
- Drywall (vapor barrier omitted for clarity)
- Rigid-foam insulation

slope of the roof. Attach planking to the bottom edges of the trusses to cap the cavity. To avoid having roof trim the same width as the trusses, attach jet blocks to the box.

Rigid-foam roof insulation

In this system, sheets of rigid-foam insulation are laid over 2x6 planks within a box built around the roof perimeter (see the top drawing at left). Planking is used instead of drywall because the interior roof sheathing must be able to support its own weight between timbers without sagging.

The planks are applied directly to the roof timbers, and the roof box is built from stock that is as wide as the insulation is thick. A vapor barrier is tacked to the planks, sealing the sides of the box. All seams should be sealed or taped. The insulation is then installed in the box. Choose insulation thickness by analyzing the relative values of the foam; to prevent crushing or deflection in high-load situations, the foam should have a density of 1½ lb. to 2 lb. It is certainly possible to use foam not much thicker than 3 in. or 3½ in.

After installing the insulation, caulk all voids or fill them with expanding foam and tape the seams. To make an airspace between the foam and the exterior sheathing, attach 2x3 or 2x4 nailers 24 in. on center, perpendicular to the roof timbers. Nail through the foam to the frame using the guidelines suggested for panels on p. 111. Then put on the exterior sheathing. Roof overhangs can be established using the planks and/or the nailers for support.

Foam-and-nailer roof insulation

If you want to use drywall as the interior finish instead of planking, you'll have to use a system with nailers. The nailers run perpendicular to the roof timbers (vertically over purlins and horizontally over rafters). Beyond that, the system is similar to the horizontal nailer system for walls. Apply the drywall to the frame first, then attach the vapor barrier.

Use a nailer wide enough to allow a 2-in. airspace between the foam and the exterior sheathing—if you were using 3½-in.-thick foam, for example, you would need a 5½-in.-wide nailer on edge. Place the nailers over the vapor barrier and toenail them to the frame with 20d galvanized nails. Then install a section of rigid foam and the next nailer. When the foam is in place and properly sealed, attach the exterior sheathing to the nailers.

While the drywall is exposed and unsupported, it presents a potential safety hazard to the installer. To help prevent accidents and damage, work your way across or up the roof, installing all the layers at the same time. This will make it possible to stand on either the sheathing or the frame while materials are being positioned and secured.

SELECTING FOAM-CORE PANELS

Some of us thought we would never submit to plastic. We saw it come in our lifetime, and when we wanted to point out what was wrong with the modern world, we pointed to plastic—tangible evidence of the great deterioration of all good things. Old cars were built like tanks; new cars have too much plastic. There might be metal somewhere in my computer, but all that is visible is plastic. We grumble and complain, but plastic is here to stay.

It is no coincidence that the timber-frame revival has moved just about as quickly as the development of foam-core panel technology. Those of us who craft timbers with mallet and chisel are often a little startled when we are reminded that the panel, a very critical component in most timber-frame building, is made mostly of plastic.

Panel specs

As I said before, the panel is only a core of foam with sheet materials bonded to either side, yet it is asked to play a major role in the construction of signifi-

cant buildings. Our expectations for panels should therefore be high; they must adhere to the following tough specifications:

• They have to be strong and stiff. The timber frame can have either purlins or rafters on the roof on approximately 4-ft. centers. Spans between horizontal timbers in the walls are usually no longer than 10 ft. Panels must be able to hold their own in these spaces. This can mean supporting as much as 100 lb. per sq. ft. on the roof and resisting a 100-mph wind bearing against the walls.
• The panels must not delaminate. Delamination between the materials would be our worst fear come to life.
• None of the materials should suffer unreasonable deterioration because of exposure to time, temperature changes, or the elements. The panel should be at least as stable as wood.
• Panels should have a high R-value per inch of thickness, to achieve optimum thermal performance without creating imposing fortress walls.
• Panels should have a low perm rate because the panel core also has to act as a vapor barrier. Humidity and air pressure in tight houses are higher than normal, and it is very important to prevent the flow of humid air. If this air should penetrate the inside skin, the core material must be water-resistant enough not to soak up the excess moisture like a sponge.
• Panels should hold up well under high heat and fire. We are all concerned about flame spread and toxicity. Panels house the foam in an oxygen-free environment, putting a flammable product in the safest possible position, but we still want to know that we would have a chance to leave the building safely should a fire start.
• The core material should have a sufficient molecular bond to resist creep. Even though the panels are nailed to the frame, creep could cause a more rapid deterioration of the panel system, especially on the roof, where the panels are unsupported at the base and tend to carry a greater load.

• The panels must allow practical, efficient installation.
• Cost must be reasonable or, like many other exotic building products, foam-core panels will be saved for commercial and public buildings and for the very rich.

Panel core

As I said, current commercially available panels are made using either urethane or EPS as the core material. The choice between EPS and urethane should be based on an analysis of the attributes and deficiencies of each material (for more information about EPS and urethane, see pp. 113-115). Panel manufacturers tend to specialize in one foam type or the other, and they battle to claim the perfect product. In an attempt to settle the dispute, I hereby pronounce them both in need of further development—the best manufacturers are those who recognize this. Rigid foam has value only in relation to the role it plays as one of the panel components and should be judged on the basis of performance, safety, durability, and cost.

Exterior and interior skins

For the exterior and interior skins, most manufacturers offer several options, and the best option is not necessarily clear. Luckily, the problems inherent in each of the options are not necessarily severe. The most important concern should be whether or not the manufacturer has tested the specific panel to meet the buyer's local structural codes. With this aside, there are good and better choices, depending on local conditions and the requirements of the building. A house on the shore of Nantucket Island, which must endure high winds and high humidity, should be treated differently from a house in the mountains of Colorado, which will be subjected to heavy snow but low humidity. Large loads and long frame spans might suggest the strongest panel; enclosing a swimming pool or a hot tub might force the decision to turn on moisture protection. Remember, too, that while it is in the best interest of the manufacturer to make and sell identical panels to keep the price down, it is often in your interest to get panels made to your specification.

In general, the exterior skin should be strong, especially under compression. It should have good nail-holding capacity for the application of siding, roofing, and trim. It should be dimensionally stable, not expanding and shrinking abnormally in wet and dry cycles. Finally, it should be a capable vapor barrier, helping to prevent moisture penetration.

The usual options are chipboard, OSB, and plywood. Inevitably, there are trade-offs. For strength and moisture resistance, marine plywood would be wonderful, but the cost is prohibitively high. Some of the prefinished plywood sidings, such as Texture 1-11, might be durable enough, but it doesn't make sense to use a great thermal panel with a poor thermal joint—it's almost impossible to have both the expanding foam seal necessary for optimum energy performance and good looks in prefinished panels. Regular exterior plywood is not bonded as well as it should be and tends to delaminate. Because the panel leaves no airspace between the plywood and the core, moisture gets in, stays in, and the plies split apart. So that leaves chipboard and OSB. Chipboard is nothing more than compressed flakes of wood held together with glue. OSB looks like chipboard, but the grain of the wood chips is aligned and compressed into sheets with the fibers cross-laminated in a manner that gives it better strength and nail-holding capacity. The advantage of OSB and chipboard over plywood is that they can't delaminate. OSB is stronger than chipboard, has better nail-holding capacity, and is about the same price; it has therefore been our preference.

The interior skin should have good tensile resistance to loads and should serve as a vapor barrier to keep moisture from penetrating the core from the inside. It should also serve as a fire barrier, isolating the panel core from the

Blueboard is generally the interior panel surface. When the panels have been installed, interior finish, insulation, and exterior sheathing are completed.

house interior, and must either be the interior wall surface or be able to support it. The alternatives are usually drywall, blueboard (plaster-based drywall), greenboard (moisture-resistant drywall), and type-X (drywall with a half-hour fire rating). Blueboard is our first choice because it is stronger than regular drywall and holds up well when rain gets to the site before we get the roof on. Blueboard also gives our clients the option of either plastering or painting.

The exterior sheathings listed previously can also be used for the interior skin, with the finish interior surface then applied as another layer. We call these panels "doublechips." Although more expensive, doublechips have several advantages. First, they're stronger and have a better nail-holding capacity for attaching trim, cabinets, and other finish elements. Second, the greater strength of the interior skin helps keep

the panels from warping when the exterior skin expands in high-moisture conditions. Finally, they may be required for certain structural conditions of the building. When we use doublechips, we specifically request the interior skin be made with little formaldehyde in the glue. Don't forget that a combination of interior panel skins might also make sense. For example, where there are high-wind conditions but little snow, drywall panels can be used for the roof and doublechips for the walls. Or doublechips can be used just in the area where cabinets need to be hung and drywall panels used for all other areas.

Panel joints

There are about 50 major panel manufacturers across North America (see Sources of Supply on p. 232), with the numbers growing as the use of foam-core panels proliferates as an independent form of construction. All panel manufacturers use some variation of the techniques discussed later in this chapter. Read that before deciding on the type of panel that's appropriate for your job. Aside from the differences in manufacturing technique, there are a number of manufacturer-suggested panel-to-panel connections. Several of the most common are shown below. Panel connection is just as important a consideration as the way a panel is made, because the seams are the areas most prone to infiltration and weakness, and are where expansion and contraction are most likely to show. Unfortunately, there is a prevalent tendency to overlook the critical fact that insulation must be tight to be effective. Just because the panels have been pushed together does not mean a seal has been made—in fact, in almost every circumstance, a good seal has not been made. You just can't expect 90 to 200 linear inches of sheathing edge to be joined without some pretty big gaps. Think of the panels as you would sheets of glass for an aquarium—the glass alone is not enough.

Ease of installation is a big concern for panel manufacturers, many of whom use molded joints or tongue-and-groove joints for precisely that reason. But I've found that these systems don't give a reliable seal, so I prefer to use the

SOME PANEL-JOINING OPTIONS

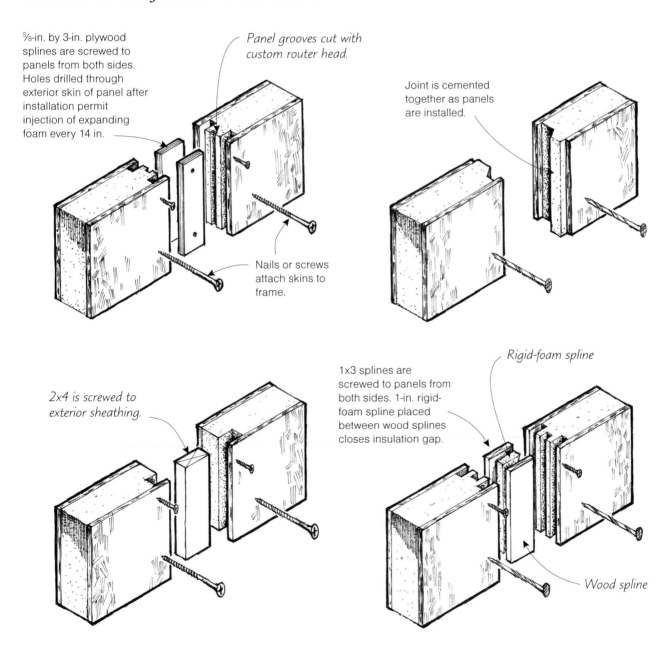

⅝-in. by 3-in. plywood splines are screwed to panels from both sides. Holes drilled through exterior skin of panel after installation permit injection of expanding foam every 14 in.

Panel grooves cut with custom router head.

Nails or screws attach skins to frame.

Joint is cemented together as panels are installed.

2x4 is screwed to exterior sheathing.

1x3 splines are screwed to panels from both sides. 1-in. rigid-foam spline placed between wood splines closes insulation gap.

Rigid-foam spline

Wood spline

option shown in the top left drawing on p. 105. The panels arrive with square edges, which are then routed to accept two ⅝-in. by 3-in. plywood splines. We use a custom router head designed to take out a little extra insulation at the foam edge between splines to create a cavity into which we can spray expanding foam. This is done after the panels have been installed by drilling a ¼-in. hole approximately every 14 in. through the splines to accept the nozzle of the foam can. We fill all roof joints as well as the wall joints. In addition, where panels join over a timber, we leave a deliberate gap of at least ¼ in. during installation, to be filled with foam later. We also foam at the base between the 2x8 and 2x12 sills, at all outside corners, at the eave and rake seams between wall and roof, and at the ridge. It may seem like a lot of bother, but these extra steps make the difference between good and great performance.

INSTALLING FOAM-CORE PANELS

In theory, installing foam-core panels is similar to installing other types of exterior sheathing except that the panels are thicker, heavier, and a whole lot more expensive. I will describe in the following pages a process for planning, cutting, and installing foam-core panels that will work with different types of panels and a number of panel suppliers. All of the details may not be applicable to your situation, so check with your suppliers to find out what they offer and to learn about their specifications for panel spans and attachment. In general, panels come in two widths—either 4 ft. or 8 ft.—and lengths between 8 ft. and 24 ft. The most commonly available sizes are 4x8, 4x12, and 4x16. But many panel suppliers will precut panels based on your plans. Some will even provide installation services. In any case, you should know what sizes are offered.

The location of the timbers in the frame determines the final lengths, widths, and cuts for the panels.

Panel layout

To make installation efficient, it is important to map out a strategy prior to getting started. Because panels are attached to the timber frame, the location of the timbers determines the final lengths, widths, and cuts for the panels. Therefore, use a blueprint of the frame plan as the basis for the panel plan. You'll need a plan for each wall of the house and for the roof surfaces. Locate the rough openings for windows and doors using the architectural plans for reference—don't draw in any panels yet. The rough openings should be the same as those specified by the door and window manufacturers for stud-frame construction. All locations for openings should be referenced from the edges of the timbers, because the panel installers will have nothing else from which to measure.

After locating the rough openings, draw in the panels. Laying out the panels is a matter of juggling several considerations—strength, panel waste, rough openings, and roof overhang. Here are a few guidelines to follow before you begin.

First, check the requirements of the local building code and the loading characteristics of the chosen panel. Most manufactured panels are engineered to span 8 ft. to 9 ft. on the walls and 4 ft. on the roof. Be wary of a manufacturer that cannot provide documentation.

Second, don't risk inordinate panel waste by forcing the spans to work out perfectly. For example, suppose the distance from the 2x12 sill to the centerline of the girt is larger than the 4x8 panels. You could certainly cut 4x12 panels to fit, but you'd be creating a lot of debris. A better solution would be to position the 4x8 panels from where they had adequate nailing (2 in. minimum) on the rim joist to where they had adequate nailing on the girt. To do this, snap a line along the face of the rim joist and nail a ledger to the line to support the panels during nailing.

When the panels will not reach from the sill to the girt, nail a ledger to the rim joist to support the panels. Then use panel offcuts to fill in over the rim joist.

Then fill in over the rim joist with off-cuts (see the photo at left).

Third, panel joints that fall between the edges of rough openings should be reinforced with a 2x4 spline (see the drawings below). (I use 2x4s generically here; the splines would be different dimensions if the panels were thicker or thinner.) Window openings that are wider than 3 ft. 6 in. and taller than 5 ft. and all door openings should be reinforced with a 2x4 on either side that runs from sill to girt. Smaller windows can be cut directly into the panels without a need for this reinforcement. If the window is small enough, try to locate it toward the middle of the panel, leaving 6 in. to 8 in. on either side. But if the window has to be closer to a panel edge, move the panel edge to the edge of the rough opening to put the joint in a place where it can be strengthened with a 2x4. In other words, you don't want just a little bit of insulation between the edge of the rough opening and the

edge of the panel because this would create a weak area.

Fourth, nonsupported overhangs on the rakes should be limited to 1½ ft. beyond the wall panel, and 1 ft. should be the limit at the eaves. Using doublechip panels allows an increase in overhang to 2½ ft. on the rakes and 2 ft. at the eaves. Some trim details support the eave panels, making it possible to use greater overhangs with the standard panel, as discussed in Chapter 10. Doublechip panels are also useful in high-load situations, because the nail-base sheathing is so much stronger in tension than drywall. When using doublechips, you can avoid infilling the interior finish sheathing by nailing it to the outside of the frame before panel installation.

Here are some other things to consider when laying out the panels on the plan: Panels should run vertically on the walls, unless the spacing of the posts is closer than the spacing of the horizontal girts and plates. Next, plan

REINFORCED DOOR OPENING

2x4 gives continuous sill-to-girt reinforcement when panel seams break at window and door openings.

Timber girt

Timber post

Plywood subfloor

2x8 sill

2x12 sill

2x4 nailers

Panel splines (hidden)

REINFORCED WINDOW OPENING

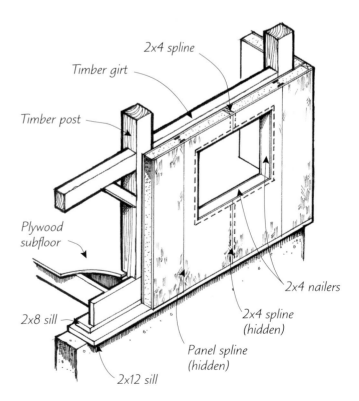

2x4 spline

Timber girt

Timber post

Plywood subfloor

2x8 sill

2x12 sill

2x4 nailers

2x4 spline (hidden)

Panel spline (hidden)

to fill in above and below window and door openings with panel pieces. Work hard to have the tapered factory edges of the drywall meet at all seams, though you won't be able to achieve this everywhere. Use the same procedure on the roof, laying out full panel sections on either side of roof, window, or chimney rough openings. You will have to juggle all these factors in an attempt to reduce waste. Dot in the panels over the frame plan, making sure each panel and offcut is clearly marked (see the drawing below).

Cutting and installation

Once the plan is drawn, the panels can be cut and installed. During these stages, try to satisfy the requirements of all three panel components. Interior sheathing must be handled with proverbial kid gloves. The foam core is tougher, but it must be well sealed at all cracks and crevices before installation is finished. The exterior skin is primarily a nail base, and you must make sure it provides solid, dependable nail-

TYPICAL PANEL PLAN

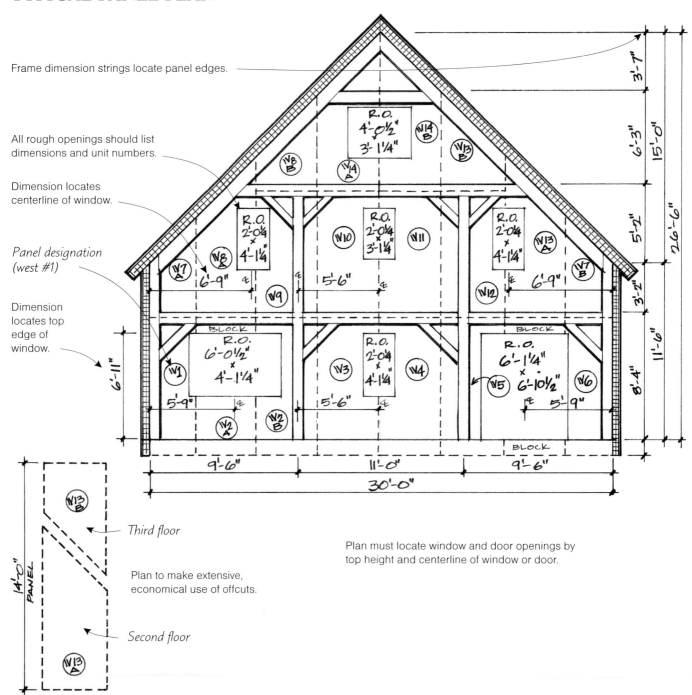

Frame dimension strings locate panel edges.

All rough openings should list dimensions and unit numbers.

Dimension locates centerline of window.

Panel designation (west #1)

Dimension locates top edge of window.

Third floor

Plan to make extensive, economical use of offcuts.

Second floor

Plan must locate window and door openings by top height and centerline of window or door.

Foam-core panels for walls are laid out and cut one at a time, after measurements and layout lines have been double-checked. The window opening in this panel has been routed to receive a 2x4. (Photo by Sarah Knock.)

ing for all materials applied. Good installation procedure requires vigilance on all these fronts at once.

Although it's not a rule by any means, we usually attach the wall panels first. It is much easier to lift the wall panels into place without the roof panels in the way, particularly if an overhead winch or crane is used to help with lifting, as is typically the case. There are also some situations in which it would be extremely difficult to fit the wall panels under the eave panels and over the 2x12 sill simultaneously. If the eave panels extend over the upper plate or girt, nailing the top edge of the wall panel would be difficult, if not impossible. But the obvious disadvantage of installing the wall panels first is that they will be unprotected and thus vulnerable to the elements until the roof is on. You can see the need for good planning and tight scheduling. (The tools you'll need for panel installation are discussed briefly in the sidebar above.)

Begin by marking panel breaks and the rough openings for windows and doors on the outside face of the sill and beams. Check that openings coincide with the frame as depicted on the plans. Then string a line along the eave to accurately represent the eave intersection. Using a chalkline or a large T-square, draw lines on the panels for the rough openings and all other cuts. Check all measurements before cutting. We usually lay out and cut the wall panels one at a time and precut the roof panels in preparation for crane assistance. The benefit to this system is that you can check your work on the walls as you go, whereas the possibilities of making a mistake on the roof are pretty slim, as there are usually few openings. Always use a mask and goggles when cutting. Panel dust and chips are inorganic and ugly, and should be cleaned up often. My most disturbing experience with panel debris was when a client's beautiful cranberry bog was fouled with a frost of panel dust. The house needed insulating, not the bog.

The panels are heavy, so make all the cuts in a panel at the same time. Panels that will span the full height of the wall should be sawn about ⅜ in. short to make room for the foam. If your saw isn't capable of cutting through the thickness of the panel, cut in halfway from each side—any remaining foam in the middle will break off easily. Tilt the saw base to cut the roof angle at the top of the wall panels (see the left drawing on p. 110). Then cut a ½-in.-deep notch in the top outside edge through the exterior sheathing and the depth of the foam, leaving only the interior panel skin intact. This notch is to be filled with expanding foam to seal this joint. With the grinder equipped with the spline-cutter head, rout all seams that do not fall on posts; panel edges falling on posts are sawn to allow a ¼-in. gap at the seam for the foam. Rout the perimeters of all rough openings for windows and doors to accept nailers (usually 2x4s)—do this with the nailer-cutter head in the grinder set to full depth. Also rout the outside panel edge on each building

PANEL DETAIL AT EAVE

1-in.-high by ½-in.-deep notch receives expanding foam seal.

PANEL DETAIL AT CORNER

PLAN VIEW

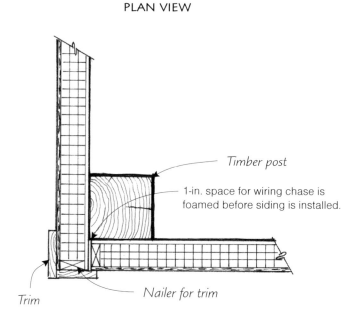

Timber post

1-in. space for wiring chase is foamed before siding is installed.

Trim

Nailer for trim

All seams that don't fall over timbers are routed using a grinder with a special spline-cutter head. Goggles and a mask should be used when cutting. (Photo by Sarah Knock.)

Before the panels are lifted into position on the frame, nails are started in the exterior sheathing. In this oak frame, spiral galvanized nails were used to avoid a tannic-acid reaction with bare metal. (Photo by Sarah Knock.)

corner for a nailer (see the right drawing on the facing page). Where the panel edges need reinforcement, as with wide windows (see p. 107), the nailer-cutter head is set to one-half the width of the nailer, so the nailer can bridge the joint between panels.

After the panels have been cut and while they're still on the sawhorses, install and secure the splines to one edge of a pair of mating panels. Attach the splines first on the exterior side with 1½-in. galvanized screws and then use regular drywall screws on the other side. Screws should be approximately

8 in. on center. The nailers on the corners of the house may be put in while the panels are on the ground, but don't put any nailers in window and door openings until the panels are installed, because the nailers should span the panel seams for extra reinforcement.

Attaching panels to the frame

Panels can be attached with either nails or screws. Good-quality screws have become available for this application (see Sources of Supply on p. 232). We now prefer the use of screws because they hold well, are driven with less brute effort, and can be removed. The nails

used depend on the frame material. For softwood frames, use a ring-shank (pole-barn) nail that will penetrate the timbers by at least 2 in. For hardwood frames, use spiral galvanized nails long enough to penetrate the wood by 1½ in. Both nails and screws should be 8 in. to 10 in. on center around the perimeter and 16 in. on center for midpanel attachment.

Before positioning the panels, start the nails or screws through the exterior sheathing. Then apply a bead of construction adhesive onto the faces of the posts, beams, and 2x12 sill (or face of

A spline is being driven into place from above. If the panel were over 10 ft. long, this maneuver would not be possible.

These two panels were attached to the frame without preinstalled splines. With splines in place, the panels often have to be driven together. (Photo by Sarah Knock.)

This window opening has been routed to receive 2x4 nailers. The splines are screwed to the interior and exterior sheathing. The gap between the splines will be filled with expanding foam.

The first roof panel is laid to a chalkline snapped on the frame. Roof-panel edges are routed for a nailer, installed when all the roof panels are in place. The notch in the wall panel enables the foam to make a good seal with the roof panel.

Nailers are fixed to the window and door openings and to the roof edges after all panels are positioned. Regular drywall screws are used for the interior sheathing; galvanized screws are used for the exterior. (Photo by Sarah Knock.)

the rim joist) that the panel will be attached to. Starting with an outside corner, lift each panel into place. Slide the panels together horizontally. When installing the top panels in the wall, lift them to the eave string by prying with a flat bar. Drive in the nails or screws.

After the first panel on each wall is in position, you will need to drive subsequent panels together to engage splines. Sometimes it is necessary to do this with a mallet, protecting the panel edge with a block of wood. If the panel length is not greater than 10 ft., it is often easier to drive the splines from above rather than mating the splines

edgewise, another reason to put on the wall panels first. In places where panels are stacked on top of each other, use ¼-in. plywood spacers to create a cavity for foam. Make sure to allow at least 2 in. of nailing surface in the timbers for the panel edges. Gable-end wall panels should be shy of the roof panels by the same amount for foaming.

Before installing the roof panels, snap a line on the purlin or rafter that will be at the first panel seam (see the left photo above). Following the line will help ensure that the eave or rake will be straight for the trim. Place a bead of construction adhesive on the roof

timbers and on the top of the beveled edge of the eave panels prior to placing the roof panels. With the nails or screws already in position, attach the panel when it is aligned with the chalkline. Most roofs require few spline joints because the timbers are 4 ft. on center. Space the panels ¼ in. from each other with plywood spacers, creating a cavity for foam. If you choose to ignore my instructions about foaming the wall seams, don't carry the illogical thinking up to the roof, for you'd certainly be disappointed with the resulting energy performance.

Skins and Frames

When all the panels are in position and completely nailed to the frame, install the nailers in all the window and door rough openings and around the perimeter of the roof (see the right photo on the facing page). Use long, straight material for the roof nailers and set their edges precisely to a string line. This will make installing the roof trim infinitely easier. Secure all nailers with 8d galvanized nails from the exterior skin and screw with drywall screws from the interior skin. Also make sure all the spline joints have been properly screwed and nailed.

Now fill all the roof and wall seams with expanding foam. At each spline joint, drill a ¼-in. hole approximately every 14 in. to insert the nozzle of the foam can. Work your way up, not down, the joints. Keep the cans warm and experiment on some scraps before you start because climatic conditions affect foam expansion. We have found that a two-second count on a 14-in. spacing generally fills to the next level quite nicely, but be prepared to adjust

the spacing and the count as necessary. After the foam has completely expanded and hardened, scrape the excess from the surface.

EPS PANELS AND URETHANE

EPS and urethane are alike in that they both are rigid-foam plastics used for insulation. Thereafter, they are mostly different from each other. Following are some advantages and disadvantages of each and a discussion of manufacturing techniques. This information is meant to help you decide which material is best for your situation.

Advantages of EPS

• It is easy to manufacture. Polystyrene beads are compressed together under heat and pressure to make a large block, or "bun." The bun is then slabbed with a hot knife to the required thickness to create panel cores.
• EPS is light and easy to work with.
• When hot wires are used instead of a

router to make cuts, there isn't a problem with dust.
• EPS accepts various glues and mastics, and generally bonds well to the skins.

Disadvantages of EPS

• Because EPS panels are so easy to make, some are produced in uncontrolled conditions. Panels fabricated under the apple tree are sold alongside those made in well-tooled facilities with good quality control.
• EPS is a hazard in high heat and fire. It loses its structural integrity at about 180°F and melts at 300°F. In a fire test I witnessed, heat from the fire quickly melted the panel into a volatile liquid. Therefore, consider using type-X drywall (half-hour fire rating) as an interior skin for EPS panels.
• EPS panels have potential for radical molecular creep. Tim Johnson, a technical researcher at Massachusetts Institute of Technology, reports that over a 16-ft. span loaded to 40 lb. per sq. ft. for 90 days, EPS panel samples shifted 6 in. because of creep. This is a big load

Roof panels are usually lifted into place with a crane. Holes are drilled through a top spline to fill a deliberate gap between panels. (Photo by Bill Holtz.)

and little time; I worry about small loads and lots of time.

• Most panel manufacturers keep costs down by using 1-lb. instead of 2-lb. density EPS. Yet a 2-lb. density foam would give better compression strength, a higher R-value, and a lower perm rate. EPS panels are generally the least expensive, but not because they are on sale.

• Low R-value per inch means more inches of thickness are necessary for good performance. The lower price of the material is offset when the R-values are equivalent. Window and door jambs and roof edges require more lumber for framing and finish.

Advantages of urethane

• Urethane foam has a very high R-value. A panel made to a typical 2x4-stud thickness has an R-value of about 24 to 28.

• Urethane is typically manufactured at a 2-lb. density. When properly formulated, it is stiff and resilient.

• Because the panels are fairly thin, they are relatively easy to install. Nailers needed around windows and doors and at roof edges can be 2x4s instead of 2x6s or 2x8s.

• With a perm rate of 1 or less per inch, the urethane itself acts as a vapor barrier.

• Panels can be made either by laminating skins to slabbed bun stock or by injecting liquid urethane between the skins (called pouring). Panels made from other materials can only be laminated.

• Good urethane formulations will not support flame. However, they will eventually burn if the fire is fueled by another source.

Disadvantages of urethane

• Urethane foams are complex. There are hundreds of different formulas, and both the manufacturing environment and technique must be precisely monitored. It is rather like Grandma's cake recipe: Leave out one little ingredient and the cake tastes terrible; open the

Foam is injected into all seams. Panel installation is only as good as the quality of the seal between panels.

oven for a peek at the wrong moment and it falls flat; and only Grandma knows how to make it right anyway. An increase or decrease in the blowing agent (usually Freon) that causes the foam to expand can greatly affect density. If the temperature is too low during manufacture, the foam could be too brittle. There is no generic foam; physical properties change greatly from one company to another. If your supplier hasn't heard of words like isotropic, polyol, and isocyanate, you are probably purchasing from the wrong company.

• Although some formulations do not support flame, most urethane is flammable, and the smoke is toxic.

• Urethane loses some of its R-value as the gases are lost from the cellular structure. Over a period of four or five years, the panel could lose 5 points of R-value. Again, this depends on the particular formula and on the manufacturing system.

EPS panel construction

EPS panels can be made only by laminating the skins to the slab stock. It's a simple process that helps keep the price down. This panel can literally be made by spreading glue over the surface of the foam, applying the skins, and putting weight on it while it sets.

Laminated-urethane-panel construction

The advantage of lamination is that it isn't technologically as difficult as pouring, and the slabs of foam can be precured, meaning the foam should be dimensionally stable and the initial outgasing of propellant should be completed. On the other hand, pouring eliminates the potential deterioration of the adhesive and is much quicker. But because pouring technology is still new, the most important thing for consumers is to buy from reputable manufacturers.

As with EPS panels, a laminated urethane panel can literally be made by spreading glue or contact adhesive over the foam surfaces, applying the skins, and putting weight on the assembly while it sets. Contact adhesive is used for speed; glue is used when finer technology does not exist. One company I visited used a corps of high-school kids to construct giant piles of panels. The kids would mop glue on a skin, place a foam slab on the top, spread more glue and another skin, and so on, until they could no longer reach the top and were ankle deep in glue. Unused buckets of glue were then placed on top to hold down the mountain of sandwiches. The panels actually weren't bad, and though the company went out of business, it wasn't for want of glue.

I have a homespun test for panels. I put samples measuring 4 in. square on the wire cage in a canning pot with several inches of water, and bring the temperature up to 155°F. I leave it there for 12 hours—100% humidity at 155°F, and while not as harsh as what time and weather could do to a panel, it's still a pretty good test. The glue-mopped panels described previously survived the test well, but samples made with contact adhesive failed miserably.

The disadvantages of laminated panels are several. For example, precuring often causes tension to build up in the bun stock, resulting in warping. In addition, cutting urethane slabs from the buns leaves a film of dust on each surface because the cellular structure is somewhat brittle. Trying to bond a material to a dusty surface has predictably poor results. In one of the assembly-line gluing processes, the panels are run under a high-pressure pinch roller while contact cement is setting. The pinch roller crushes the cells on the slab surface, making even more dust. It is no wonder that this type of laminated panel almost always falls apart in my canning-pot test in less than four hours. More disconcerting than my private laboratory conclusions have been those occasions when I have found scraps of the material left on the building site that were completely delaminated after only a few weeks of exposure.

Poured-urethane-panel construction

There are two ways to pour panels: vertically and horizontally. In vertical pouring, liquid urethane is injected between two skins set on edge in a form. Vertical simply means that the 4x16 or 4x8 skins are standing on edge with the 4-ft. side vertical. This system requires simple technology and relatively inexpensive equipment, but it is necessarily slow. The skins are placed in the form manually, and the foam has to rise 4 ft. before the panel is completed. Because the form has no top, vertically poured panels often show uneven cell structure and therefore would exhibit uneven strength and stability properties.

A bigger disadvantage is that the foam cells rise vertically and tend to be elongated in the same direction. Considerable compressive strength in the flat direction is lost because of this cellular shape. Think of the cells in the foam as a cluster of eggs. We know eggs to be much stronger in length than in width, and if they were all lined up lengthwise, this cluster would be easy to crush. When cells are elongated like this, the foam is said to have anisotropic properties, resulting in more strength in the direction of the rise than perpendicular to it. To prevent anisotropism, the foam must have more than 2-lb. density, must be made using the proper amount of blowing agent, and both the urethane and the manufacturing environment must be at the correct temperatures.

In horizontal pouring, liquid ingredients are sprayed between two horizontal skins, one held at the bottom of a form, the other at the top. The foam is thus required to rise only the width of the panel, 3½ in. to 5 in., instead of 4 ft. Cell rise and formation occur in the same direction in which compressive strength is required. Because the foam rise is measurable and consistent, it is possible to make precise adjustments, achieving an isotopic foam and a panel with an excellent bond.

Horizontal pouring also lends itself to automation. Panels can be made on a belted assembly line, giving some assurance that the price will stay reasonable.

A timber-frame built to last hundreds of years should stand on a foundation designed with the same commitment to longevity. (Photo by Bill Holtz.)

CHAPTER 6

GETTING OUT OF THE GROUND

Construction of a house begins with bulldozers and ends with 220-grit sandpaper, proceeding from rough to fine, from larger to smaller tolerances. It's a sensible progression. But an unfortunate corollary is the thinking that brawn is needed at the beginning of a job and brains at the end, that it's okay for dirty work to be accompanied by muddy thinking. The roar of heavy machinery, the splash of concrete, and the crude piles of dirt are all uninviting and tend to keep the project planners on the periphery until the "good" work begins. In addition, excavation and foundation work contribute little to the aesthetics of a house, so people are generally less concerned about these stages of the job. This attitude isn't surprising, but it is shortsighted, because the longevity of a building is directly related to the way it sits on the earth. A foundation is a one-shot deal: Once it is in, the die is cast. The building either has a chance to endure or it doesn't. If brains and craftsmanship are applied nowhere else in the house, they should be used to get out of the ground.

A spate of hurricanes and earthquakes in recent years has magnified the significance of this point. Millions of people have now seen for themselves by way of TV broadcasts that the awesome power of natural forces ought never to be underestimated. In response, building officials are toughening their standards, the code itself has been revised throughout the country, and most of the competent professionals have become more conservative and diligent. What was "good enough" 10 years ago is no longer adequate today.

When foundations are taken for granted, their designs are produced for the sole purpose of satisfying base code requirements, and the job is usually contracted on the basis of price. On the site, critical decisions are often made by people who are not in a position to know all the criteria that should bear on design and construction. My own experience concerning faulty foundations includes a lesson or two learned the hard way. The excavation for one of my company's early projects in northern Massachusetts began in the late fall, well into the time when frost penetration becomes a factor to consider when preparing a site. It was my job to lay out the foundation and set the benchmark (the reference point for the top of the wall). Because the site was 70 miles from my home, I left it to the homeowner and the subcontractors to see to it that the work was performed according to our plans and specifications.

On a bleak and forbidding day, a man and a bulldozer worked without enthusiasm, prudence, or guidance. When

they left, the area for the house was roughly excavated, but the tough digging through hard soil and cold weather resulted in an inaccurate job of grading the base of the excavation in preparation for building the footing forms. And nobody thought to protect the newly exposed earth from frost.

When the crew showed up to build the footings two days later, they were faced with hard frost, hard soil, and uneven terrain. What to do? I can hear them talking: "Why spend the rest of the day working like convicts with picks and shovels because of Bull Dozer's mistakes, when what we need most of all are warmer derrieres and fatter wallets?" So they set the formboards without regard for anything or anybody: not for our plans, for the client's house, for the building code, for the laws of physics—not even for their own reputations.

At its best, the footing was fully 12 in. deep, as called for in the plans. At its worst, the "footing" was only a 1-in.-thick concrete skim; most of it was between 2 in. and 6 in. thick. These guys had simply nailed some formboards together on top of the uneven, frozen soil and leveled out the concrete in between. To make the story even more tragic, in the next two days another crew came in and poured a wall on this footing. I discovered the crime only after the forms had been stripped. When I went into a rage about the disaster, the owner shrugged, the wall crew pointed to the footing crew, the footing crew pointed to old Bull Dozer, and he pointed back at me. Needless to say, we did not build until the problems were resolved, and I gained some of what you might call "experience."

In a timber frame, the overall high standards and unique structural considerations demand that particularly close attention be paid to both foundation design and construction. Don't assume that foundations typically used with stud construction will satisfy the requirements of a timber-frame building. Unlike a stud-framed house, in which

building loads are evenly transferred through hundreds of closely spaced members, a timber frame exerts point loads on a foundation through a few principal posts—between 12 and 16 in a medium to large building. The design of the foundation and the placement of the reinforcing rod within it are geared toward coping with these point loads. In this chapter I'll discuss some basic foundation considerations, as well as the modifications to conventional foundations required by timber frames. I won't go into detail on general foundation information that may be obtained elsewhere. I'll finish by discussing stick-framed and timber-framed floor-deck framing systems.

FOUNDATION DESIGN

Soil, climatic, and geologic conditions, structural and design features of the building, and site conditions are important factors in foundation design and are some of the reasons why foundations are not the same everywhere. Building on a delta in Louisiana suggests an entirely different approach from building on a hilltop in Vermont. If the house is to be built in California, it must be designed for earthquakes; if in Minnesota, it must be designed for deep frost. As in buildings, in foundations there are no standard solutions. Instead there is a range of methodologies and options to be weighed against house design and site conditions.

The soil
The real foundation for all buildings is the earth. What we put between the structure and the earth is intended to transmit the load, not support it. Support, or the lack of it, comes from somewhere in the ground beneath the building. To prevent the soil movements from damaging or destroying the foundation, the building must be placed on terra firma, never on loose soil or new fill because settling will cause the foundation to crack. It is important to dig down to fully compacted, undisturbed earth. Once you get

there, you need to determine what the soil is composed of and the best way to build on it.

The quality of the soil is critical in foundation design. Soft soils require that the foundation have a larger bearing area (which means a broader footing) than hard soils or rock would need. The chart at right lists some types of soils and their bearing values. Bedrock has a bearing capacity of 25 tons per sq. ft. or more, while soft clay or loose sand might be able to hold only a ton or less. Because they hold water, clay and silt are the bane of good foundations and require careful treatment. The potential for excess moisture in these soils reduces their ability to compact and allows them to expand if the moisture freezes. Loose sand, which is difficult to compact, is a problem, too. A mixture of materials is best, such as a gravel having enough clay to allow it to compact well and enough sand to allow moisture to percolate through.

Solid bedrock can be great under a foundation, but it too has some special requirements. First, a rock surface is not generally tidy and level, so its peaks and valleys have to be carefully cleaned of dirt so that the footings won't shift or slide. Second, holes must be drilled and rebar inserted to link the foundation to the bedrock. Third, if you hit bedrock in one corner of the foundation, you should usually dig to bedrock for the entire excavation, so the entire foundation will be on the same type of material. (The exception to this is when compactible soils are in a rock basin, because there the soil is contained and can't shift.)

In most cases, general local soil conditions have been well studied, and standard foundation specifications for various circumstances are established as part of the code. But don't fall into the trap of allowing a standard specification to fit your nonstandard situation—foundations should be specific, not generic. In an urban area, you can learn about soil conditions by looking at the foundations of adjacent build-

BEARING VALUE FOR SOME SOILS

Type of soil	Approx. load in tons per sq. ft.
Soft clay or silt	1
Loose, medium sand	1
Compact, fine sand	2
Coarse gravel	4
Hardpan or partially cemented gravel over rock	10
Sedimentary rock, including sandstone and conglomerates	20
Solid bedrock: granite, slate gneiss	25

ings. In the country, use the information gathered for the percolation tests done in preparation for designing the septic system. Better yet, attend the tests to see for yourself the soil the foundation will rest upon. You don't have to be an engineer to use common sense. If you can make a mud ball that holds together in your hand, the soil contains quite a bit of clay. If you can wring water out of that mud ball, or if water fills the test hole on a dry day, an engineer should be consulted before the foundation is designed. Designers and architects sometimes neglect the bearing capacity of the soil; if you have such a professional involved in your project, question him or her. Frank Lloyd Wright never visited the site of his house known as Fountainhead. The building was nearly torn apart by soil expansion and needed complete restructuring in a recent renovation.

Climate and geology

Most of the very early timber-frame buildings in this country had foundations that were inadequate for New England winters. Having come from a more temperate climate, the colonists simply did not know how to deal with the deep penetration of frost that moved and heaved whole buildings. Primarily for this reason, there are few timber-frame buildings left from the first years in this country, while many examples have survived from the 14th

and 15th centuries and earlier throughout Europe. Putting a building on top of the ground in harsh New England weather is almost like launching it out onto a rolling sea of ice and mud.

The most obvious concern is freezing, because freezing soil will heave even the heaviest buildings and crack even the most massive foundations. A stable foundation requires the footing to penetrate deeper into the ground than the frost. In other words, the footing must bear upon soil that will never freeze. Local building codes generally have reliable information and good regulations regarding footing depth. Some extremely cold regions demand a depth of at least 6 ft., while some warm areas require only 1 ft. or so. People from the South often wonder why so many New Englanders have full basements, thinking perhaps their breeding encourages things subterranean. Actually, it's a matter of practicality. Because they have to dig 4 ft. to 6 ft. anyway, it often makes sense to go a few extra feet and gain living or storage area.

Structural standards for foundation design are generally predicated on worst-case scenario. Faded memory, then, causes standards to droop, and yesterday's disaster pushes them upward again. Recent earthquakes and hurricanes have escalated building standards nearly everywhere. There have been earthquakes in the mountain states and in New England, and hurricanes have struck in places previously considered safe. The lesson is clear: Nature is chaotic and unpredictable; assume a visit from its dark side.

Foundation design is usually specific to anticipation of certain natural calamities, such as earthquakes, tornadoes, or hurricanes. Local codes in areas prone to such potential disasters usually give good guidance regarding standards nec-essary to resist expected forces. For example, buildings in quake zones require foundations that are heavily reinforced to resist shearing forces. The idea is that the foundation walls should act like a set of rigidly interconnected beams. In the event of an earthquake, the whole building is intended to respond as a unit; it should not separate or crack. I've never experienced a significant earthquake, but people who have been through one tell me that no amount of reinforcement seems like enough in those hair-raising moments of turbulence.

In preparation for earthquakes or high winds, a foundation also needs a good system for keeping the house firmly attached to it. This is not an overreaction to Dorothy's trip to Oz: Every year there are stories about buildings that are blown off their foundations. Some attachment systems are described later in this chapter.

A building should be designed for the topography, geography, and soil of the land it will sit upon. Foundation detailing is a key to the success of site-specific integration. This home tucks into a hilltop.

For the design potential of this long, low house to be fulfilled, the building needed to sit low in the land.

Building design and site conditions

The foundation is the building's roots, not just a mass of masonry beneath it. So in addition to responding to the site and climate, the foundation must also meet the design and construction requirements of the building. For example, if the house is intended to conserve energy, so should the foundation. If the house has any odd loading situations, they need to be directed through the foundation. Also, how the foundation is treated can drastically change the look and feel of a building. A Victorian home perched on poles would be an absurdity, but elevated on a foundation with a brick facing, it could appear lofty. Likewise, a traditional design perched on a tall foundation can look unconnected to its environment.

Foundations very often are stepped to follow the contour of the land. When houses are well designed, finished grades, terraces, and a landscaping scheme are all addressed at the same time as the foundation. Homes built on hillside sites are commonly designed to take advantage of the terrain by gaining living area and outside access at the lowest grade level.

FOUNDATION SYSTEMS

As a preface to the discussion of the various foundation systems that follows, here are a few personal prejudices. I favor a system with a full perimeter wall rather than one with slabs or piers. If buildings are going to be well protected from the elements and well insulated, it is practically mandatory to begin with a good seal at the base. In addition, a perimeter foundation takes advantage of the relatively constant temperature of the earth (about 55°F), making the building much easier to heat than when cold exterior air is rushing beneath it.

I dislike shallow crawlspaces used with a perimeter wall. They are dark, dank, and forbidding. People just don't like getting down on their bellies and crawling under houses, so this area usually gets little attention and maintenance. With not enough room for good air movement, mildew is encouraged, along with the subsequent deterioration of framing members. If there is going to be a space, it should be large enough for people to move around freely, and the ceiling should be high enough to allow comfortable walking.

Concrete is key to durability

I like poured concrete—a mixture of portland cement (lime, silica, and alumina), aggregate, and water. The concrete we use today is similar to the material first used by the ancient Romans. Some of their concrete buildings and roads have survived, demonstrating the durability of the material.

Concrete is, I think, one of the most important developments in the building field. Because it is reasonable in cost, concrete makes durable buildings possible for everyone. It can be molded to fit even the most irregular contour, it hardens to a degree we can calculate and control, and it gives strength and design flexibility with few limitations. The timber-frame buildings we construct today have an opportunity to exceed the expected life span of those made by our predecessors in the craft, not because of any greater skill in joinery but because of better foundations. Concrete is the key.

The richer the cement, the stronger the concrete will be. Density is increased by adding more cement to the mix. Common concrete for houses is rated at 2,500 lb. per square inch (psi); exotic new formulations have made 15,000 to 20,000 psi possible. For our timber-frame homes, we have established 3,000-psi concrete as the minimum standard.

Properly mixed and poured, concrete is very strong in compression. A poured concrete wall does not have the shear planes inherent in a concrete-block wall, so it has much more resistance to lateral loads. But concrete is not an elastic material and is fairly weak in

With good design attention and lots of hard work, a home can sit comfortably in its natural setting.

POURED CONCRETE FOOTING

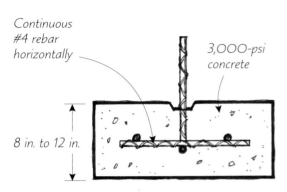

Continuous #4 rebar horizontally

3,000-psi concrete

8 in. to 12 in.

Keyway helps tie wall to footing and also helps prevent moisture seepage.

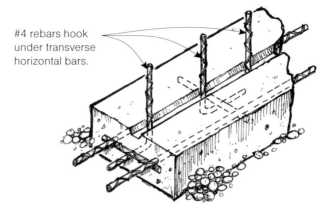

#4 rebars hook under transverse horizontal bars.

Poured footings on undisturbed soil below frost line. Footing dimensions are dependent on soil conditions, building load, local geology, and other factors. Consult local building code and/or an engineer.

FORMWORK FOR POURED FOOTINGS

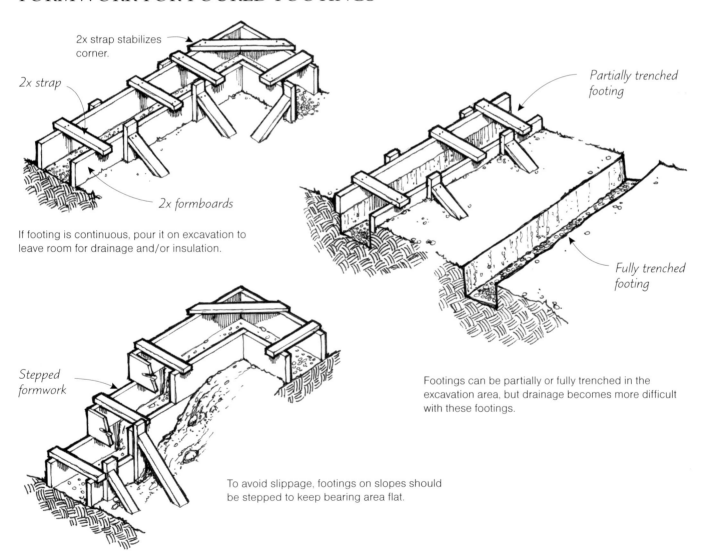

2x strap stabilizes corner.

2x strap

2x formboards

If footing is continuous, pour it on excavation to leave room for drainage and/or insulation.

Partially trenched footing

Fully trenched footing

Footings can be partially or fully trenched in the excavation area, but drainage becomes more difficult with these footings.

Stepped formwork

To avoid slippage, footings on slopes should be stepped to keep bearing area flat.

shear strength. Strength can be increased many times, however, by placing metal reinforcing bars (rebar) into the forms before the concrete is poured. Rebar comes in sizes designated by numbers 2 through 8. Each number represents $\frac{1}{8}$ in. A #2 rebar is $\frac{2}{8}$ in., or $\frac{1}{4}$ in.; a #5 rebar is $\frac{5}{8}$ in., and so on. For residential construction, #4 and #5 rebars are the most common. Wire mesh is used as a reinforcement for flatwork such as slabs, walkways, and patios.

Continuous footings

Most foundations are constructed in two parts: footings first, then walls or piers. The footings allow the building load to be distributed to the earth over a larger area and provide a more or less level surface for forming the rest of the foundation (see the drawings on p. 121). A continuous footing is used for a perimeter-wall system. Many of the rules for continuous footings apply to footings for pier foundations and the systems they support.

The width and thickness of the footings are determined by analyzing the weight of the building (including the concrete walls), the way loads are distributed by the structure, and the type of earth upon which the building will sit. Most codes have some general standards for footing size, concrete density, and reinforcement. But these regulations should be seen for what they are—a minimum standard—and should not be applied blindly to every circumstance. Verify the situation by adding up the load that will be distributed to each timber post. It will probably fall in the range of 3 to 5 tons at each location, including the weight of the foundation. Compare this with the bearing capacity of the soil. If the soil is soft, the footings may have to be broader and thicker to distribute the load over a larger area.

Footings must be accurately positioned and roughly level. Other than this, building the formwork for them is not necessarily precise work, although it can require creativity because the rough excavation often doesn't offer an accurate base. Footing forms are typically made of 2x stock, and a few building options are shown on p. 121. Remember that the real foundation is the earth and that the footing must be on undisturbed ground. I once visited a project while footings were being formed and found a "professional" filling in the footing area with loose soil from the excavation to make leveling the formboards easier. His surprise and anger that I would question him about this gave me much to think about. Obviously, I was criticizing his standard practice. Such ignorance in this critical trade is an unnerving reality.

Poured concrete foundation

A poured concrete foundation system is the one we use most. In timber-frame house construction, the foundation wall must distribute the point loads from the frame to the larger area of the footing (see the top drawing on the facing page). To improve the wall's capacity to withstand the weight and distribute the load, we commonly specify an arrangement of reinforcement intended for both greater shear strength and better load transfer (see the bottom right drawing on the facing page). It's also important to allow for good drainage to protect the foundation from excessive moisture penetration and soil expansion (see the bottom left drawing on the facing page).

It's possible to make your own foundation, either by making site-built forms of 2x4s and plywood or by using one of the many new rigid-foam form systems, which remain in place, acting as insulation after the pour. But because of the labor and materials savings, most concrete work is still done by professionals. Get bids from firms recommended by other professionals, and hire the one who doesn't argue about your desire to improve on the generally accepted standards. The typical poured concrete foundations for timber-frame buildings should not be compromised.

Concrete-block foundation

A concrete-block foundation is made of individual precast units (called concrete masonry units, or CMUs). While easy to lay, with their mortar joints and hollow cavities, this type of foundation has an inherent shear problem and, without reinforcement, has about one-quarter the compressive strength of an equivalent poured concrete foundation.

A concrete-block foundation is unsuitable for timber-frame construction unless it has been strengthened to handle the point loads of the frame and the shear forces of the earth. To that end, long runs of block wall, subject to buckling from soil pressure, are commonly reinforced at every principal post with wall extensions called pilasters (see the drawings on p. 124). The pilasters strengthen the wall against shear forces and increase the bearing area of the wall at the critical point-load positions. A common dimension for a pilaster is 16 in. by 24 in. so that typical 8x16 blocks can be woven into the wall without cutting. The pilasters are reinforced by filling all the cores with concrete and running four pieces of #5 rebar vertically through the cores. The footings for pilasters are formed and poured along with the wall footings. In normal soil, footings should be 6 in. larger in each direction than the proposed pilaster—and even larger in soft soils. Because the pilasters are designed to take the full load of the building, the sections of wall between pilasters are essentially non-load-bearing, serving to resist the lateral pressure of the soil and to tie the pilasters. These walls must be reinforced with horizontal and vertical rebar tied at their intersections.

Because of its structural limitations, I think the use of concrete block should be avoided, but sometimes there is no easy alternative. Often, a preference for using concrete block reflects regional eccentricities or characteristics that make poured concrete difficult to use. For instance, in areas where aggregate material, which is essential to the con-

POURED CONCRETE FOUNDATIONS

This is a typical poured concrete wall designed for a timber-frame building. This is intended as a minimum standard. Increased capacities may be necessary. Check codes and be aware of local soil conditions.

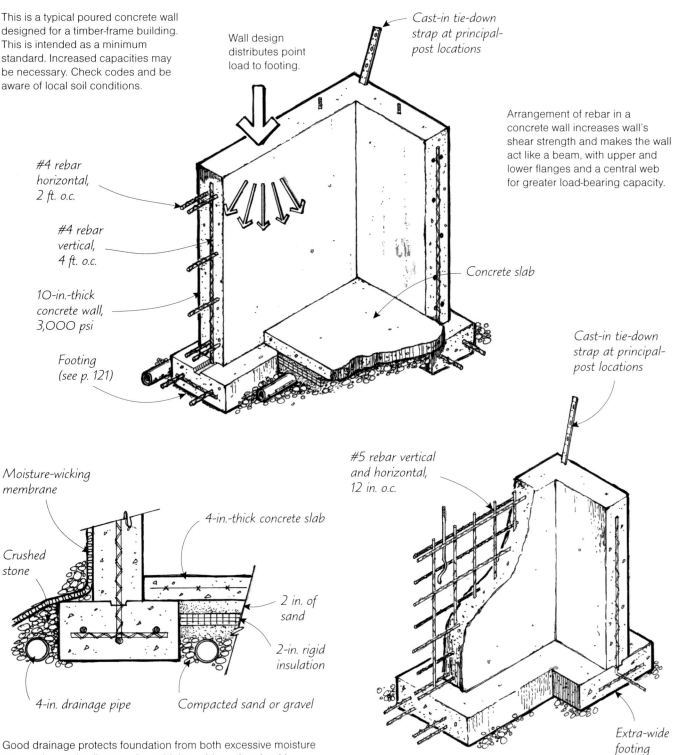

Wall design distributes point load to footing.

Cast-in tie-down strap at principal-post locations

Arrangement of rebar in a concrete wall increases wall's shear strength and makes the wall act like a beam, with upper and lower flanges and a central web for greater load-bearing capacity.

#4 rebar horizontal, 2 ft. o.c.

#4 rebar vertical, 4 ft. o.c.

10-in.-thick concrete wall, 3,000 psi

Footing (see p. 121)

Concrete slab

Cast-in tie-down strap at principal-post locations

Moisture-wicking membrane

Crushed stone

4-in.-thick concrete slab

2 in. of sand

2-in. rigid insulation

4-in. drainage pipe

Compacted sand or gravel

#5 rebar vertical and horizontal, 12 in. o.c.

Extra-wide footing

Good drainage protects foundation from both excessive moisture penetration and soil expansion, which could crack or buckle foundation wall.

In areas prone to expansive soils or earthquakes, footing and reinforcement standards are significantly increased. Here, footing is widened to make an increased bearing area, and rebar is a tightly woven mat of steel.

CONCRETE-BLOCK FOUNDATIONS

Without reinforcement, wall is susceptible to shear forces from soil pressure and point loads from timber frame.

Point load of building

Shear forces of soil

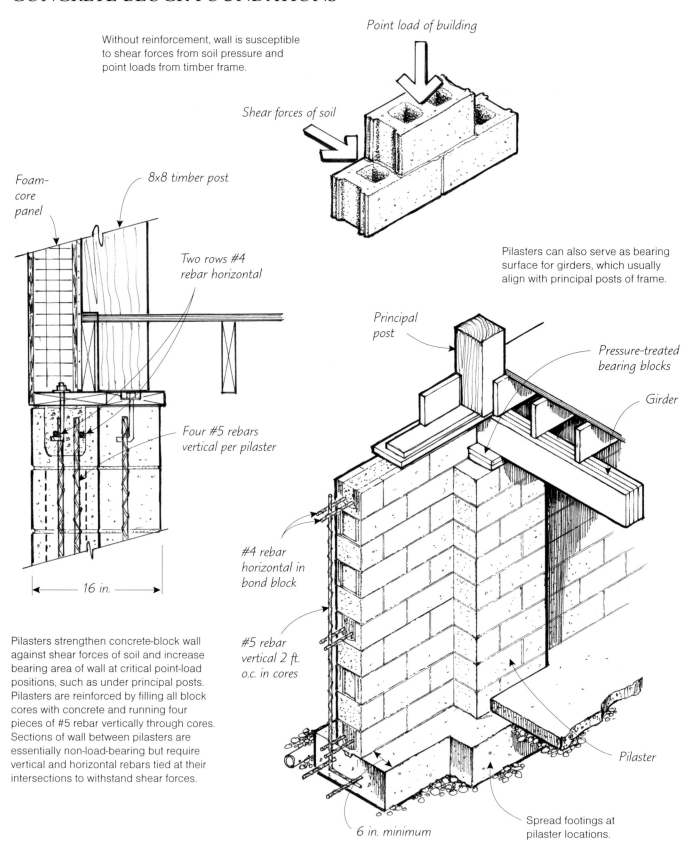

Foam-core panel

8x8 timber post

Two rows #4 rebar horizontal

Four #5 rebars vertical per pilaster

16 in.

Pilasters strengthen concrete-block wall against shear forces of soil and increase bearing area of wall at critical point-load positions, such as under principal posts. Pilasters are reinforced by filling all block cores with concrete and running four pieces of #5 rebar vertically through cores. Sections of wall between pilasters are essentially non-load-bearing but require vertical and horizontal rebars tied at their intersections to withstand shear forces.

Pilasters can also serve as bearing surface for girders, which usually align with principal posts of frame.

Principal post

Pressure-treated bearing blocks

Girder

#4 rebar horizontal in bond block

#5 rebar vertical 2 ft. o.c. in cores

Pilaster

6 in. minimum

Spread footings at pilaster locations.

crete recipe, is scarce, the price of poured concrete is sometimes prohibitive. Good examples are parts of upper New York state and Florida, where clay and sand, respectively, predominate. Remote rural regions and islands might not have a concrete mixing plant because the economy cannot support it. Concrete for a poured foundation can be mixed by hand, but the work is labor intensive. In addition, the end product isn't as strong as a foundation made with a continuous pour, because cold joints (incomplete bonds) are created in the wall between areas that cure at different times. There are even areas where there is plenty of material for great concrete but the tradespeople demand what seem to be excessive prices. In these cases, concrete block becomes a practical alternative.

Slab-on-grade foundation
Perimeter wall foundations, whether poured concrete or concrete block, can also be used for slab-on-grade construction (see the drawing at right). But because there is fill on both sides of the wall, the forces exerted upon the wall from the earth are equalized, and there is less need for reinforcement against lateral pressure—pilasters on a concrete-block wall would not be necessary, for example. Excavation for this type of foundation proceeds quite differently, for instead of a bulldozer to level the entire area, only a backhoe is needed to create a trench for the walls. As usual, footings must extend below the frost line. Although it is expensive to put this much effort into making a foundation that is almost entirely hidden from sight, it offers the surest strength and the most complete protection of any slab-on-grade system.

Grade beam and pier foundation
In this type of foundation, a reinforced concrete beam (called the grade beam) is built over a trench filled with crushed stone and is supported by reinforced concrete piers. The system is perfectly suitable for timber frames because its piers and beams easily align

with the loading points of the timber structure. Although labor intensive, it uses materials economically and can be installed without professional assistance. Probably the biggest drawback, however, is that this foundation is hard to insulate. Because the grade beam does not extend below the frost line, a lot of heat may be lost from the house at the bottom of the wall, where frozen soil could be close to the heated house interior.

The design of the timber frame determines the number of piers and their locations. To control potential heaving in cold climates, spans greater than 12 ft. require intermediate support from additional piers.

The building area is excavated to remove the topsoil, then it's roughly leveled to a grade beneath the slab, allowing for insulation and drainage fill. The perimeter is trenched another 1 ft. deep and 2 ft. wide, with the approximate center of the grade beam being the center of the trench.

The piers around the perimeter should align exactly with the principal posts in the frame and should extend below the frost line. In this system, the piers are a minimum of 10 in. in diameter. If the soil is good, it may be possible simply to flare the pier hole at the bottom for a larger bearing area. If not, it may be necessary to prepare a larger footing and pour it separately from the pier.

SLAB-ON-GRADE FOUNDATION

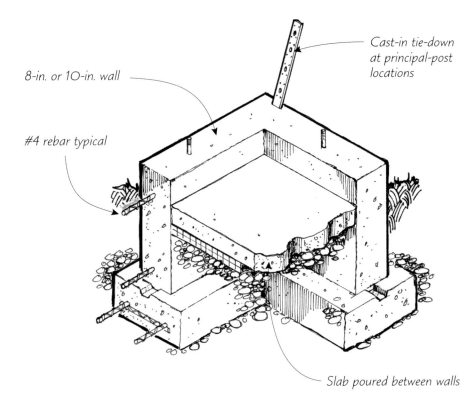

8-in. or 10-in. wall

#4 rebar typical

Cast-in tie-down at principal-post locations

Slab poured between walls

Because this type of continuous poured concrete foundation is buried on all sides, it requires less reinforcement. System would be used when crawlspace or basement is not desired, but benefits of complete perimeter wall is important.

GRADE BEAM AND PIER FOUNDATION

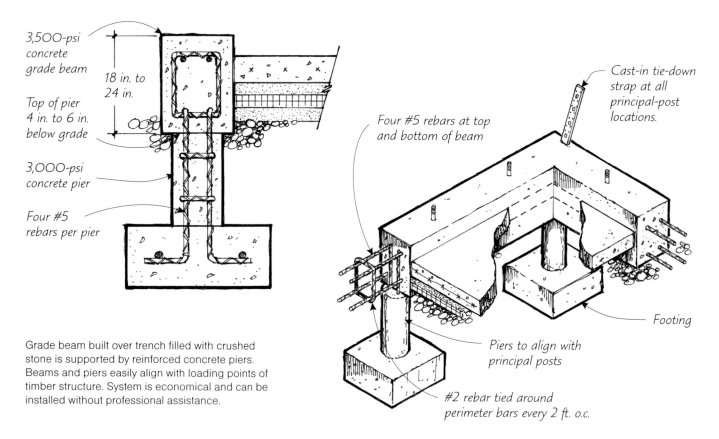

3,500-psi concrete grade beam

Top of pier 4 in. to 6 in. below grade

3,000-psi concrete pier

Four #5 rebars per pier

18 in. to 24 in.

Grade beam built over trench filled with crushed stone is supported by reinforced concrete piers. Beams and piers easily align with loading points of timber structure. System is economical and can be installed without professional assistance.

Four #5 rebars at top and bottom of beam

Cast-in tie-down strap at all principal-post locations.

Footing

Piers to align with principal posts

#2 rebar tied around perimeter bars every 2 ft. o.c.

The top of the piers should be about 6 in. below finished grade. Most important, they must be level with each other. Forms for the piers could be round cardboard tubes made for this purpose or simple square forms made from framing stock and boards. One advantage of cardboard tubes is that they can be backfilled before the pour, so they do not require bracing. Use 3,000-psi concrete for the piers. Each one should have at least four lengths of #5 rebar that extend about 2 ft. above the top of the proposed grade beam (see the drawings above).

After the piers have been completed, the perimeter trench is filled with 1½ in. of crushed stone for drainage and then compacted. In poor soil, it may be advisable to put drain tile in the trench to carry away excess water. The bed of crushed stone should initially be leveled to the top of the piers to support the beam; more stone will be added later.

Grade beams are typically 12 in. wide by 18 in. high, but dimensions depend on the specific site. Forms can be built with 2x framing stock for the sides and 1x3s for stakes and strapping. The beam should be made of 3,500-psi concrete and must be reinforced well—four #5 rebars running in two parallel rows at top and bottom is usually adequate. The perimeter rebar is spliced lengthwise and tied in a loop (called a stirrup) 2 ft. on center with #2 rebar. Vertical rebars from the piers are bent over at the top and tied to perimeter rebars. Tie-down straps are cast in the grade beam at all principal-post locations to tie the structure to the foundation.

The slab is poured, using conventional procedures, after footings for the interior posts are installed (see the sidebar on p. 128).

Thickened-edge slab foundation

In areas where freezing is not a concern, monolithic slabs can be poured in which the outer edge is thickened to increase strength and bearing area. In the some parts of the country, slab foundations such as this are predominant. Thickened-edge slabs are normally used with buildings that have evenly distributed loads; the dimensions of the thickened edge tend to be constant around the perimeter. But for this system to be suitable for timber-frame buildings, it is necessary to create large concrete pads at each post location along the thickened edge and in the slab. These pads will distribute the point loads of the frame (see the drawings on the facing page). If the frame will be insulated with stress-skin panels, plan for the completed foundation to be 3 in. to 4 in. larger than the timber frame in each direction.

To build the foundation, the area is first excavated to a level below the slab

THICKENED-EDGE SLAB FOUNDATION

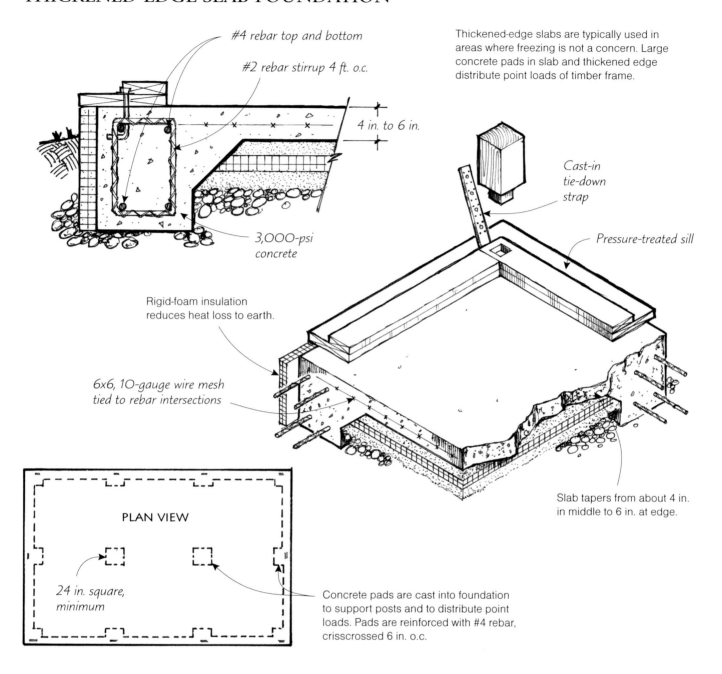

#4 rebar top and bottom

#2 rebar stirrup 4 ft. o.c.

Thickened-edge slabs are typically used in areas where freezing is not a concern. Large concrete pads in slab and thickened edge distribute point loads of timber frame.

4 in. to 6 in.

Cast-in tie-down strap

Pressure-treated sill

3,000-psi concrete

Rigid-foam insulation reduces heat loss to earth.

6x6, 10-gauge wire mesh tied to rebar intersections

Slab tapers from about 4 in. in middle to 6 in. at edge.

PLAN VIEW

24 in. square, minimum

Concrete pads are cast into foundation to support posts and to distribute point loads. Pads are reinforced with #4 rebar, crisscrossed 6 in. o.c.

(including insulation and drainage soil). Then the perimeter for the thickened edge is trenched. This requires some handwork, because the transition from the slab to the trench is gently sloped—the slab thickness in the middle should be about 4 in., pitching to 6 in. toward the outside of the foundation. Trench dimensions are generally about 12 in. deep and 18 in. wide before tapering to the slab. Four lengths of #4 rebar are run parallel around the

perimeter of the trench, two on the top and two on the bottom. Linear splices are overlapped and tied. The #4 rebars are tied with #2 rebar stirrups every 4 ft. on center.

Then the forms for the pads are prepared at each post location. The pad size depends on the building loads and soil type (often pads are 24 in. square or more). Each post pad is reinforced with a mat of #4 rebar, crisscrossed

6 in. on center. The mat should be tied to the lower perimeter rebar to help distribute the loads.

When the excavation has been completed, a one-sided form is built around the outside in preparation for a continuous pour of concrete for the slab, the trench, and the pads. The slab area is reinforced with 6x6, 10-gauge wire mesh, which should be tied to the rebar intersections.

SUPPORTING INTERIOR POSTS

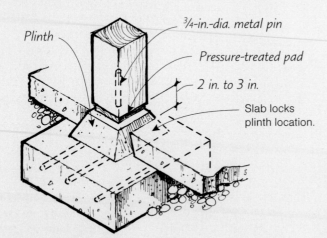

Plinth

¾-in.-dia. metal pin

Pressure-treated pad

2 in. to 3 in.

Slab locks plinth location.

Concrete-filled steel column

Slab keys column foot in place.

All the foundations described in this chapter also need a series of footings to transmit the loads at interior post locations. These footings—located under the slab—are generally between 10 in. and 12 in. thick and approximately 24 in. to 28 in. square. The forms are made using 2x framing stock and stakes. Reinforcement is usually wire mesh, but a mat of welded or tied rebar is better. These footings should also be poured on undisturbed soil with 3,000-psi concrete.

Either wood posts or concrete-filled steel columns are placed on top of the footings to support the first floor. Capped steel columns can be set directly on top of the footing before the slab is poured. (Do not use hollow, telescoping jack posts because they are not strong enough.) When the concrete sets, the column is locked into position.

When a wood post is used, choose straight-grained material with few defects. Posts are usually at least 7 in. by 7 in. under most loading situations. A tapered, concrete plinth topped with a pressure-treated wood cap keeps the post off the concrete; otherwise, the post would draw moisture from the concrete and rot. Plinth dimensions are determined by the base of the post and the proposed thickness of the slab. The plinth top should be the same size as the post bottom, and the taper should be about 20° outward to the base. A ¾-in.-diameter metal pin in the plinth protrudes about 4 in. into the post to key it to the plinth.

CONCRETE-PIER FOUNDATION

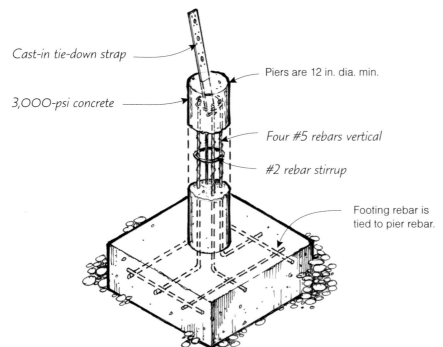

Cast-in tie-down strap

3,000-psi concrete

Piers are 12 in. dia. min.

Four #5 rebars vertical

#2 rebar stirrup

Footing rebar is tied to pier rebar.

Concrete-pier foundation

For buildings such as vacation homes and workshops, where energy efficiency is not a priority, a concrete-pier foundation can be used. Lack of integration between the piers makes this system inherently weaker than other foundation systems, but some people like its easy installation and economy. Follow the guidelines for constructing piers on p. 126, with these changes: Increase the minimum diameter to 12 in., and don't extend the rebar beyond the pier top. Even with reinforcement, these piers are weak against shear forces, so they should not extend more than 2½ ft. above finished grade.

FOUNDATION INSULATION

There's no magic formula for building a house with good energy performance, but we can be certain that all our efforts with insulating and sealing would be misspent if we neglected the foundation level. As in the foundation itself, use the best materials. Insulation placed under a slab or outside a foundation is not likely to be replaced, so do it well the first time. For most situations, there should be 2 in. of rigid foam (R-value of 12 to 16) on the exterior of the walls and under the slab. In very cold climates, more than 2 in. may be required above grade.

But wall insulation shouldn't always be installed on the outside. For instance, if the basement is unheated, I can't see how the concrete walls can be used for heat storage; additionally, if the area is heated only occasionally, the cool concrete walls would have to be warmed before the room would be comfortable. Therefore, we often specify insulation on the inside of the foundation walls, especially for living areas or basements that may serve a primary use.

FLOOR DECKS FOR TIMBER-FRAME HOUSES

To cap the foundation and form the base of the timber frame, you can use either timbers or conventional stick-framing materials. Compelling arguments can be made for the latter option. Wood placed close to the ground needs to be rot-resistant, and the species with the best natural resistance, such as white oak, chestnut, cypress, and redwood, are not as available in timber dimensions as they once were. Good materials for capping the foundation, including pressure-treated lumber, are much more available in stick-framing dimensions than they are in timber dimensions.

For strength, it's no longer necessary to use a system made from timbers. In the heyday of timber framing, houses were usually supported with stone foundations of dubious dependability, which racked, heaved, and settled, often subjecting the floor system to incredible stresses. But with sills fully supported by the best sort of modern foundation, the only force encountered by the platform is compression. A stick-framed floor system therefore offers little compromise in strength. Also, when the basement area is not used as a living space, the workmanship of the first-floor frame does not contribute significantly to the aesthetic quality of the home. The previous considerations and the realities of building costs and budgets often lead to the use of conventional construction for the floor deck of a timber-frame house.

Having said all this, there are some good reasons to use a timber deck. Sometimes it seems easier simply to prepare the framing members and install them than to communicate the details to a disinterested subcontractor. The standards of workmanship in the trades is often disappointing, causing both frustration and disharmony. It is not unusual to find a deck to be neither square nor level and the post pockets in the wrong places or the wrong size. In the time it takes to fix these mistakes, we often feel we could have cut the timber deck in our shop and installed it on site. Whether or not this is precisely true, it can certainly be argued that a timber system offers good value for certain situations.

It's hard to beat the durability and heirloom quality of a timber-framed deck.

So, if it is possible in the constraints of the budget, it may well be worthwhile to continue the heirloom quality of the frame right through to the deck. Still, if a stick-framed deck is chosen for economic reasons, and the area beneath it won't be used as a primary living area, it should be considered a minimal compromise. The largest advantage of the more conventional stick-framed deck is the ease of running mechanical systems and better sound-deadening. Following is a discussion of a few stick- and timber-framed systems.

Stick-framed floor deck

Only a few refinements are necessary to adapt a conventional floor-framing system to a timber frame. First, the arrangement of girders should coincide with the linear arrangement of posts in the frame, either parallel or perpendicular to the bents, depending on post layout. Doing this means the piers that support the girders can then also be located beneath principal posts—a system necessary to transfer the point loads to the footings. The decision regarding how girders are run in relation to frame and foundation is based on giving each interior timber post direct pier support while keeping the floor-joist spans as short as possible by overlapping them on the center girder (see the drawings on the facing page).

Sometimes girders are to be supported with steel columns instead of wood posts. In most situations, the columns not only bear a portion of the first-floor load, but they also bear a significant load from the weight of the frame, all other floor loads above the first, and loads from the roof and all the other building materials. Many tons of weight have to be supported at that one point. It is important to design and select a column that will support these significant loading points, and, additionally, to design the bearing area so that it's large enough to transfer the load efficiently from the beam to the column. I have seen a situation where

both a steel column and its flimsy metal cap were crushed into a girder by nearly ½ in.—perhaps a large enough column, but inadequate bearing and load transfer. Caps for steel columns should be made from ⅜-in.-thick plate metal, usually about 7 in. by 7 in., for a bearing area of about 50 sq. in.

Concrete-pier foundation framing

When the timber frame is supported by a pier foundation, it is necessary for the deck framing to have integrated beams to span from pier to pier (see the drawing below). The beams can be laminated on site, as you would an interior girder, by nailing and gluing dimensional stock. A pressure-treated sill is laid onto the pier first, almost certainly requiring props to keep the sills from sagging until the beams can be built on top. The outside dimension of the sills

should be planned to create a shelf for the foam-core panels, while the outside edge of the perimeter beam will be decided by the dimensions of the frame.

The perimeter beam can then be built in place with nails and construction adhesive. While building the beam, pockets should be left open at the post locations for the posts to bear directly on the pressure-treated sills on top of the piers. Because the beam is laminated, the pocket can be created simply by leaving out the middle members at the post locations. Keep the outer two laminations intact, but otherwise create the largest possible bearing area for the post to sit on the pier. Also remember to allow for the corners to overlap when constructing the beam. After the beams have been constructed, the pressure-treated sills can be nailed up to the beams from below.

CONCRETE-PIER FOUNDATION FRAMING

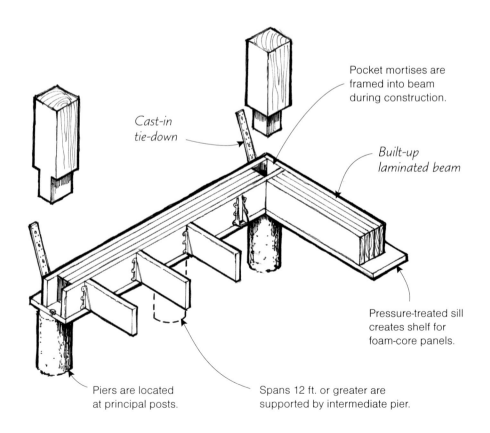

Cast-in tie-down

Pocket mortises are framed into beam during construction.

Built-up laminated beam

Pressure-treated sill creates shelf for foam-core panels.

Piers are located at principal posts.

Spans 12 ft. or greater are supported by intermediate pier.

STICK-FRAMED FLOOR DECK

Deck girders should align with principal posts to provide support.

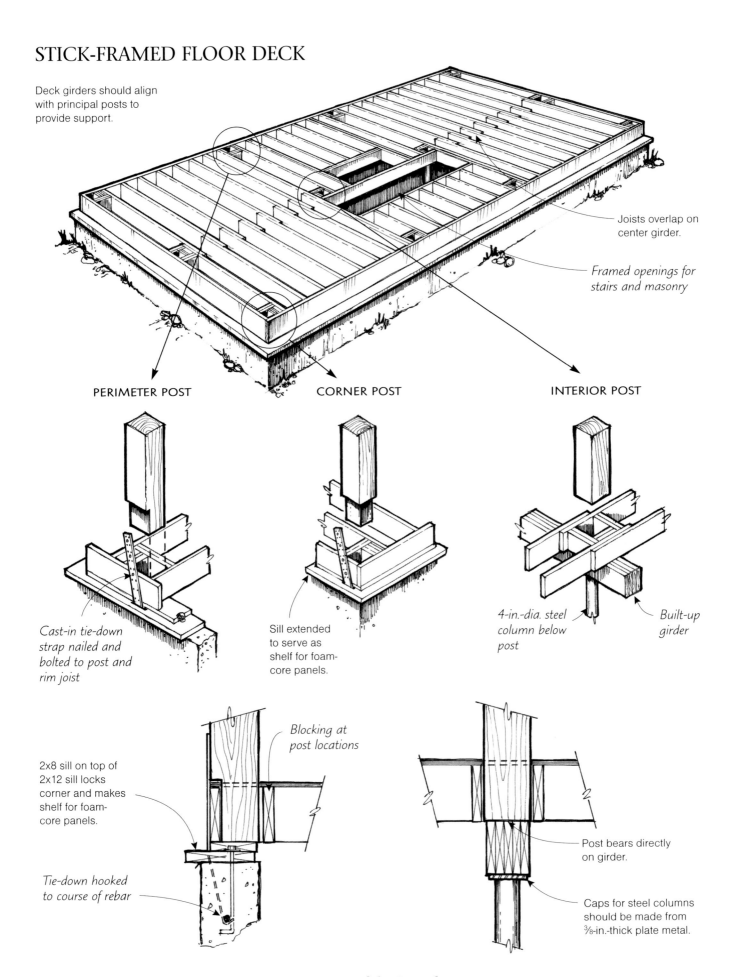

Joists overlap on center girder.

Framed openings for stairs and masonry

PERIMETER POST

CORNER POST

INTERIOR POST

Cast-in tie-down strap nailed and bolted to post and rim joist

Sill extended to serve as shelf for foam-core panels.

4-in.-dia. steel column below post

Built-up girder

2x8 sill on top of 2x12 sill locks corner and makes shelf for foam-core panels.

Blocking at post locations

Tie-down hooked to course of rebar

Post bears directly on girder.

Caps for steel columns should be made from 3/8-in.-thick plate metal.

SLAB-ON-GRADE SILL FRAMING

Slab-on-grade foundations have no interior floor framing, though there is still a need to receive the perimeter posts and provide a nailing base for the enclosure system. The very simplest system is to use a typical 2x12 pressure-treated sill and a 2x8 sill on top of that. Because there is little depth to secure the post, this system requires the use of tie-down straps.

After the 2x12 sill is bolted to the foundation, the frame is raised onto it. Then the 2x8 sill is placed on top of the 2x12 (if a wire chase is needed, use two 2x4s). At post locations, the 2x8s are notched to key the posts into position. Finally, the tie-down straps are attached to the posts as a critical connection to the foundation. The shelf created by the two sills provides a good surface for the foam-core panels.

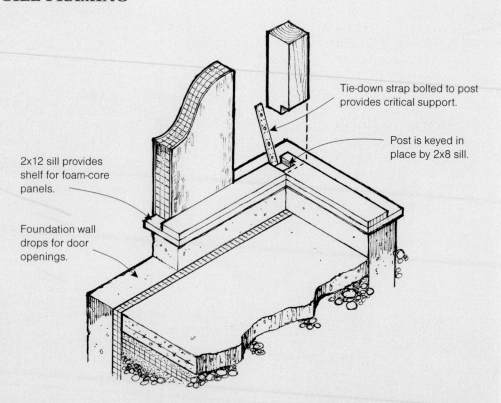

Tie-down strap bolted to post provides critical support.

Post is keyed in place by 2x8 sill.

2x12 sill provides shelf for foam-core panels.

Foundation wall drops for door openings.

For this addition to the Thoreau house in Concord, Massachusetts, a slab-on-grade system was used. Note that the pressure-treated sill is in place. The cap sill will be installed after the frame is up. The tie-down straps are critical for this system. (Photo by Jeff Adams.)

Building on a sloping site

If a house is built on a sloping site or uneven terrain, the top of the foundation might actually be on two or three levels to follow the contour of the land (see the drawing below). You then need to build walls between the lower foundation levels and the first-floor level. There are two options. You can use a timber at each post location, insulating the wall the same way as the timber-frame walls above. Or you can frame conventionally with 2x studs, but with this strategy it might be necessary to go to extreme measures to keep the insulation value the same as that provided by the foam-core panels (assuming you use that system) on the rest of the house. Also, to support the girders and principal timber posts, you would have to fabricate posts by laminating framing members together. Because there's so much complicated work in trying both to support the posts and to match the insulation level of the rest of the house, there's no real time or money savings in this method—we've found it makes much more sense just to use timber posts and continue the foam-core panels from the frame down to the sill.

If you use posts between the lower foundation levels and the first-floor level, you'll have to make some changes in the typical sill system. Eliminate the sill overhang where the post wall on the first-floor level begins, since the panels continue to the base sill. Where the foundation drops to a different level, it is necessary to use a solid timber or a built-up, laminated beam to span from support to support. For the lower sill, use a built-up beam, like that used in a slab-on-grade foundation (see the sidebar on the facing page).

SUPPORTING FRAME WITH STEPPED FOUNDATION

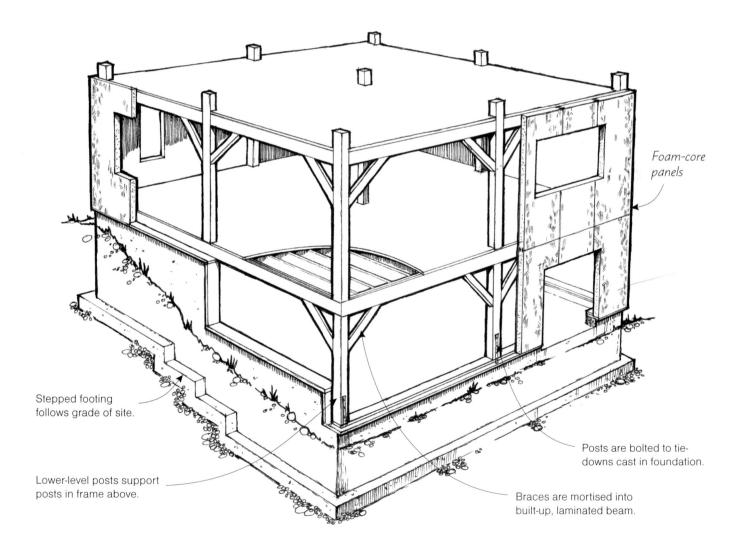

Foam-core panels

Stepped footing follows grade of site.

Lower-level posts support posts in frame above.

Posts are bolted to tie-downs cast in foundation.

Braces are mortised into built-up, laminated beam.

Timber-framed floor deck

Using a timber-framed floor is the surest way to maintain the integrity and strength of the rest of the frame. When the ground-floor level is used as living area (a family room, for example), the beauty of the timbers is an obvious advantage.

The system begins with a 2x12 sill and a 2x8 sill in the same manner as for a stick-framed deck (see the drawings on the facing page). These members cap the insulation and protect the timber sill from moisture. Historically, chestnut and white oak were widely used for sills, but chestnut is now nearly extinct, and good white oak is hard to find. Most of the woods good for tim-ber framing are not especially moisture resistant. Redwood and cedar would be good choices for the timber sill, but quality, availability, and cost can be problems. Getting a suitably moisture-resistant sill in lumber dimensions is obviously much easier and less expensive. When a timber sill is used on a continuous foundation, it doesn't need to be very large because it doesn't have to carry the weight of the floor in an open span. It need only be thick enough to allow good connections to floor joists and girders, and wide enough to transfer the weight of the posts to the foundation (a timber sill for average circumstances might be about 5 in. thick by 8 in. wide). A wire chase can be created by making the sill slightly narrower than the posts.

The foundation is the building's anchor to the earth. It is one of two major determinants of structural integrity. The other is the frame. Though not glamorous, usually not as beautiful as it could be, and sometimes not even visible, it never pays to under-build the foundation. Choose to dislike it, if you wish. Or to be bored by it. But do give it some respect and attention. A firm foundation is fundamental to the security your home provides and essential to its durability. Unless you intend to build a sturdy and durable foundation, don't bother with the timber frame.

A timber-framed floor system gives the basement area continuity, beauty, and strength. Concrete plinths protect the posts from absorbing moisture from the slab. (Photo by Gordon Cook.)

TIMBER-FRAMED FLOOR DECK

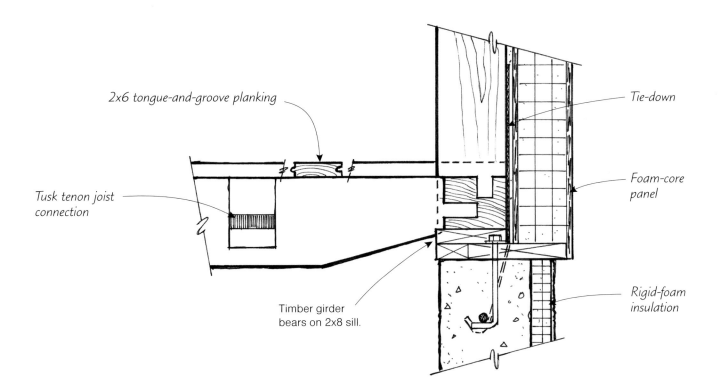

2-in. stub tenon

Timber girder

Foam-core panel

2x8 sill

2x12 sill

Cast-in tie-downs are bolted to all posts.

Timber sill beam

Cast-in tie-down wraps over sill beam.

Rigid-foam insulation

2x6 tongue-and-groove planking

Tie-down

Tusk tenon joist connection

Foam-core panel

Timber girder bears on 2x8 sill.

Rigid-foam insulation

The warm colonial atmosphere of this area is achieved by using soft lighting and stained wood.

CHAPTER 7

WIRING AND LIGHTING

Sprawled throughout our rooms like sleeping snakes, wires are an umbilical cord to the accessories of the 20th century. In my small home office alone, there are wires for two lamps; three wires for the computer; one for the telephone; two for a radio and headset; one for a drill waiting for a job in the corner; and another dangling overhead, begging for a light fixture. Thousands of linear feet of wire course through our walls, pulsing with energy people feel they can't live without. Linking us to all the things considered necessary to a civilized lifestyle, often including heating and plumbing, the electrical system is the central nervous system of the modern home. We are hooked on electricity, and although we may occasionally begrudge the price that's paid for it and perhaps even argue philosophically that life is really not finer for it, not many people would trade it in for a life unfettered.

In timber-frame home building, the issue of wiring often causes puzzlement and frustration in homeowners, builders, and electricians alike. Many clients want to know how we get wires through walls built of 6x8 and 8x8 timbers enclosed with foam-core panels. When I explain the process, these clients are usually surprised at its straightforward logic, having expected that they would live amid coils of exposed wires or pay for techniques of incomprehensible complexity.

Still, no matter how simple wiring a timber-frame house is in theory, there is bound to be misadventure. Many of the procedures for wiring timber-frame structures fall outside conventions of the trade, and new rules and guidelines are not yet clearly established. Timber-frame designers and builders therefore sometimes neglect to take the time to consider the electrical system, waiting until it's too late to solve problems creatively. Caught up in the excitement of building their house, homeowners often ignore the entire question of electricity, with the result that their rooms are not illuminated in the way they would have liked and that outlets and switches are inconveniently located. Confused electricians, relying on intuition rather than on systematic procedures, are often driven to poke at the timbers with their drills as if the frame were a giant voodoo doll.

Wiring a timber-frame house is further complicated by the fact that there is no one right way to do the job. Instead, there is a wide selection of options, some more appropriate than others, depending on the particular condition. In studying electrical systems, the goal therefore is to cultivate a way of thinking that will allow flexibility in evaluating each situation individually and to choose the very best option possible.

Only with a thorough understanding of the basic principles can we make intelligent choices.

In this chapter, I will discuss the techniques of wiring a typical timber-frame house that uses foam-core panels as its enclosure system. The foam-core insulating system is the focus because most timber-frame houses today use it. (When the built-up insulating systems are used, conventional wiring practice can be employed to a greater degree.) Bear in mind, as you proceed through this chapter, that timber frames and the systems used to enclose them do not change the theories of electrical wiring or the rules governing circuit design. Nothing about the timber-frame building system alters decisions about wire size and type, switching options, safety, or any other matter related to what it takes to move electrical current properly from the generating utility to the consuming appliance in the home.

PLANNING THE ELECTRICAL SYSTEM

During the design stages of the building process, it is in everyone's best interest to devote sufficient time and energy to planning the electrical system. This includes considering everything from the types of electrical devices and fixtures that will be in each room to the path of every single wire in the house.

There are several strong arguments for good planning. Running extra wires is almost impossible once the frame is enclosed, so thorough planning can help guarantee that outlets and fixtures will be exactly where they're needed. Also, a set of good plans makes it easier to communicate with the electrician; therefore the job usually will run more efficiently and economically. And because good planning makes it possible for the timber framer to make the nec-

Electrical fixtures that will be mounted on the timbers must be planned and specified well in advance. In this home, the wire routes for the track lighting and the ceiling fan were determined before the timbers were cut.

essary cuts for the wires while the timbers are still on sawhorses, the amount of drilling the electrician has to do will be minimal—the surest way to prevent the unnecessary marring of timbers.

My company once dealt with a contractor who refused to plan or to follow our plans, and the results of his bullheadedness seriously damaged the timber frame. This fellow personified the almost universal adversarial relationship between designers and contractors—he refused to acknowledge our blueprints as anything more than a rough example of what a building of the size and shape shown might look like. And the plans for the electrical system? Well, he didn't need them, because he already knew how to wire a house. We repeatedly told him that our electrical plans were critical, given that the local building code demanded that all wires be encased in conduit, but he somehow convinced the panel crew that he had a better plan, so they enclosed the house with no consideration for where the wires would go. As it turned out, his plan was simple: By eliminating all of the inaccessible lighting locations and riddling the timber frame with notches and holes large enough for a fire hose, wiring would be a cinch. Lest you think that such matters are always properly resolved, in this case there was no cure for the damage.

Planning begins by locating lights, outlets, appliances, stereos, televisions, telephones, and all other wire-dependent equipment on the floor plan. The designer or architect will need a great deal of input from the homeowner on this, and the homeowner will want to anticipate alternate locations for equipment that is likely to be moved occasionally, such as televisions and stereos. Running all the wires during the construction stage will provide greater flexibility later. By code, outlets will have to be about 6 ft. on center around the perimeter of the room. This is a good regulation, but it should not dictate the exact location of the outlets. While planning the electrical system, it's smart to have as many

outlets and switch boxes as possible installed on the interior walls, which will minimize penetrations in the insulation. In homes with high standards of energy efficiency, even small leaks can have large significance, like a pinhole in a balloon. However, because timber-frame houses commonly have open floor plans and few partition walls, it is inevitable that outlets will be on exterior walls, but do your best to reduce the number of them.

Use a copy of the floor plan to create the electrical plan. As you will see later, the position of timber posts and ceiling beams are critical in determining wire paths and the lighting scheme, so these should be indicated on the electrical plan. (To keep the plan uncluttered, draw in the beams lightly or with dotted lines.) After all the fixtures are located, the designer draws the electrical plan, including wire paths. If the electrical system is simple, a designer often will leave the circuitry to the electrician after determining the paths, but in complicated situations with few or no path options, the designer will determine the circuitry as well. In the rare instances where tradesmen are contracted early in a project, I have found it valuable to involve the electrician in planning. The electrician often has helpful input and always appreciates being a part of the decision-making process and not just a victim of it.

House plans are drawn to deliver information about how an intended result will be achieved. To be effective, all the participants need to understand the role they play in implementation; the electrical plan won't do much good as just another blueprint in the set. The joiners need to understand what the plan means to the frame. Are there timbers to notch? Holes to drill? Panel installers should be prepared for the wires that will run through panels or panel joints. Carpenters must understand the accommodations necessary for wires or fixtures. In other words, it is critical that the construction crew, the designer, and the homeowner act as a team and communicate precisely about even

the small details of the electrical plan. Only in this manner can a good wiring plan be transformed into a good electrical system.

THE WIRING PROCESS AND PREWIRING

Basically, electrical wires carry currents of energy the way a pipe carries water. A single large wire brings the electricity to the house, where it is attached to a service panel, or circuit box. From the service panel, the current flows through smaller wires to various parts of the house. It does so in circuits—loops of current that flow from the service panel to the appliances and devices and back to the panel. The path for a circuit can be short and simple or long and complicated, depending on the number of devices and the distance back to the panel. Getting the main wire to the service panel, either overhead or underground, is done with standard procedure, but running the smaller wires through the house requires thought, because in timber-frame building, the wiring routes typically used in stud construction just aren't there.

The obvious difference between wiring a stud-frame house and a timber frame that will be enclosed with foam-core panels is that in the latter there are no cavities in the exterior walls through which to run wiring. Because of this, it's necessary to do the wiring in three stages instead of in the conventional two. With a stud-frame house, the electrician does the rough wiring as soon as the house is enclosed by the roof, windows, and exterior sheathing. Rough wiring simply means stringing the wires through the studs, joists, and rafters to the various outlet boxes. Usually, many of the final decisions on the layout of the electrical system are left to be made during this time. The electrician then comes back to do the finish wiring (attaching wire ends to outlets, switches, fixtures, and appliances) after the drywall is up.

But in a timber-frame house, the job starts with prewiring. Early in construction, just before the foam-core panels go up, the electrician will get the wires to each general area of the house by running them loosely over the outside of the sill and the timbers of the frame (see the top photo at right). Where interior partitions will intersect timber posts, the electrician drills for the wires and pulls them through. At this time the electrician also drills through rafters and purlins for track lighting, fans, or chandeliers, and mounts wires and boxes for light switches.

On the first day of panel installation, the electrician will usually meet with the panel crew to review the electrical plan. It is the crew's responsibility to cut the grooves for the wires in the panels at the timber posts and to tuck the wires into place at the panel splines (see the bottom photo at right). When all the panels have been installed, but before the expanding foam and the 2x4 nailers have been applied, the electrician comes back to inspect the wiring and to run the wires for the switches next to exterior doors. All this is considered part of prewiring.

After the panels have been foamed and the interior stud-wall partitions framed, the electrician will return to the house for several days to do the rough wiring (see the photo on p. 140). By this time, the carpenter will have built the extended-baseboard chases on the exterior walls, as shown on p. 141, and the electrician will be able to mount the wires and outlet boxes in them. The electrician will also mount outlet boxes on the partition-wall studs and run the wires over the floor system. After the partition walls have been drywalled, finish wiring occurs in the conventional way.

It's the concept of prewiring that makes some electricians nervous about taking on a timber-frame job. But while it's true that prewiring requires a different strategy and different techniques, it's not true that different has to mean difficult or confusing. A

In a timber-frame house, wiring begins by stringing the wires loosely over the frame before the foam-core panels are installed.

During panel installation, the crew members cut grooves into the foam-core panels for wires and tuck the wires into spline connections. (Photo by Tafi Brown.)

Wiring and Lighting

timber-frame electrical system that is well thought out and well communicated to a responsive tradesman shouldn't be any harder to install than one for a conventional stud-frame house. In fact, electricians who have worked on several of our projects say that in many ways it's easier.

HORIZONTAL WIRE CHASES

Wires get around the perimeter of a timber-frame structure primarily through horizontal wire chases. The system most widely used is the extended-baseboard wire chase, but there are other options. Wire chases can be created in baseboard heating units, behind finished walls, behind cabinets, or on sill plates. Note: The illustrations in this chapter show both typical and doublechip panels because they are both in common use. Refer to Chapter 5 for more information about alternatives.

Extended-baseboard wire chase

The extended-baseboard wire chase is installed inside exterior walls between timber posts. Wires are mounted in a cavity created by two furring strips, and the outlet boxes are mounted in the front face of the baseboard (see the drawings on the facing page). The wires pass through the timber posts on their way around the perimeter of the house through a notch cut in the back of each post—ideally, these notches were planned and cut before the frame was erected. There are no notches in the corner posts because it's too difficult to feed the wires around corners. Instead, wires are fed down through the floor and up again on the adjacent side.

While commercial surface-mounted wire chases can substitute for the extended baseboard, I don't think they are attractive enough to be used undisguised in high-quality homes. A possible exception is Wiremold's Access Baseboard Raceway. This is an extruded PVC baseboard wire-chase system with two separate cavities, one for power and the other for low-voltage wires. It is designed with many fittings to solve a range of installation situations and has removable covers to allow easy access for changes or upgrading.

The extended-baseboard wire-chase system actually begins at the sill. If the frame is attached to a timber sill, during prewiring the electrician will mount wires in a chase created with furring strips on the outside of the

After the foam-core panels have been installed and the interior partition walls built, the electrician can complete the rough wiring.

EXTENDED-BASEBOARD WIRE CHASE

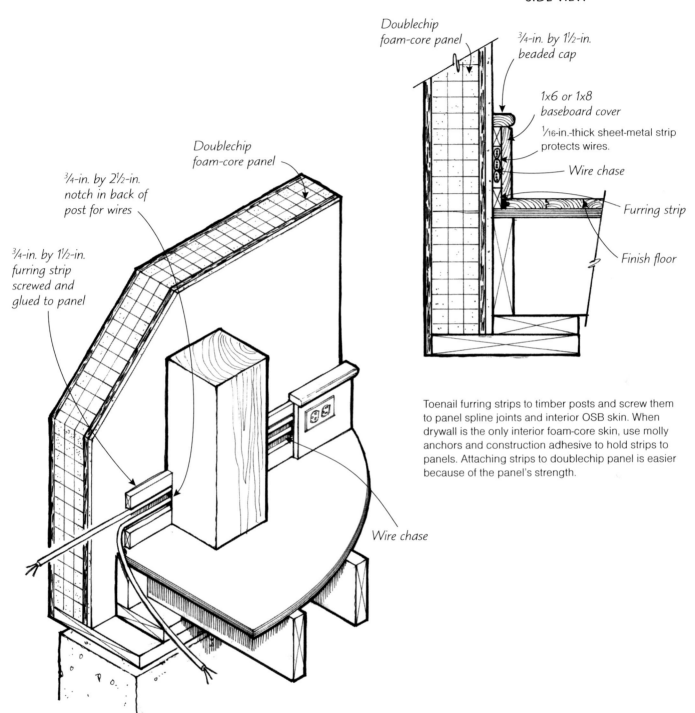

SIDE VIEW

Doublechip foam-core panel

¾-in. by 1½-in. beaded cap

1x6 or 1x8 baseboard cover

¹⁄₁₆-in.-thick sheet-metal strip protects wires.

Wire chase

Furring strip

Finish floor

¾-in. by 2½-in. notch in back of post for wires

Doublechip foam-core panel

¾-in. by 1½-in. furring strip screwed and glued to panel

Wire chase

Toenail furring strips to timber posts and screw them to panel spline joints and interior OSB skin. When drywall is the only interior foam-core skin, use molly anchors and construction adhesive to hold strips to panels. Attaching strips to doublechip panel is easier because of the panel's strength.

System keeps wiring on interior side of foam-core panel, which eliminates cutting through foam and resulting heat loss.

sill (see the drawings below). This keeps the interior of the timber floor system from being ruined visually by strings of wire running in all directions. Although simple, this system consumes a great deal of wire because all wires have to pass around the perimeter. Sometimes it is acceptable to find one place for wires to pass through the house, perhaps using a dropped ceiling between joists (similar to the plumbing chase discussed on p. 165). To feed an electrical device or series of outlets in the wall, the electrician pulls a tail, or wire end, into the extended-baseboard area through a gap left in the top sill furring strip. After all the wires have been mounted in the sill chase, a ¹⁄₁₆-in.-thick sheet-metal strip is screwed or nailed over the chase to protect the wires. This may not be required by the building inspector, but it certainly can help prevent a problem in the event of a misplaced nail.

If the timber frame is on a stick-framed floor deck, during prewiring the electrician runs wires to and from the service panel in the cavities between joists. To access the extended baseboard, the electrician drills a hole on a diagonal from the top outside corner of the subfloor toward the inside face of the rim joist (see the left photo on the facing page). One hole is drilled for each wire needed between posts. The wires are then pushed up from

TIMBER-SILL WIRE CHASE

When using timbers for sills and joists, create space around perimeter by holding sill to inside by ¾ in. and then use furring strips to make wire chase. Wires must pass around perimeter or move across at strategic locations so as not to be visible from inside.

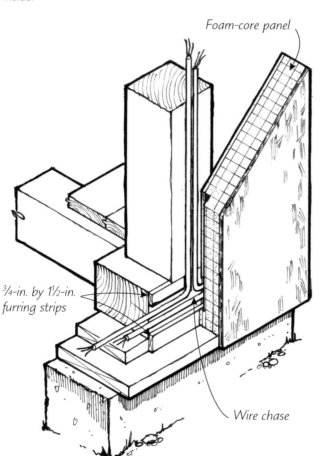

Foam-core panel

¾-in. by 1½-in. furring strips

Wire chase

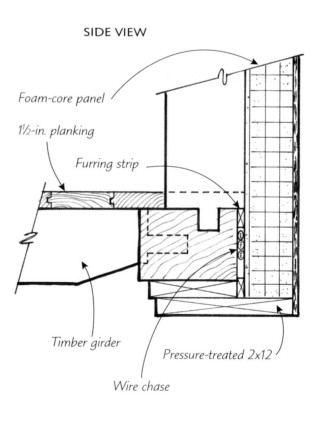

SIDE VIEW

Foam-core panel

1½-in. planking

Furring strip

Timber girder

Pressure-treated 2x12

Wire chase

If the deck is stick-framed, holes are drilled between each pair of posts from the top outside corner of the subfloor to the inside of the rim joist (left). Wires can then easily pass from the basement joist area to the extended-baseboard chase.

Wires are run between furring strips (below). Outlet boxes are placed in holes in the baseboard and panels.

below at a later date, usually during rough wiring. From there the wire can be run from outlet to outlet inside the chase.

Once the frame has been prewired, it's time to assemble the extended-baseboard chases. This is basic carpentry. To begin, snap a line on a wall to show the top of the baseboard minus the cap. If a 1x6 or 1x8 is used for the baseboard cover, this dimension will be 5½ in. or 7½ in., respectively. Then cut the top and bottom furring strips to length, using more than one piece for each run, if necessary. Apply a bead of construction adhesive to the top furring strip and fit it between posts with its top edge on the chalkline. Toenail it to the timber posts and screw it to the panel splines. Repeat the process with the bottom furring strip, but toenail it

to the subfloor as well as to the posts. To draw the furring strips tightly to the wall, use molly anchors and screws every 2 ft. where there isn't a spline or nailer.

Using the electrical plan as a guide, next cut the holes for the outlet boxes in the baseboard cover, which is then used as a template to mark the holes on the wall. Obviously, because the space between the furring strips is narrow, duplex outlets are run horizontally. Make the cuts in the baseboard precise, because overcutting will show up as gaps around the outlet cover. Then test-fit the baseboard between the timbers and mark the box locations on the wall between the furring strips. To keep the outlets well above the finish floor, locate the boxes directly against the bot-

tom edge of the upper furring strip. Remove the baseboard and cut a housing in the wall for each box, keeping it as shallow as possible; you don't have to cut to the full depth of the box because of its placement in the baseboard cover. (Outlet boxes should be selected on the basis of minimal penetration of the insulation. It's easier for the electrician if the boxes are deep, but better for the energy performance of the house if they're shallow.) Then pry the drywall and foam block loose with a flat bar or screwdriver, pulling out excess foam with a hard, sharp tool.

When all this has been done, the electrician runs the wires through the chase and secures them with staples at the panel splines. If necessary, electrical tape will corral several wires until the baseboard cover goes on. The carpenter then mounts the cover between timber posts, pulls the wires through the holes for the outlet boxes, and attaches the baseboard to the furring strips with 8d finish nails about 16 in. on center. The electrician mounts the boxes on the baseboard and attaches the outlets. For the benefit of safety (or for the building inspector), a $\frac{1}{16}$-in.-thick strip of sheet metal is screwed or nailed behind the baseboard cover to protect the wires.

Some codes require electric outlets to be 14 in. off the finish floor, although the reasons for this have more to do with the convenience of the homeowner than with safety. If this issue is pressed, the extended baseboard can still be used for a wire chase while the outlet boxes are mounted higher in the wall (see the drawings below). Set up the chase as usual, leaving the cover off until the outlets are installed. Mark the outlets on the wall no more than 16 in. off the floor, using a sample outlet box to scribe the lines. Cut the holes for the boxes as shallow as possible. Then ream a hole through the foam-core panel from each box opening to the chase area with a $\frac{1}{2}$-in.-dia. bar or pipe (rebar works well). Stay as close as possible to the interior sheathing. Intersect that hole with a hole drilled out from the chase. When you push a wire down from the outlet box, it should be easy to pull it through from the chase. Pull the wire into the outlet box and mount it in the drywall with switch-box supports. Before closing up the box, fill any voids in the insulation with spray foam. Keep in mind that there is extra heat loss when the outlets are outside the wire chase, because more insulation is removed to accommodate the depth of the box.

EXTENDED-BASEBOARD WIRE CHASE WITH RAISED OUTLET BOX

Extended-baseboard wire chase can still be used with raised outlet boxes. Boxes can be located in panel, with hole reamed through panel core to bring wire from chase to box.

SIDE VIEW

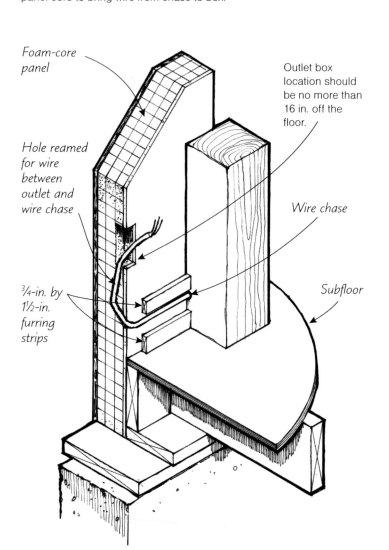

Foam-core panel

Hole reamed for wire between outlet and wire chase

$\frac{3}{4}$-in. by $1\frac{1}{2}$-in. furring strips

Outlet box location should be no more than 16 in. off the floor.

Wire chase

Subfloor

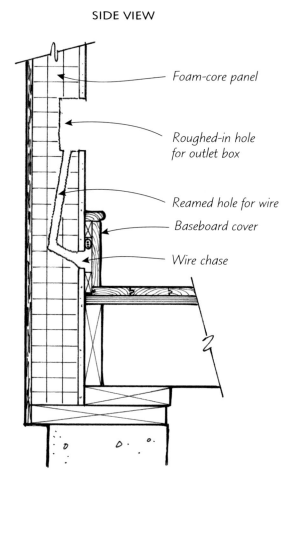

Foam-core panel

Roughed-in hole for outlet box

Reamed hole for wire

Baseboard cover

Wire chase

Baseboard heating unit wire chase

Some commercial baseboard heating systems are designed with a built-in chase for one or two wires to supply outlets in a circuit. Some brands even offer inserts that include a mounting for a duplex outlet. But if the chase needs to accommodate wires for other circuits, it will probably make more sense to use the extended-baseboard wire chase behind the baseboard heating unit, as shown in the top drawing at right. The heating unit is then mounted on the furring strips. In this case, you can use either the outlets in the heating unit or outlets mounted in the extended baseboard between sections of the baseboard heating unit.

Finish-wall wire chase

Other interior finish elements can also be used as wire chases without substantially altering their function or design. For example, if wainscoting is intended or if a wall is to be completely paneled, the furring strips needed to attach the wainscoting or paneling to the walls create a natural wire chase (see the bottom drawing at right). The furring strips are installed in the same way as in the extended-baseboard system (see p. 141). In the case of paneling, where the entire wall is set up with furring strips, the vertical wires for switches and wall lights can be run as part of the same system, but make sure all the wires are in a safe position or are protected with a strip of $1/16$-in.-thick sheet metal.

Cabinet wire chase

Cabinets in kitchens and baths offer another opportunity to set up a wire chase if you mount them to furring strips. Install the furring strips on the wall about 12 in. on center, locating a strip approximately 6 in. from the top and bottom of the cabinet. Because outlets for kitchen and bath cabinets tend to be located just above the cabinet back, it's necessary to leave a gap in the furring strips so that a wire can be brought up from behind the cabinet. A built-up backsplash is then constructed using the method for making an ex-

BASEBOARD HEATING UNIT WIRE CHASE

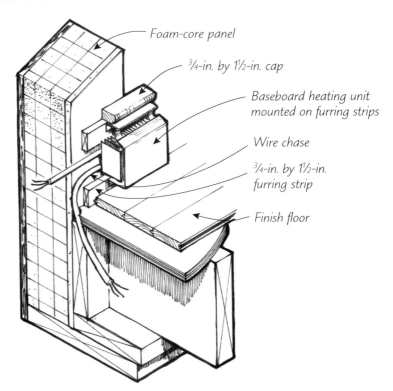

Foam-core panel

$3/4$-in. by $1 1/2$-in. cap

Baseboard heating unit mounted on furring strips

Wire chase

$3/4$-in. by $1 1/2$-in. furring strip

Finish floor

FINISH-WALL WIRE CHASE

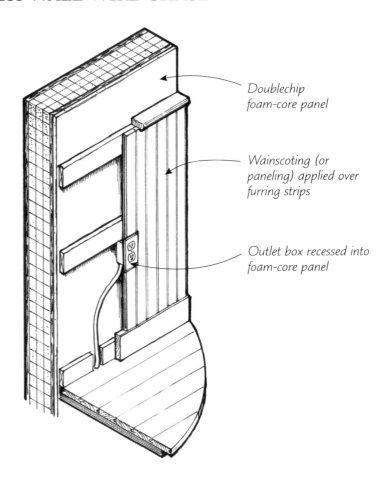

Doublechip foam-core panel

Wainscoting (or paneling) applied over furring strips

Outlet box recessed into foam-core panel

CABINET WIRE CHASE

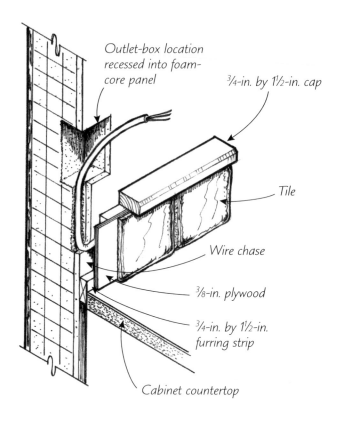

Outlet-box location recessed into foam-core panel

¾-in. by 1½-in. cap

Tile

Wire chase

⅜-in. plywood

¾-in. by 1½-in. furring strip

Cabinet countertop

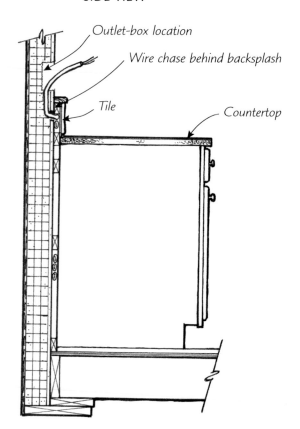

Outlet-box location

Wire chase behind backsplash

Tile

Countertop

SILL-PLATE WIRE CHASE

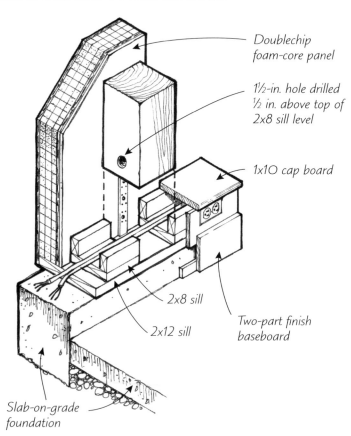

Doublechip foam-core panel

1½-in. hole drilled ½ in. above top of 2x8 sill level

1x10 cap board

2x8 sill

2x12 sill

Two-part finish baseboard

Slab-on-grade foundation

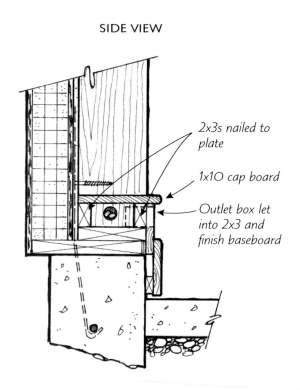

SIDE VIEW

2x3s nailed to plate

1x10 cap board

Outlet box let into 2x3 and finish baseboard

Wiring and Lighting

tended baseboard, except that ⅜-in.-thick plywood is attached to the furring strips to back the tile. Another variation is to use tile just above the counter and a more typical wire chase just above that. Using tile as the backsplash is attractive and gives better moisture protection, but to prevent accidental electric shock, code requires that ground-fault circuit interrupters be used in bathrooms and in areas close to the kitchen sink.

If it is necessary to have outlets higher than the backsplash area, use the space behind the cabinets for the chase and mount the outlet in the foam-core panel not more than 16 in. above the cabinet, as shown in the top drawings on the facing page. Remember to foam all the voids around the outlet boxes.

Sill-plate wire chase

The sill system used with slab-on-grade foundations (described in Chapter 6), can easily be used to make a wire chase. Start by drilling a 1½-in. hole in the posts for the wires to pass through. This hole should be located about ½ in. up from the 2x8 cap sill. Then, nail 2x3s on edge on top of the 2x8. Locate one against the foam-core panel and the other on the front edge of the 2x12 and 2x8 sills. This will not only provide enough room for all the usual wires but also for the outlet boxes. For the protection of the wires, staple them to the center of the cavity. Using a circular saw, cut an opening for the outlet boxes through the outside 2x3. Run the wires through the chase, leaving adequate tails for the outlets. When all the wires are in place, precisely cut the outlet holes in the finish baseboard, holding the baseboard over the sill and the 2x3 to transfer the outlet locations. Feed the wires through the baseboard and nail them to the sills and to the face of the 2x3. Finally, attach the 1x10 cap board to the 2x3s and the lower baseboard to the finish floor (see the bottom drawings on the facing page). If possible, screw the cap board on to allow for future access.

WIRING UNDER DOORWAYS

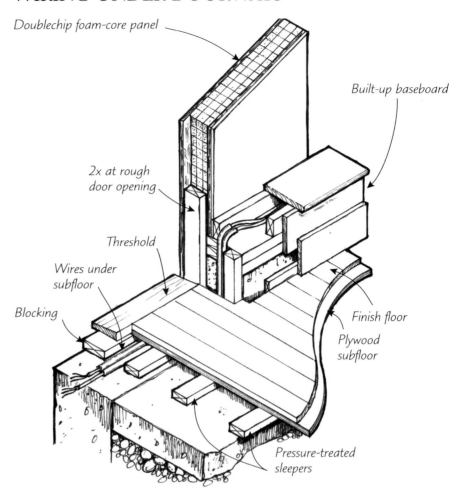

Doublechip foam-core panel

Built-up baseboard

2x at rough door opening

Threshold

Wires under subfloor

Blocking

Finish floor

Plywood subfloor

Pressure-treated sleepers

In this system, exterior doorways can present a problem because the sill is lower than the rest of the foundation wall and the rim joist cannot travel around the perimeter of the house without interruption. The most common solution is to block up the door threshold 1 in. to 1½ in. from the slab to allow electrical conduit to pass underneath. The blocking is attached to the concrete toward the inside and outside of the threshold using concrete nails or expansion bolts, and the wires are run through conduits between. (Allow a few extra inches in the width of the concrete rough opening so wires have room to drop from the foundation wall down to threshold level.) If a wooden floor is to be laid over the concrete, this technique would not alter the typical relationship between the threshold and the finish floor.

When the house is on a slab instead of on a wooden structure, it is usually necessary to have several conduits embedded in the concrete to get wires across the building. Otherwise, all the wires would have to run around the building in the chase, wasting wire and time. It would have to be clear from the plan which wires would need to be in the conduit, and the conduit would need to have a vertical riser at the ends to bring the wires to the future wire chase. This technique is familiar to almost all electricians because the situation is commonly encountered in house building.

WIRING THROUGH PARTITION WALLS

Except for the last method, which is specific to a particular foundation type, the wire chases described previously can be used on any exterior wall. They will work as conveniently on the second-floor or third-floor levels as on the first. But for interior walls, it makes sense to switch to more conventional wiring methods. Interior partition walls are framed with studs after the exterior walls are in place, and wires and boxes can be installed in them as usual.

Partition walls usually intersect exterior walls at timber posts, but if a partition and an exterior wall intersect between posts, the wires can be passed into the partition from the extended-baseboard chase as shown in the drawing below.

Where a partition wall is located at a post, the electrician must drill through the post to allow the wires to pass from the chase to the stud cavity. This happens during prewiring, before the foam-core panels go on, and I'm always surprised at how many times these holes don't get drilled for lack of thorough planning. Without them, it can be quite difficult to get to the partition, requiring either passing the wires through the floor system or drilling completely through both the foam-core panel and the post. The holes should be located in the posts at the level of the wire chase in the extended baseboard and drilled from the inside, which makes it easier to align them precisely with the center of the partition wall. The wires are fed through the post from the outside to the outlet or switch boxes. Because partitions are usually not framed at this stage, it's necessary to notch the first stud around the wire and the hole drilled through the post. Subsequent studs are drilled in the conventional manner.

When it is necessary to bring a wire to an interior partition wall that does not intersect an exterior wall, bring the wire back to the floor system and drill through to the partition from the basement or crawlspace. For timber floors, which are usually exposed to view, plan even further ahead and run this wire in a groove routed into the top of a timber.

WIRING PARTITION WALLS

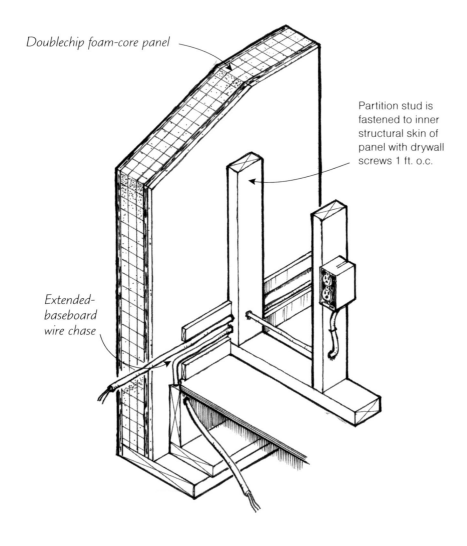

Doublechip foam-core panel

Partition stud is fastened to inner structural skin of panel with drywall screws 1 ft. o.c.

Extended-baseboard wire chase

VERTICAL WIRE CHASES

In a timber-frame house, the seams between foam-core panels make convenient chases for vertical wires. Wires can be run either in the joints between panels over timber posts or at the panel splines. A panel joint will not always fall conveniently on a post requiring wires, but the problem is easily solved by cutting a whole panel to make a joint at the post. No structural integrity is lost, and wiring is made substantially easier. At panel splines, a cavity is created that is meant to be filled with foam, but before it is filled, it's an excellent way to bring wires to the extended baseboard between posts.

Timber-post wire chase

Remember that during prewiring, the wires were strung loosely in position on the timber posts, their ends directed toward horizontal wire chases or run through posts toward interior partition walls. During panel installation, the crew makes a chase for the wires by notching the inside edges of the panels meeting over posts. The first panel is nailed to the frame as described in Chapter 5, with the wires pulled away to avoid damage. When that panel is

BUILT-IN CEILING FIXTURE

Ceiling fixtures can be built in between timber joists to provide downlighting. The translucent panel is cut ⅜ in. smaller than the opening between timbers and end trim pieces, so it can be easily tilted into position.

SIDE VIEW

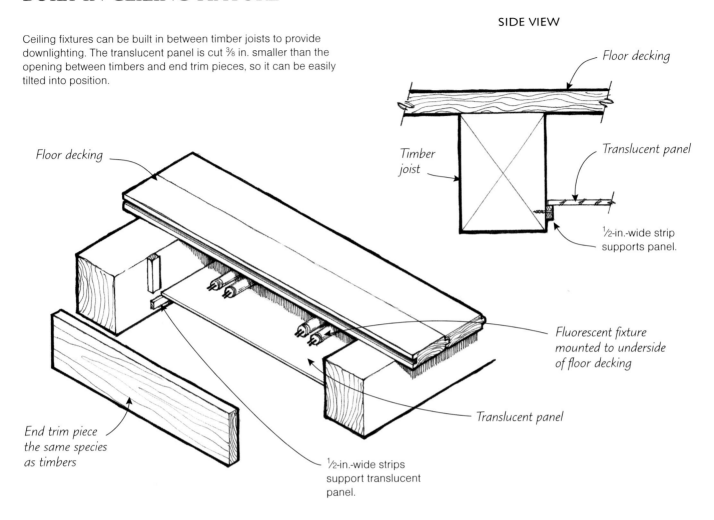

Floor decking

Timber joist

Translucent panel

½-in.-wide strip supports panel.

Floor decking

Fluorescent fixture mounted to underside of floor decking

Translucent panel

End trim piece the same species as timbers

½-in.-wide strips support translucent panel.

RECESSED LIGHT FIXTURE

Dropped ceiling creates cavity for recessed light fixtures. Check with lighting manufacturer for clearance and ventilation requirements.

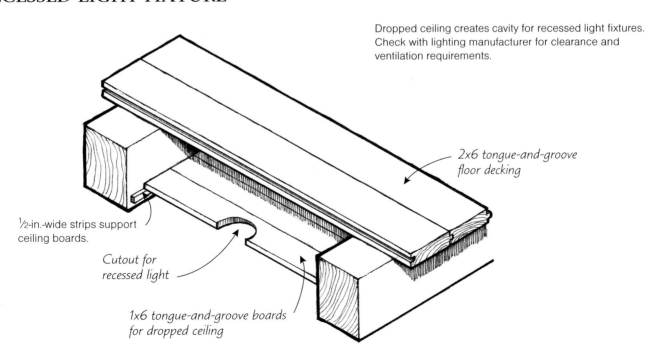

2x6 tongue-and-groove floor decking

½-in.-wide strips support ceiling boards.

Cutout for recessed light

1x6 tongue-and-groove boards for dropped ceiling

Wiring and Lighting

155

room. Track lighting can be used creatively to wash walls with indirect light or to focus on an object.

The upper sides of roof purlins in open areas also provide good mounting for track lights. When track lights are used this way, be sure to get fixtures that can turn down past 90° or else the options for directing the light will be limited. With a full range of movement, the lights can be directed toward the ceiling to illuminate the frame or pointed down for general lighting or to highlight artwork or furniture.

Frames for large areas often have hammer beams or king- and queen-post trusses, which can provide a mounting surface for individual fixtures of track lights. It is best in these situations if the fixtures have flexible heads, to allow the light to be focused in a number of directions. To recess fixtures, dadoes can be cut in the timbers before the frame is raised. When the tops of the timbers are not visible, it's even possible to hide a tubular light in a dado.

When houses have been well designed, the living spaces receive the natural light appropriate to their use during daylight hours. Artificial light is often intended to imitate daylight, but remember that activities and moods change during evening hours, and there are new requirements involving entertainment, relaxation, and romance. The easiest way to achieve the desired results while maintaining flexibility is to overlight and then employ a dimmer. Additional fixtures could also be installed to provide extra light when needed.

The kitchen and dining areas of this house feature hanging lamps mounted on the ceiling between timbers.

The timber-frame building system leaves few natural cavities for pipes—especially those that run horizontally. In this case, the horizontal pipes are hidden in the platform beneath the tub.

CHAPTER 8
PLUMBING

I made a commitment to get more involved with the design of timber-frame houses one afternoon many years ago when I learned of a disaster caused by plumbing. A few months earlier, my company had completed a project in one of the local communities. We had helped with design, but on a very minimal level. When the frame was finished, we gave the clients a few words of advice, told them to call if necessary, and went to work on cutting another frame.

Later on, I happened upon the plumber for the project and asked him how things were going. He told me everything was fine, but, "Boy, I had trouble finding a 6-in. drill bit." I was puzzled. "What 6-in. drill bit?" I wondered. "Well, I had to go all the way to Boston and spend $90 to find a 6-in. drill bit to make a hole through your 8x8 timber for that waste line by the first-floor bath." I feel certain the color of my face and my open mouth said more than words could have. The plumber had acquired a new bit, and our frame had lost an important timber. It was too late to argue or place blame, but I knew that from then on things would have to change. In a way, that plumber did me a favor. He helped me understand that I would have to address the construction idiosyncrasies inherent in timber-frame building, and that I could not expect people in the various trades to solve problems foreign to their experience. As a result, I was forced to become more involved with the design of timber-frame houses and the way in which certain jobs, such as plumbing, were handled.

The problem with plumbing a timber-frame house is not so much how to do it, for the standards and techniques are essentially the same as those used in conventional construction, but how to house and conceal the pipes. In this respect, wiring and plumbing are similar. Much of the task is to create spaces in which to install the workings of the system and then to camouflage those spaces. This may sound simple in principle, but you'd be surprised at how often the principle is mishandled. By far the most common problem we see in completed plans for timber-frame houses is unresolved plumbing situations. It's as if in the concentration of working out the floor plans and the aesthetics of the building, the designers (who are often registered architects) simply forgot that plumbing fixtures must be attached to pipes to operate. When we ask how the problems will be solved, we're often told, "Oh, we'll just box the pipes in somehow." But while this may be an appropriate solution in a laundry room or closet, it could ruin the looks of a living room, a dining room, or a bedroom.

The secret to a successful plumbing job in the timber-frame home is early and careful planning. This is then followed by an intelligent selection of the best options for each particular situation. For the options to make sense, however, it's important to have at least a basic understanding of a few simple plumbing concepts, which I'll discuss first. Then I'll look at planning and creating hidden spaces for pipes.

SOME BASIC PLUMBING

The fundamental aim of every plumbing system is to pump clean water in and to drain used water out. Water usually comes from either a city supply (most often a lake or reservoir) or from a well on the site. When water leaves the house, it is directed to either a city sewage-treatment center or a septic system near the building.

Water is brought through the house by a network of pipes called the supply system and flows out after use through a network called the drainage system (sometimes called DWV, for drain, waste, and vent).

Supply system

In the supply system, water is pumped through a main trunk line to the basement or designated utility area, where one major branch pipe connects to the water heater. From there, smaller branch pipes carry hot and cold water to various parts of the house, feeding into even smaller pipes for individual fixtures.

Many code officials require supply pipes to be copper, although various kinds of plastic piping are gaining acceptance. Because the water in the supply pipes is under pressure from the city water main or well pump, no air is required to assist the flow. This means that the pipes can be smaller than drainage pipes (which are merely conduits for water to flow by the force of gravity)—generally no larger than 1 in. dia. and no smaller than ⅜ in. dia.

In addition, the pipes can be run in any direction on their way from the source to the fixture.

Drainage system

The drainage system is more complicated than the supply system and therefore is the focus of all our planning. When the space requirements of the drainage system have been satisfied, the requirements of the supply system will almost always automatically be satisfied as well.

The drawing on the facing page shows the anatomy of a typical drainage system. Basically, it works like this: When you pull the drain plug on your bathtub, gravity pulls the water down a short vertical section of pipe to the trap, where some is captured in the loop to prevent gases in the line from rising into the living area. (Toilets don't need traps because they always contain water.) When the water passes through the trap, it drops into a pipe that is slightly pitched, called a branch drain. The branch drain directs the water to a larger vertical pipe, called the soil stack. A vent pipe connected to the branch drain just beyond the trap allows air into the branch drain and releases the sewage gases. This branch vent rises vertically to a point above the fixtures and then pitches upward toward the upper part of the soil stack, which is called the stack vent. Essentially, drainage occurs in the lower portion of the stack while the upper part brings air to the branch vents and allows the sewage gases to escape. Meanwhile, the bath water drops through the soil stack until it reaches the main building drain, which carries all of the household waste water and sewage to a septic tank or sewer.

Because the water in the drain pipes is not pressurized, the pipes must be oversized to allow air in the lines. The smallest drain for an individual fixture would have a diameter of 1½ in., and the largest pipe, the soil stack, would have a diameter of 4½ in. (This pipe won't even fit within a typical stud wall.) Drainage pipes are commonly

TYPICAL DRAINAGE SYSTEM

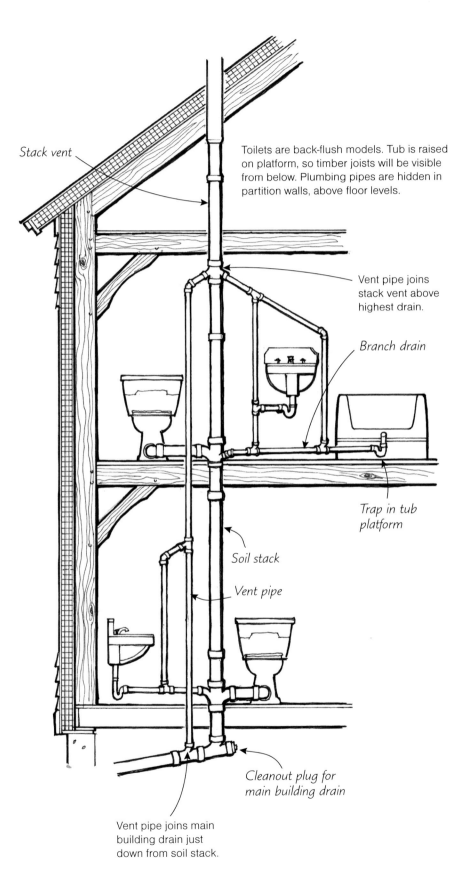

Stack vent

Toilets are back-flush models. Tub is raised on platform, so timber joists will be visible from below. Plumbing pipes are hidden in partition walls, above floor levels.

Vent pipe joins stack vent above highest drain.

Branch drain

Trap in tub platform

Soil stack

Vent pipe

Cleanout plug for main building drain

Vent pipe joins main building drain just down from soil stack.

made of ABS plastic, although cast iron is often better for the stack because it helps muffle the sound of the water as it rushes downward. Branch drains must be pitched all the way to their stacks; codes require a minimum pitch of ¼ in. per foot. Tubs, showers, and toilets require the most planning because their drains are usually underneath the fixture, requiring space in the floor system. For most situations, the minimum space required beneath fixtures for drains is 6 in., but it can be more with a long run from the drain to the stack. For instance, if a pipe were pitched ¼ in. per foot and had to run 12 ft., an additional 3 in. of space would be required from the point of connection to the branch drain. Sinks are simpler to deal with because their traps and drains are above the floor. If the stack is not too far away, sink drains can be run to it without a special cavity.

DESIGNING THE PLUMBING SYSTEM

Plumbing design should begin at the earliest stages of house design, when there is only blank paper and a full bank account: You will want to know that everything has been done to avoid unnecessary complications. No doubt, even after careful planning there will still be situations calling for imaginative thinking, but keep these several rules of thumb in mind.

• The most important rule is to consolidate plumbing areas wherever possible. Primary plumbing facilities (bath, laundry, and kitchen) should be clustered in one section of the house, with plumbing areas on different floors stacked atop one another. The benefits are that pipe runs will be kept short, and there will be more opportunities for shared drains and stacks. Fewer feet of pipe minimize potential problems with the plumbing system; fewer vents passing through the roof reduce the potential for water leaks or heat loss and make roofing easier. Consolidation of plumbing areas also saves money. Hotel designers have this down to a science and always place bathrooms back to back and stack them one over another.

• After the plumbing areas are clustered, consolidate further by trying to get supply and drain lines to share a single chase in a common wet wall (a wall with plumbing). If this isn't possible, use more than one wet wall for supply and drains but attach the drains to only one stack. Keep working toward the simplest and most compact arrangement until the number of wet walls and the lengths of pipe required have been reduced to a minimum.

• To reduce noise, avoid locating wet walls adjacent to major living areas. Wherever possible, run the plumbing through secondary partitions, such as those that enclose a bathtub or shower stall or the partition between a bathroom and laundry.

• Likewise, when plumbing areas can't be stacked floor to floor, avoid locating wet walls over or under open areas or primary rooms. Remember that drains go down and vents go up. When a bathroom on the second floor falls over a dining room on the first floor, hiding pipes immediately becomes difficult. Creative solutions, even design innovations, can arise from such situations, but more often the result is disappointment. I know of a house with a hollow fake post, a camouflaged mastery that gurgles from time to time. And I've heard about an eccentric with an interest in the details of his household effluent—he required Plexiglas drain pipes that would be revealed to the living room. When the suggestion came, my bet is that the designer wished he had located the second-floor plumbing somewhere else. Exposed pipes are an option, and recently there has been a movement among some avant-garde architects to reveal all the mechanics of a building, but so far this "warehouse architecture" hasn't gained much momentum. I, for one, don't mind seeing good-quality copper plumbing in supply lines, but I am still a little old-fashioned about the drainage pipes.

• Partition walls that align with beams cannot be used as wet walls because it would then be necessary to drill through the timbers. (This principle conflicts with the one established in Chapter 4, which says timbers should be used to define rooms, but supports the idea that wet walls should not be adjacent to primary living areas.) Instead, try to use secondary partitions, such as closet and bathroom walls, for wet walls. These secondary walls seldom have interference from timbers and are separate enough from the rest of the house so that their treatment need not match the decor of the primary living areas (see the discussion in this chapter on vertical pipe chases). Wet walls should align on each level so that pipes can run uninterrupted from the first floor to the roof.

• In any plumbing area, position the fixtures as close as possible to the soil stack. When there are several fixtures, try to arrange them so that those with the most critical drainage requirements (usually the toilet first, then the tub) are closer to the stack. It would not make sense to back the sink up to the soil stack and locate the toilet in the far corner of the room because its drain would have to travel far to the stack. Draining water from the sink is much less difficult than draining waste from the toilet, and the branch drain from the sink can be run to the stack without interaction with the floor.

• Don't run plumbing through exterior walls. It would compromise insulation and possibly allow pipes to freeze.

These guidelines may sound like a lot to keep in mind, but they actually dovetail nicely with good house design; therefore, many of them come rather naturally. Consider the following example of plumbing layout in the three-bay timber-frame house we used as an example in Chapter 4. The major living areas, such as the living and dining rooms, are gathered in one end of the house (for the sun, view, and/or privacy). The secondary areas, such as the laundry room and bathroom, are

pushed to the opposite end, toward the north (see the drawing on the facing page). The kitchen is located near the utility entrance for convenience when bringing groceries into the house—part of the plumbing has therefore automatically been located. People doing household chores shouldn't have to run from one end of the house to the other, so we try to keep the laundry (if it is to be located on this level) near the kitchen. Next, we attempt to back up the bathroom to the laundry. In the best possible arrangement, the wall that contains pipes for the laundry is shared by the bath. This not only makes plumbing easier but also removes the wet wall from the living areas. So, by following some natural design inclinations, all of the plumbing is in one bay. The rest of the house is open and unencumbered by partitions, and yet the bathroom is convenient.

The second floor would follow the pattern of the first. Bedrooms would be located toward the view or the sun, with closets and bathrooms pushed toward the opposite end. By stacking the second-floor bath over the first-floor plumbing area, the difficulty of creating spaces for pipes will be minimal.

Planning

In residential construction, the set of plumbing plans itself is not usually very complicated or precise. Plan views are drawn as overlays on the floor plan. The plans show the location of wet walls in relation to fixtures, and though they show pipe routes, the plans do not necessarily show pipe connections. Typical building sections and sections specific to the plumbing area give the plumber and the carpenter an exact description of each plumbing chase. These plans and elevations should show hot and cold supply lines, drains, stacks, and vents, but again it's not usually necessary to be specific about pipe connections. The plans should be drawn by the designer and reviewed carefully with both the plumber and the carpenter before work commences. Here it's critical that the separate trades work together. The de-

PLUMBING LAYOUT IN SAMPLE THREE-BAY HOUSE

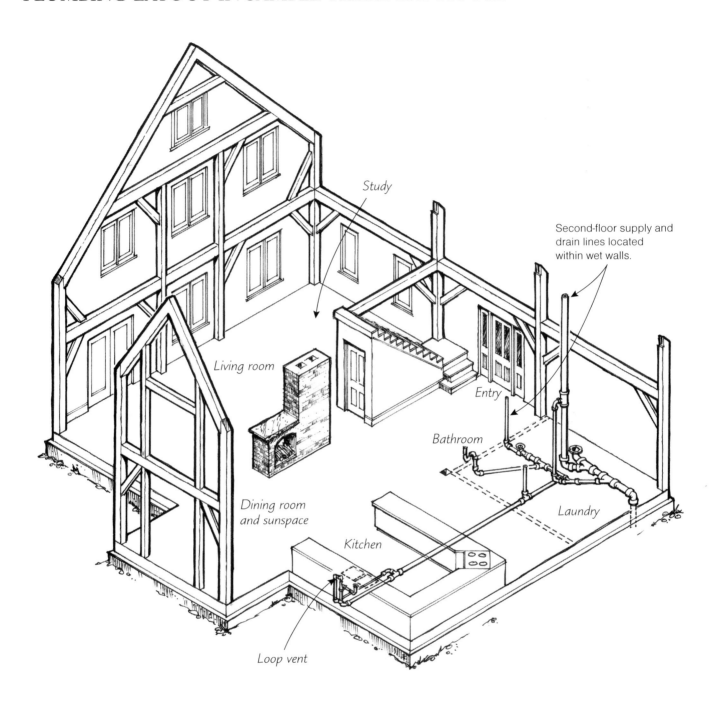

Study

Second-floor supply and
drain lines located
within wet walls.

Living room

Entry

Bathroom

Dining room
and sunspace

Laundry

Kitchen

Loop vent

signer plans the spaces for plumbing, the carpenter builds the spaces, and the plumber uses the spaces. Together they can accomplish near miracles of deception. As separate forces, they can touch off a small war.

It would take a large budget, and a very skilled carpenter and plumber, to rescue a project if the design criteria I've

listed are neglected. Yet even if you give planning the plumbing system your best shot, house design includes a consideration of many factors, and often it will not be possible to adhere to each guideline. Final decisions on frame design and room layout will inevitably include compromises that will affect the complexity of the plumbing system. To be properly prepared for planning, it is

therefore necessary to have a small arsenal of solutions for the various problems that may arise. Although vent pipes often angle diagonally upward and drain pipes always pitch toward the stack, pipe chases are always oriented either vertically or horizontally. Let's look at some typical solutions in terms of these requirements.

VERTICAL PIPE CHASES

The most obvious and common vertical chase is an interior partition. But as I've mentioned, the difficulty is that in a timber-frame house, there should be a deliberate alignment of partitions and beams—a goal that conflicts with creating pipe chases. To allow the unimpeded passage of pipes, it is necessary to design wet walls to stand away from beams. This idea needs to be conceived in the planning stage; if it is, execution is easy.

When framing wet walls, remember that partitions in a timber-frame house exist only to separate rooms. They have no load-bearing function, so there need be only enough structure within the walls for stiffness and to support the finish surfaces. Therefore, try to anticipate where pipes will fall within wet walls and eliminate or reduce structure as much as possible. For instance, if the wall is being built in sections anyway, consider constructing it so there will be no obstruction to the soil stack. There certainly isn't any reason to have top and bottom plates in the wall when the hole for the stack will eliminate any structural usefulness the plates might otherwise have had.

When wet walls fall by necessity at beam locations, there are three choices, none of which calls for drilling through the timber. You can hide the plumbing by building either a double or single wet wall adjacent to the timbers, or you can build a boxed chase in a partition (see the drawings at right).

Double walls
The first choice is to build two parallel walls that will conceal the plumbing—one wall between timbers and the other in the plumbing area (see the top photo on the facing page). In this case, each wall supports sheathing on only one side, and the structural requirements are almost nil. To reduce the cost of lumber, you can frame each wall with 2x3s. Hold the inside wall away from the beam far enough to contain

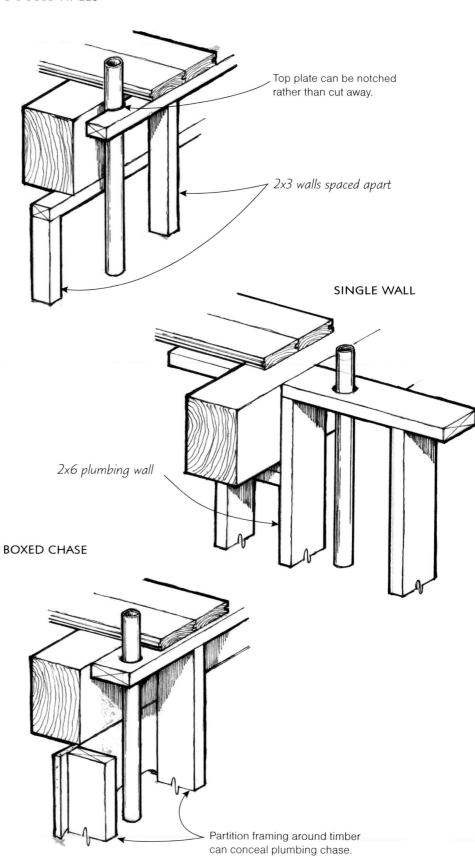

DOUBLE WALLS

Top plate can be notched rather than cut away.

2x3 walls spaced apart

SINGLE WALL

2x6 plumbing wall

BOXED CHASE

Partition framing around timber can conceal plumbing chase.

the pipes. The advantage of this method is that the reveal of timber to the living area is kept consistent throughout the house. The disadvantage is that the aesthetic value of the timber is lost to the room with the wet wall. In a bathroom or laundry area, this may be an easy compromise.

Single wall

The second choice is to build only one wall and to locate it completely on the plumbing-area side of the timbers (see the bottom photo at right). The timbers are then concealed from the plumbing area, and their full depth is completely exposed to the living area in the same manner as those on the exterior walls. This is most acceptable in a house having no other first-floor partitions besides those surrounding the plumbing areas (as in the floor plan on p. 161). Otherwise, the relationship of timbers to walls will be noticeably inconsistent. The walls can be created the same way as built-up exterior walls (see Chapter 5) by applying the drywall first and the framing members afterward. Because nothing has to be fitted between timbers, this technique is easy.

Boxed chase

The third choice is to box the pipes in a corner or in a specially designed chase, which allows the timbers to be revealed to the plumbing area as well as to the living area. This works well if the plumbing can be run in the wall at the end of a shower stall or in the back of a cabinet. The partition wall is then built between timbers as usual, with a chase for drains, stacks, and supply located on the inside of the wall. Bathrooms and kitchens are sometimes especially full of cabinets and closets, and it is occasionally possible to camouflage pipes on the inside of a room (see the top photo on p. 164).

Despite the best intentions, it is not always possible to prevent plumbing from falling over or under living areas without convenient wet walls. The first order of business is to look for an opportunity to make an unobtrusive vertical chase from some other design

This bathroom employs double walls to allow pipes to pass between them. The headers for supply lines take advantage of their non-load-bearing function.

This plumbing wall is built on the bathroom side of the timbers to allow pipes to be run without hiding or compromising the timbers.

The partition wall behind the tub conceals a plumbing chase. It falls to the side of the timber so that pipes can be installed easily.

Raising the floor need not inhibit the proper functioning of household systems. In this bathroom, the sink (not shown) is on the same level as the hallway, while the toilet and shower are a step up.

element in the house and then to use horizontal runs, described in the next section, to get the pipes to the chase. The chase can be a closet, a built-in cabinet, or even a chimney. In the latter case, all that is usually necessary is to make a masonry partition within the chimney to isolate the pipes from the flues. (Check local code before proceeding.) If no enclosure is available, it may be necessary to design a built-in cabinet or shelving unit to serve the purpose. The trick is to make the built-in look natural while still providing adequate space for pipes. (See the photo on p. 73—the built-in cabinet in the dining room conceals plumbing.)

To keep drain-pipe noises from disturbing the living area, make the chase large enough so that there's room to pack the pipes with fiberglass insulation. As I mentioned earlier, using cast iron instead of plastic for vertical drains can also cut sound transmission.

HORIZONTAL PIPE CHASES

The basic issue with horizontal pipe chases is to find a way to run pipes in the floor, given the absence of a cavity. In a timber-frame house, the floor material is usually the ceiling for the living area below, consisting either of planks over beams or a thin, built-up membrane of flooring and ceiling materials (see Chapter 10). These floor systems provide aesthetic and economic benefits, but the lack of space for plumbing is a significant obstacle. With good planning, however, the problem (and the pipes) can disappear.

Assume that through careful design, the plumbing areas have been consolidated and convenient vertical chases for supply pipes and stacks have been provided. The next step is to arrange the fixtures so they have an efficient relationship with the wet walls. As I mentioned earlier, by far the most difficult fixtures to accommodate are toilets, tubs, and showers. The drains for these are usually in the floor, and in the case of the toilet, there is both solid waste and water. Obviously, if these fixtures are located a great distance away from the wet walls, the required length and slope of the pipes create difficulties. If at all possible, the toilet should be the closest fixture to the soil stack, the tub or shower next, and the sink farthest away. Furthermore, all fixtures should be as close as possible to the wet wall and stack. The natural extension of this rule is that vertical and horizontal chases are designed simultaneously and for the benefit of each other.

After wet walls have been determined and fixtures arranged, you must devise a way to get the horizontal pipes to connect with the vertical pipes. In most cases the horizontal pipes run in a chase built either above the floor level or below it. In a few lucky situations, no chase will be required, such as when supply and drain pipes can be passed directly from the fixture to the wet wall. This is quite possible with all sinks and with back-flush toilets. A back-flush toilet has an outlet in the rear instead of underneath. It's more expensive but worth it if it eliminates the carpentry involved in creating a chase. In the basement, it just might make sense to let the pipes run through the floor and under the timbers in the typical helter-skelter manner. If this area is not used for living, it is impractical to spend money and effort to hide what will seldom be seen. Anyway, it's often helpful to have the pipes exposed in the basement for maintenance, especially at the points where water enters and leaves the house.

But, more likely than not, there still will be a need for a horizontal chase. There are four options here. You can build a raised platform, you can run the pipes between timber joists or 2x joists, or you can build a dropped floor.

Raised-platform chase
The simplest, least-compromising solution is to place some of the fixtures on a raised platform while leaving most of the floor level unaltered. Doing this separates the bathroom into distinct

HORIZONTAL PIPE CHASES

TIMBER-JOIST CHASE

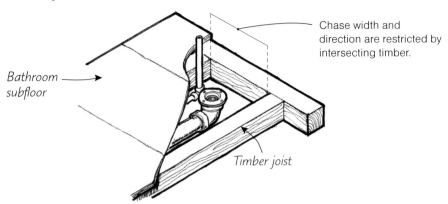

Chase width and direction are restricted by intersecting timber.

Bathroom subfloor

Timber joist

STICK-FRAMED CHASE

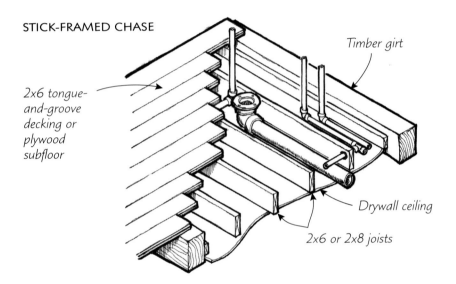

Timber girt

2x6 tongue-and-groove decking or plywood subfloor

Drywall ceiling

2x6 or 2x8 joists

DROPPED-CEILING CHASE

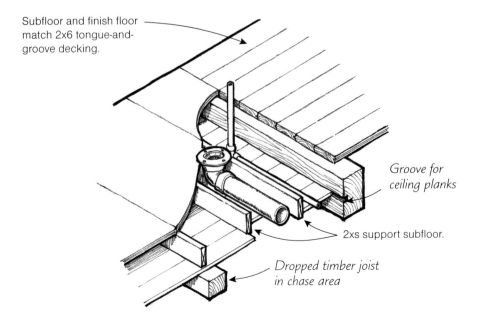

Subfloor and finish floor match 2x6 tongue-and-groove decking.

Groove for ceiling planks

2xs support subfloor.

Dropped timber joist in chase area

The floor joists have been lowered in this oversized bent girt to make room for a false floor above the joists. The routed groove in the girt will receive the floor planks.

areas, making it a design device as well as a way to conceal pipes (see the bottom photo on p. 164). If the sink is close to the entrance and the tub and toilet farthest away, the sink would remain on the common-floor level, and the other fixtures would be raised. A raised tub is considered something of a luxury, and a raised toilet doesn't necessarily affect comfort or convenience, unless there is a handicap consideration. Or the sink and a back-flush toilet could be hooked directly to branch drains in the wall, with just the tub elevated. Often, it will be necessary to build a chase that continues around most of the perimeter of the room, with a platform only for the fixtures. Technically, the chase for the sink plumbing has to be just large enough for its pipes, while the tub and toilet chase has to be large enough for both the fixtures and the pipes. But after fulfilling this requirement, the chase area can be increased to whatever size benefits room design.

The structure of the platform is simple because it has little load-bearing re-

sponsibility. Construct it using conventional floor-framing standards. Joists are typically 2x6s placed 16 in. on center, but if the plumbing run is long, wider joists (and therefore a deeper chase) may be required to allow the proper pitch from the fixture to the stack. The finished ceiling for the room below is installed first, and then the joists are toenailed on top, perpendicular to the timber joists. Before beginning, check the manufacturer's specifications and be sure that the fixture will have adequate support.

Timber-joist chase
If raising the floor is awkward or not desirable, the plumbing can be run in a cavity between timber joists (see the top drawing on p. 165). But because this system has severe limitations, I usually don't recommend it. Because plumbing can fall only between joists, the direction of travel is restricted, and the distance of travel is limited by the next intersecting beam; this means that the branch drains running between a pair of timber joists must connect with a vertical chase before they meet up

with the next perpendicular beam. The distance a branch drain can run between timber joists is also limited by the relationship between the depth of the joists and the drop of the drain as it pitches toward the stack. If the drain drops too low, the timber ceiling will be lost. Yet another problem is that it is unlikely that all fixtures will be located over the same joist bay, causing multiple branch drains where they wouldn't normally be necessary. Of course, this sort of chase has an impact on the room below. It is usually desirable to finish the entire ceiling in the same manner as the area with the plumbing chase, to keep the look consistent. This does not necessarily present a problem, but it does add expense.

Stick-framed chase
When plumbing is consolidated, as discussed earlier, optimally there will be a bathroom or two on the second floor located directly above the plumbing on the first floor. With such dense plumbing, it is often prudent to allow these areas to have different aesthetics from the rest of the house. The most practical solution might be to eliminate the timber joists and replace them with 2x joists, as shown in the middle drawing on p. 165. This is desirable only if all the plumbing is localized and if the area is properly isolated. These joists could even be located below the principal timbers, but the timber ceiling must be high enough to allow this dropped ceiling to fall below their level.

Dropped-ceiling chase
When it's important to maintain the timber ceiling, and you can't build a raised platform (for instance, if there are height restrictions imposed by the roofline), you can design the frame with the timber joists dropped in the area of the plumbing (see the bottom drawing on p. 165 and the photo above). The idea is to keep the timbers revealed below and the floor level consistent above by laying a built-up floor over a lowered timber ceiling—the cavity above the timber joists is the plumbing chase. This works particularly well if the area below benefits from the spa-

Plumbing a kitchen is usually simple enough to make it possible to eliminate wet walls by running pipes between floor joists.

tial or design outcome a dropped ceiling produces: The only division between a living room and study might be the point at which the ceiling becomes lower. (The ceiling must meet code requirements for height, so it usually can't be any lower than 7 ft.) To keep the perimeter timbers exposed as they would be in other parts of the frame, use deep beams (typically 12 in. to 14 in.) to receive the joists. Join the joists far enough below the tops of the timbers to leave room for the chase. A common height for the chase is 5½ in. to fit a standard 2x6 (or 2x4, if no accommodation need be made for the 4-in.-dia. waste line from a toilet). Make sure the drain pipes have an escapement from the timber-floor system at the point where they will be directed toward the vertical chase; the timber adjacent to the vertical chase should be dropped to allow the pipes to pass through. Include the finish ceiling material when considering the depth of the chase. Whether drywall or planking, it should run over the top of the joists as it does in the rest of the house.

If the frame is designed with this feature, creating the plumbing chase is easy. First install the ceiling material over the timbers as discussed in Chapter 10. The built-up floor and plumbing chase is then constructed with conventional materials and techniques, with the finish floor level maintained from the timber floor to the plumbing-chase area. This system is an example of how a problem can be transformed into a design asset.

SINK VENTS

Kitchen plumbing often poses a problem in timber-frame houses because the kitchen is the one space that is not easily isolated from the primary living areas. In addition, an attempt is usually made to design the kitchen spacious and open, which further reduces the opportunities for convenient wet walls.

In the kitchen, the items of concern are usually the sink and the dishwasher. Supply and drainage pipes aren't often a problem for these, because the kitchen is usually located on the first floor, and plumbing can run between joists directly to the basement (see the photo above). Because the sink and dishwasher are almost always side by side, they can share a drain and vent, which reduces the plumbing to a single hot and cold supply line and a single branch drain and vent. But when the sink is on an exterior wall or in an island, where do you put the branch vent? You don't want to run a vertical pipe chase in an exterior wall because this would compromise the insulation, and you certainly don't want to run pipes directly up from an island through the room.

TWO SINK VENTS

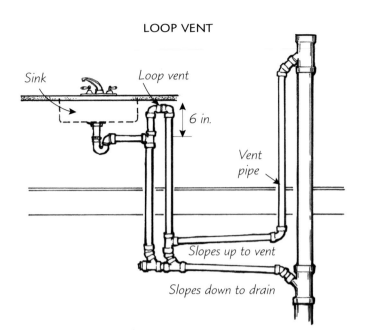

LOOP VENT

Sink

Loop vent

6 in.

Vent pipe

Slopes up to vent

Slopes down to drain

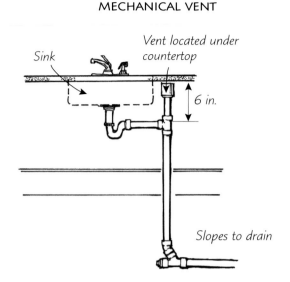

MECHANICAL VENT

Sink

Vent located under countertop

6 in.

Slopes to drain

There are two common solutions to this problem—the loop vent and the mechanical vent. But before choosing either, check local code.

Loop vent

With the loop vent (also called a dry vent), the pipes form a long, upside-down U up to just under the top of the counter and then go back down to a vent pipe, as shown in the left drawing above. The loop vent must rise at least 6 in. above the sink drain to prevent siphoning waste water. The system is simple to install, uses normal plumbing fittings, and usually works well. But the vent does take up space in the cabinet, and some codes don't allow it.

Mechanical vent

The mechanical vent is a device that is installed into the top of a pipe that extends 6 in. above the sink drain. It uses water pressure to open and close a valve that lets air into the line when water is draining and reseals when the drain is not operating. The disadvantage here is that the device can wear out; many codes don't allow it anyway.

The advantage is that it's easy to install and easily replaced if a problem arises.

If neither of these options can be used, a vertical plumbing chase may be fabricated in a kitchen cabinet. This solution is often used but seldom successful because the normal arrangement of kitchens and cabinets makes it difficult to hide a vertical pipe chase. The cabinet that will house the chase should reach to the ceiling and be as close as possible to the sink—examples would be a cabinet pantry or an extension of the cabinet next to the refrigerator. The cabinet would need to be modified to make room for the pipe.

NOTES ON HEATING AND COOLING

Installing heating and cooling systems in timber-frame homes is somewhat troublesome because there aren't many hidden spaces and because people are usually reluctant to commit space to ductwork. In addition, cutting into a timber-defined space for a heating or

cooling duct spoils the organization and balance provided to the room by the timber frame. The solution in large part is to minimize equipment (and fuel consumption) by making energy efficiency a top priority in house design.

Basically, heating and cooling options will be described when the floor plan, insulation levels, and location and number of windows have been determined. The energy audit we commission on our houses (see p. 96) gives us a computerized series of "what ifs" that allow us to see the relative heat performance of various combinations of insulation and glazing. Before committing to any plan, we can determine with some certainty the point of diminishing returns—when money spent doesn't mean appreciably better performance. When a strategy has been determined, the same heating engineer designs the complete system, keeping it as simple and small as possible. A problem with the conventional method of allowing the installer's supplier to lay out the system is that the resulting system is typically much larger than necessary. Let's face it, the guy pushing

furnaces has little incentive to worry about future heating bills. We have found it's better to hire a person who is trained to think—not sell—and to address the problem while there is still design flexibility.

A simple, well-insulated, three-bay timber-frame house with an open area in the middle usually requires only one small, central heat source (see the photo above). It could be the sun, a woodstove, or a small furnace. A little heat (about 30,000 to 40,000 Btus for about 2,500 sq. ft.) emanating from the cen- tral core should keep the whole house warm. If a hot-air furnace is used, the ducts run under the first floor to strategically located registers (perhaps as few as five), which bring warm air to the first level. It is usually not necessary to run the heating system to the second or third levels because the rooms on these floors use the open area as a plenum and receive heat through conduction and convection. The same thing can be done with hot-water or electric baseboard heat. Heat is supplied to the first-floor levels in the conventional way, and the next levels are heated automatically. And that, for many houses we build, is the solution to the problem of the heating system.

Should it become necessary to run heat to various parts of the house, hot-air systems, which require extensive ductwork to move air, are not generally the first choice for timber-frame houses because of the lack of spaces. Unless a convenient cavity can be found for each duct, it is too difficult to be worthwhile. Sometimes we'll choose to use a combination of hot-air heat to the first floor with a few electric-baseboard heaters where necessary on the second floor. Considering the difference in cost between running the ducts and installing the baseboards and how rarely the electric units would actually operate, this alternative can be quite successful.

To bring air to the furnace, a return air duct made from sheet metal is often housed in the masonry chimney (see the drawing on the facing page). The duct must be completely isolated from flues with a solid-brick partition and must be sized according to the specifications of the heating system. The duct should be packed around the outside with fiberglass insulation to keep it from contacting masonry and to isolate it from stray smoke and flue gases. Even if the furnace does not require return air, it might make sense to put a duct into the chimney for recycling the air. The duct can be used like a fan to even out the temperature between the upper and lower levels of the house (see the photo below). Obviously, sheet-metal ducts, unlike flues, are capped at the peak, inside the house.

Hot water and electric systems are certainly easier to accommodate in the crannies of a timber-frame house than a hot-air system. Because the pipes for hydronic systems are rarely larger than ¾ in. dia., they can be run through partitions and in some of the floor systems, using the guidelines in this chapter. For instance, avoid situations that require drilling holes through timbers. When the pipes need to pass around the outside walls, have the posts notched before the exterior insulation system is installed over the frame.

Electric heat is by far the easiest to install because all the wires can be run along with the rest of the house wiring. But unfortunately for most of the country, electric heat is also the most expensive energy source per Btu. As I mentioned before, we often use electric heat as a backup for other systems, such as in houses having good passive-solar systems and a woodstove. A few of our clients with electric backup systems have never actually used them. But bankers who finance construction still usually like to see big, impressive heating systems, even though the most successful systems are quite unimpressive. Energy efficiency is not the first concern for those who lend money.

Cooling systems are hard to disguise, but the same design concepts that keep a heating system small can make a cooling system superfluous. There are many parts of the country, however, where it is almost a necessity, no matter how well the house is conceived and built. While heating systems

The grill near the top of the chimney covers an opening to the return air duct, which brings air down to the basement for the furnace. This duct can also be used for an air-to-air heat exchanger or simply to circulate the house air.

RETURN AIR DUCT IN CHIMNEY

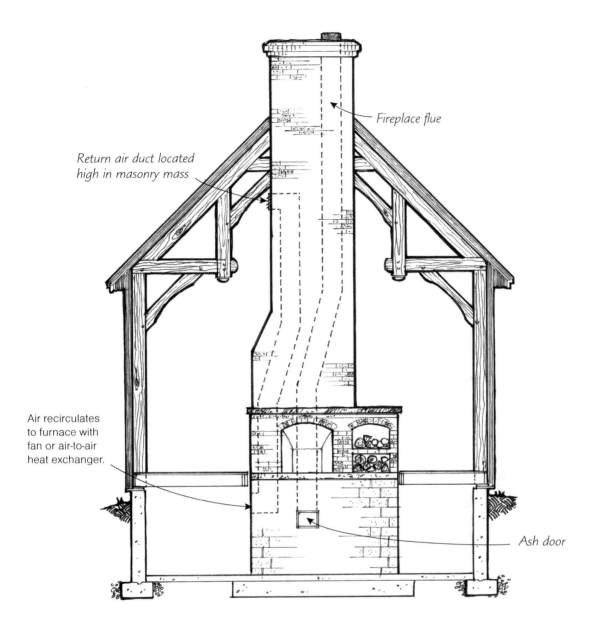

Fireplace flue

Return air duct located
high in masonry mass

Air recirculates
to furnace with
fan or air-to-air
heat exchanger.

Ash door

should be placed at the bottom of the house because warm air rises, cooling systems should be placed at the top to let the cool air drop. Air conditioners require quite a bit of room, and it is almost inevitable that space for these units and their ducts will have to be designed into the plan. One of our houses uses just one supply, located close to the peak (immediately above the collar ties) in the central bay. The cool air falls through the central area and cools the outer perimeter enough to keep the

house comfortable. If it is necessary to feed other areas, keep the unit high in the house and run the ducts down to the rooms. Closets, knee walls, and other secondary or inaccessible areas are the best places for ducts.

The preceding paragraph probably sounds like a quick dismissal of the problem of installing cooling systems. It's not, really—there just isn't much to say. Air-conditioning ducts and equipment potentially can consume large

quantities of space, so the first step is to design a well-insulated house that rejects heat. This way, only a small system will be necessary, one that does not need much space. Then specifically locate the places for equipment and ducts, knowing that design flexibility inevitably will be sacrificed to the necessities of the system. The theories and techniques described throughout this chapter for finding and creating cavities and avoiding timbers should apply to the cooling system, too.

A carved pendant embellishes the bottom of this hammer post.

CHAPTER 9

FRAME DETAILS

In any house there are many thousands of design and construction details. Most are taken for granted; if they go unnoticed, they are successful. These are the details that keep treads and risers at a consistent dimension so that people don't trip, that keep wooden posts from rotting on concrete floors, and that prevent drywall from cracking at the seams. Failure to pay attention to such detail makes for poor construction. It causes the need for constant repair and makes the house more of an annoyance than a joy. Other kinds of details can become highlights of the decor. These are the "frivolous" details that, although technically unnecessary, are undeniably important to good house construction—the frosting on the cake. Embellishing the edges of timbers is not essential, but it can change the feeling of a living space from rustic to elegant. Designing an alcove window seat might seem to be an extra expense and bother but could result in providing the most inviting place in the house. Inevitably, what anyone in house construction learns is this simple lesson: Everything matters. Good house construction requires attention to details both large and small.

In this chapter and the next (which is devoted to exterior and interior finish details), I'll take a look at both the frosting and the cake, exploring some points that were not discussed in other chapters. Here I cover frame embellishments, roof windows, dormers, chimney openings, exterior timbers (roof overhangs and porches), changes in building height and width, compound joinery, and glass. It is not my intention to explicate every possible circumstance; rather, I offer a smattering of ideas in a few critical categories associated with timber-frame construction. Don't look at any of these discussions as prescriptions to be used without thought of revision or modification. Instead, it is my hope that they will provide an outline for a way to think about details and will become a springboard to discovering the solutions best suited to your own home.

EMBELLISHING THE FRAME

Embellishments are refinements made to the edges and ends of a timber. They may be as simple as quarter rounds or bevels to soften hard timber edges, or as complex as elaborately carved pendants at the ends of posts (see the photo on the facing page). Whatever the case, determining the level, type, and location of embellishments is an important part of the design process that should occur during the development of the frame and floor plans. Even the decision to use no embellishment at all ought to be well considered. Timbers are milled to a severe rectilinear shape, and leaving them that way will affect frame design as surely as carving gargoyles on the rafter ends.

Edge treatments

For their origins, edge treatments probably owe more to practicality than decoration. Ceilings in ancient timber frames were sometimes so low that they were a problem even for our shorter ancestors. Beveling those hard timber edges was a safety precaution that grew into a design feature. In those days the work was done with a drawknife and a plane, but today typical edge treatments are executed with a single router pass that is stopped before the timber end. The drawing below shows some styles. The most popular are the quarter round and the 45° straight chamfer because their end cuts are naturally symmetrical to the timber

EDGE TREATMENTS

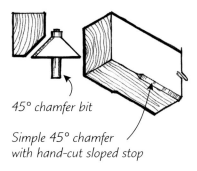

45° chamfer bit

Simple 45° chamfer with hand-cut sloped stop

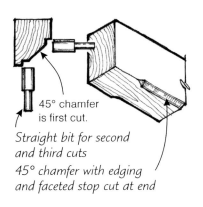

45° chamfer is first cut.

Straight bit for second and third cuts

45° chamfer with edging and faceted stop cut at end

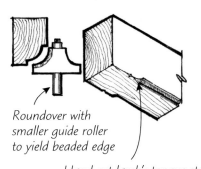

Roundover with smaller guide roller to yield beaded edge

Hand-cut lamb's tongue stop

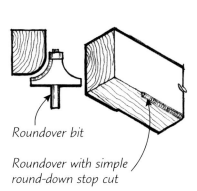

Roundover bit

Roundover with simple round-down stop cut

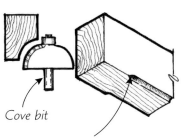

Cove bit

Simple cove with machine stop

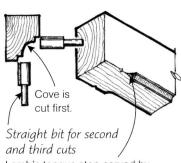

Cove is cut first.

Straight bit for second and third cuts

Lamb's tongue stop carved by hand to finish machine cuts.

This chamfered edge treatment was done with a combination of power and hand tools.

Hemlock timbers without edge embellishments were used for a house intended to have a barnlike atmosphere.

edge. More complicated edge treatments can be built up by making several passes with the router or by using hand tools to make deeper and wider cuts than those possible by machining (see the top photo at left). Working an edge by hand also produces a slightly irregular surface, which can be made to appear rustic or rich, depending on the desired effect.

Edge treatments enormously influence the look of a home. One of the houses my company recently built was intended to have the shape and feel of a barn, and we hoped to create an atmosphere that might be described as "elegant rusticity" (see the bottom photo at left). Because of their unrefined character, hemlock timbers were used for the frame; we planed them just enough to remove the saw marks and left the edges alone. Any kind of edge embellishment would not have been true to the barn idiom, and the lack of it keeps the eye moving past the frame to the volumes and shapes of the house.

By contrast, we designed another house to have some very formal rooms, which would contain chandeliers, cherry woodwork, and fine furniture (see the top photo on the facing page). To make the timbers complement this formality, we embellished them with large, hand-cut beaded-edge chamfers. We also created a subtle arch in the bottom of each summer beam by cutting a bevel from the outside edges toward the middle. Although these details are not overly complicated, they are sufficient to impart a sense of elegance. We gave the less formal rooms of this house, such as the country kitchen, a light edge treatment on the primary timbers and left the secondary timbers alone except for typical planing and oiling.

Most often we choose the middle road on edge embellishments. We frequently opt for small chamfers on all exposed edges of the secondary timbers, just enough to soften them without creating a design statement. Proportionally larger versions of the same treatment would then appear on the principal timbers. One of my favorite refinements is a simple broken edge created by whisking off the hard timber edges with a hand plane. The timbers are left looking crisp, but they feel smooth to the touch instead of splintery. (With natural edges, splinters and tears can be a real problem as the wood dries.) Another device I like for formal situations is a decorative stop called a lamb's tongue, which we normally use with quarter rounds and chamfers (see the right drawings on p. 173). This traditional timber-framing technique comes to us with a history of infinite variations to which modern timber framers have added their own interpretations. Lamb's tongues are executed by hand, using a chisel, a drawknife, and a scoop-bottom plane. We usually confine their use to hand-worked, rather than machined, edges because it's difficult to rout a chamfer that is wider than 1 in., and this is insufficient room to exercise the decorative potential of the lamb's tongue.

The timbers receive their edge embellishments while still on the ground, so when deciding on the subtlety or grandeur of each, it's critical to visualize the relationship of the frame to the floor plan and future partitions. A simple way to generate an edge-treatment plan is to develop a color code for each type of embellishment and then indicate it in that color on copies of the frame plans (both elevations and plan views). To help in planning, we adhere to a few general rules. The first is that partition walls should never encroach on edge treatments. Imagine for a moment a beam divided by a partition that separates the living room and dining room. If the timber edge exposed to the living room has a large, elaborate chamfer, the partition wall will automatically be pushed toward the dining room. If the beam is a 6x8, on the edge exposed to the dining room there will be either no room for an edge treatment or room for only a very small one. Failure to consider this during design can result in a partition that overlaps the treatment on one or both edges—a mistake

Deeply carved embellishments on beams and posts add formality to this room.

made obvious as the drywall climbs into the embellishment.

The second rule of good embellishment is that timbers defining the perimeter of a room should all be treated in a similar way. For instance, using a molded edge on a corner post suggests that other posts in the room should be molded, too. Large summer beams invariably dominate other timbers and therefore often receive larger, more elaborate edge treatments. The size and style of embellishments used on major beams should duplicate those used on major posts.

Edge treatments rarely continue to the timber end. Instead they stop (often with a lamb's tongue) at a prescribed distance from the intersection with other timbers in the frame (see the photo at right). Stopping the embell-

Edge treatments often stop at a prescribed distance from the intersection with other timbers in the frame.

The carving at the ends of timbers is an obvious way to complete the termination. It also greatly enhances the decorative influence of the frame to the living space.

Spline joinery offers a unique opportunity for embellishment. These splines are exposed and carved to repeat the detail at the ends of the hammer beams. (Photo by Tom Goldschmid.)

ishments this way is attractive, accentuates the joinery, and helps the joiner avoid complications. For example, if the embellishments weren't stopped, housings to receive timbers would have to be carved to the contour of the edge treatment at the corners. Timber joinery is hard enough with square corners and right angles, so we keep edge treatments away from all timber intersections. The stops should also be noted on the edge-treatment plan.

As a last note, choose embellishments that reflect the overall intentions of the specific house design; far too frequently, edge treatments become standardized. And make sure that they are within the abilities and time constraints of the joiner.

End treatments

Carved embellishments at timber ends typically occur where a timber passes 6 in. to 1 ft. through a joinery intersection (see the top photo at left). Leaving wood beyond the joint increases strength, but the exposed end grain is unattractive and demands further attention. To decorate the exposed end at the bottom of a post, we normally carve a pendant. The most common situations calling for a pendant are at framed overhangs, where the upper-story post passes through the second-floor girt and where a hammer post passes by the hammer beam. When the exposed end occurs at the top of a post, especially in framing around a stairway, it is called a finial. The ends of projecting beams, such as where a plate passes by the last bent post, are also usually carved, as are rafter ends that pass through the frame and support the roof overhang. Spline joints offer a unique opportunity for embellishment. The amount of wood exposed beyond the requirements of the joint can be designed to suit the embellishment, and the species of wood used for the spline can be chosen for aesthetic enhancement as well as for strength (see the bottom photo at left). Some typical end treatments are shown in the drawings on the facing page.

END TREATMENTS

PENDANT

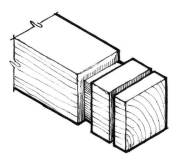

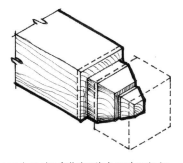

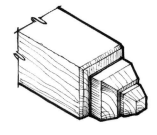

To make a pendant, first set blade depth for stop cuts or flats between beveled cuts.

Second, make full-depth bevel cuts to reveal pendant shape.

Third, pare with slick and chisel, finish bevel cuts with block plane, and seal end of pendant.

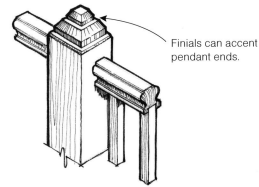

Through tenon

Pendant end cut

Finials can accent pendant ends.

DECORATIVE BEAM END CUTS

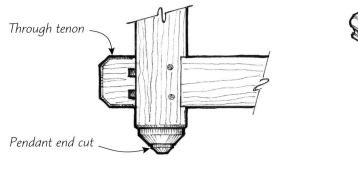

45° chamfer with steps

Cove with steps

(Special beam bandsaw is helpful for these cuts.)

Ogee curve with steps

DECORATIVE THROUGH-SPLINE END CUTS

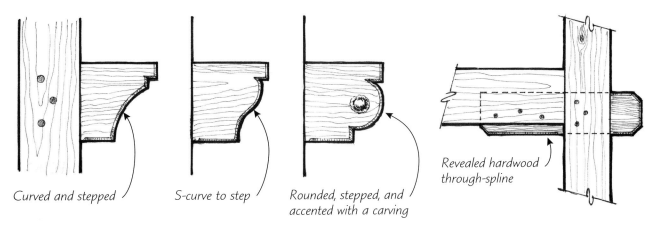

Curved and stepped

S-curve to step

Rounded, stepped, and accented with a carving

Revealed hardwood through-spline

The hammer-post detail is repeated in the stair newel finial for continuity.

Timber framers usually cut away the waste on end embellishments with a power saw, then finish the work with a chisel, a slick, and a hand plane. Work time can be reduced by simplifying the design so that it can be mostly finished with a series of power-saw cuts. Unless a portable bandsaw is available, carvings with lots of curves are time-consuming—although enjoyable—to make.

End embellishments set the tone for other details of the interior finish. A highly molded design would be out of place if every other aspect of the finish were based on square edges. Repeating elements of the end embellishments in the trim, stair parts, or even in the furniture further integrates the frame with the rest of the house.

Traditionally, and especially during the Middle Ages, an incredible range of de-

signs has been used for end embellishments, including meticulously detailed human and animal figures. A story I've heard a few times tells of a building in which the heads of saints are carved on the ends of the hammer beams, and each is identified with an inscription. One of the carvings did not have an inscription and could not be identified as a saint, but it is now believed to be a likeness of the master carpenter on the job. Good for him.

ROOF WINDOWS

In the building lexicon, "roof window" seems to be replacing "skylight," probably because almost all of the new models operate like windows. Most can be outfitted with shades and screens and cleaned from the inside—a valued convenience. But perhaps the most important advance in roof windows is that flashing systems are now sophisticated enough that they almost never leak. In a timber-frame house, the beauty of the timber work between the rafters encourages designers to use the space under the roofline for living rather than for storage, and roof windows are an inexpensive way to bring light and ventilation into these areas. The other alternative for bringing in light— dormer windows—adds considerably to the cost of construction.

Roof windows should be located for visibility (so you can see through them from a designated position) and for illumination of appropriate areas. In a bathroom, for example, you might want to locate a roof window over a whirlpool bath. In a bedroom, a roof window might be located over a work area. I have a roof window over my desk in my third-floor office. Because of their lack of horizontal members, common-rafter roofs naturally offer more choices in window placement than do rafter systems containing purlins. But most of the time, roof windows can be incorporated without changing the timber frame, since for the benefit of other building materials and roof loading, timber purlins or rafters tend to be spaced 48 in. on center. This allows plenty of space for several standard sizes of roof windows.

If you want to trim out the roof window with wood all around, choose a size that will give you 4 in. to 6 in. between the roof-window rough opening and the timbers. Try to center the window horizontally between rafters and vertically between purlins. I prefer to size roof windows to fit as tightly as possible between the timbers. The timbers then do double duty as trim (see

In this bedroom, the roof window is mounted between headers that break a purlin span to make a large vertical opening in the roof. Drywall finish extends to the sash to allow the timbers, instead of trim, to define the opening.

the photo above), while the other two sides are trimmed with wood or, better yet, left trimless by making a drywall corner return to the roof-window sash. Remember that, like wall windows and doors, roof windows are not actually mounted in the timber frame but instead are fastened to the foam-core panels above the frame with nailers (see Chapter 5).

Roof windows are installed on a slope, so it is best if the top of the opening can be trimmed level with the glass and the bottom of the opening vertical to the glass, so that maximum light can enter. Purlins at the top or bottom of an opening slightly restrict the admission of light, but in most situations it's not worthwhile to change the framing system just to avoid this problem.

Sometimes it's necessary to create an opening for a roof window by interrupting a purlin or rafter with headers, which span between two perpendicular framing members (see the drawings on p. 180). In a principal-rafter and common-purlin roof system, headers are used to locate a roof window where there would otherwise be a purlin or to make an opening larger than the span between purlins. Conversely, in a common-rafter roof, headers are used either to locate the roof window where there would otherwise be a rafter or to accommodate a window that is too wide for the opening between rafters. When headers are used, they increase the roof load on the members they span, which must be considered in sizing those pieces.

FRAMING FOR ROOF OPENINGS

COMMON-RAFTER ROOF

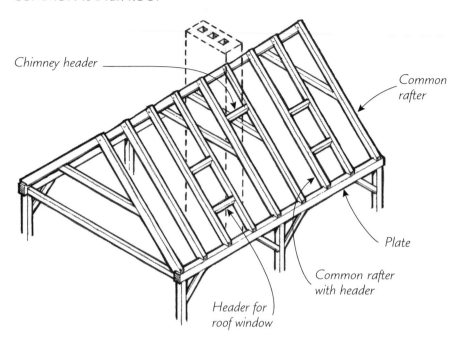

Chimney header

Common rafter

Plate

Common rafter with header

Header for roof window

PRINCIPAL-RAFTER AND COMMON-PURLIN ROOF

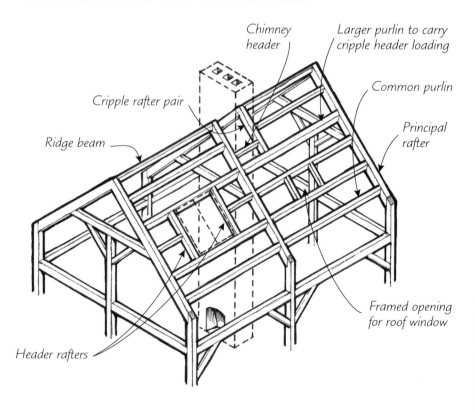

Chimney header

Larger purlin to carry cripple header loading

Common purlin

Cripple rafter pair

Principal rafter

Ridge beam

Framed opening for roof window

Header rafters

DORMERS

Dormers are really other buildings—though small—that intersect the primary building along the roof slope. They typically have at least three walls and a roof, one or several windows (or even a door), and must be roofed, sided, and trimmed to the same standards as the rest of the building. Because the area under the sloping roofline is important volume in a timber-frame building, we often rely on dormers to create space, light, and ventilation in what would otherwise be tight spaces. Dormers are very functional and can add significantly to the architecture of a home (although building them is almost always fussy, time-consuming, and expensive). This is in contrast to the current trend in conventional buildings in which computerized truss factories churn out roof facets, causing all kinds of roof bumps and gyrations to be the latest "affordable" architectural statement.

When a dormer is small, the opening often can be created in the primary roof plane in the same manner as the opening for a roof window: Timber headers break the regular purlin or rafter intervals to define an opening onto which the dormer itself can be built. This is the most common situation, simple and straightforward (see the left drawing on the facing page). With a small dormer, the next important question is whether it should be framed with timbers or built with structural panels. We have found that it is often best not to use timbers when a dormer is gabled and requires compound joinery for the valleys. It is often too expensive, and the result sometimes looks a little heavy, with large timbers making a small structure. Therefore, we often use doublechip panels to make a small dormer. The structural requirements are usually minimal, and the dormer does a better job of reflecting light because the finishes are drywall or plaster only. This is one of the few cases where the least-expensive and most-expedient option can be the best one as well.

FRAMING FOR DORMERS

SMALL DORMER

LARGE DORMER

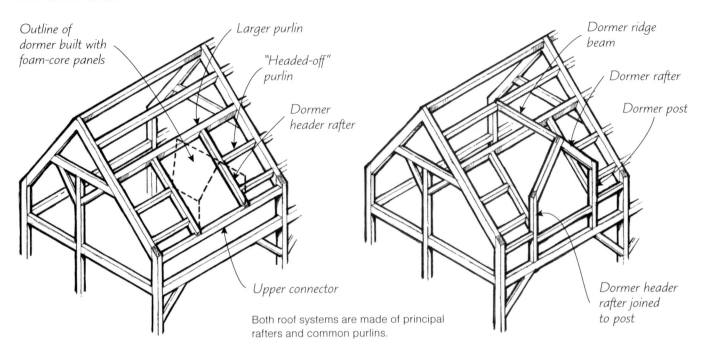

Outline of dormer built with foam-core panels

Larger purlin

"Headed-off" purlin

Dormer header rafter

Upper connector

Dormer ridge beam

Dormer rafter

Dormer post

Dormer header rafter joined to post

Both roof systems are made of principal rafters and common purlins.

Of course, once the framed opening in the main roof system has been established, it can be used as a support structure for building a timber-framed dormer. A shed dormer, which doesn't require compound joinery and has a single roof plane, is the easiest type of timber-frame dormer to construct (see the photo at right). A wall is built and mortised into the lower header or purlin; common rafters spring from the upper header to the wall's top plate. With gable dormers, however, the matter is more complicated because the peak must align with a receiving header or purlin for the ridge, and valley rafters are required to complete the interface between the roof planes.

For a large gable dormer (over 6 ft. in width), it is often beneficial to use a combination of panels and timbers. A timber frame makes up the eave wall and supports a ridge beam, which in turn supports panels that make up the roof system and the valleys. The eave wall for a large dormer is almost always constructed by joining the dormer posts into the dormer header rafters (see the right drawing above). Supporting the dormer load on the connecting

The dormer post in the frame of this shed-roof dormer extends to the top plate; the common rafters easily make the transition to the dormer.

Frame Details

181

A simple gable dormer is created in this common-rafter roof by adjusting the rafter spacing to the dormer width and mounting the dormer posts onto the rafters.

This dormer is framed by extending the posts to the bay connector and joining the ridge beam into a principal purlin.

Sometimes dormers should not be framed with timbers. In this case, foam-core panels are used to create the dormer space; the plaster finish reflects light into the room better than one created with timbers.

girt or top plate of the eave wall has structural implications that must be part of the engineering decisions for sizing these timbers.

As you can see, dormers are just small buildings mounted on the primary timber frame, so their structural demands are less significant, and the requirement for large-section timbers is less obvious. Still, you must make sure that the connections are good and that the structure and finishes of the dormers are in scale with the proportions and functions of the spaces created by them.

CHIMNEY AND FIREPLACE OPENINGS

Fire has always been an essential design consideration for houses. In the earliest timber-frame buildings, a hole was usually left in the roof to allow smoke to escape from the fire that burned in the middle of the house. As I pointed out in Chapter 1, usually there was no second floor in these buildings; they were more like elaborate tents or caves. The buildings began to resemble our notion of a home only after chimneys were designed to exhaust the smoke.

Here, the chimney opening in the roof—yet to be cut out—is visible in the top left of the photo. A header receives a purlin, creating the opening. Also note the framed opening for the chimney in the foreground at the bottom left.

The first thing to say about a chimney is that it must be completely independent of the timber frame; if you were to strip away the house, the chimney should stand entirely on its own. I don't know why this is, but in the preliminary plans we review, a common mistake is locating the chimney where it would pass through a bent or an exterior wall. Wooden structures move a bit, and masonry structures should not. Never use the masonry to support the frame or the frame to support the masonry. Like so many other things in a timber-frame house, it is important to plan the chimney in some detail before the frame is cut. You must know the size and location of the chimney at each floor level and where it passes through the roof. If there are fireplaces attached to the chimney, it is necessary

to know how they will affect the size of the chimney opening. It's not possible to explain every detail of masonry construction here, but allow me to provide a few tips.
• First, know enough about typical masonry details to communicate with the professional you hire. Read some books on masonry building; *Audel's Guide to Masonry Construction* is a particularly good reference. Then, rely heavily on the advice of a mason you trust. If you can retain this person to help you in the design phase, you'll be a lot more confident when the timbers are being cut. After you have described all the things affecting chimney dimensions, the mason will be able to provide precise measurements based on personal construction techniques. And believe

me, every mason is different. Two masons setting out to make a chimney with exactly the same specifications and using the same materials could wind up with completely different measurements, and each would tell you it was done exactly the right way. I don't pretend to understand this.
• Despite your confusion and lack of knowledge, speak up. On one of our jobs, I argued weakly with a mason who was putting in the flues without brick partitions between them. I told him it didn't look right. He argued eloquently and persuasively that "the latest befaddle on counterflow air currents and retroactive heat flow has it that the weight of the mass is inversely proportional to the ability of the flues to do headstands," or some such gibberish.

FRAMING FOR THE CHIMNEY

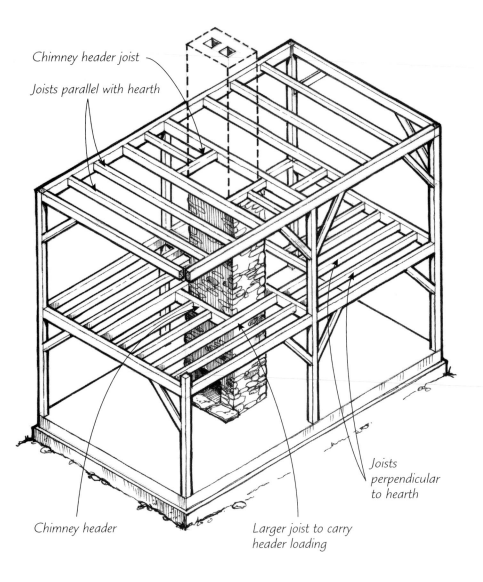

Chimney header joist

Joists parallel with hearth

Chimney header

Larger joist to carry header loading

Joists perpendicular to hearth

• Beware of the use of stone for interior masonry because of the possibility of bringing radon into the house.

Framing for the chimney

For fire safety, the usual code requirement is that the chimney should be at least 2 in. away from framing materials on all sides. This means that the chimney opening in the frame will have to be a total of 4 in. larger than the proposed chimney in width and length. (This rule also ensures that the chimney will be far enough away from the frame so that it won't be damaged by wood movement.) The finish flooring should be held back by ¼ in., but the trim can be cut to fit tightly to the chimney.

Often, the chimney imposes no special framing requirements on the floor system because the spacing between joists is frequently as much as 32 in., which allows more than enough room for the width of a typical chimney. Sometimes, however, the flooring requires support around the chimney. A small timber header on either side of the chimney, perpendicular to the joists, will keep the flooring stiff. If necessary, frame between these two headers with a third header to bridge the gap between the adjacent joist and the chimney, as shown in the drawing at left. Try to use as few timbers as possible to keep the opening uncluttered.

Where the chimney has to interrupt the joists, use headers to create an opening in the floor. Particularly if the opening is large, it may be best to plan the joist layout around the chimney. If it can be done symmetrically, start by designing a joist on two sides of the chimney and then put headers between those joists on the other two sides of the chimney. Then divide the headered space equally, putting a joist in the middle. Remember that half the load borne by the headers will be transferred to the joists on either side of the chimney, so they will have to be sized to handle the increased load.

I looked at the four wobbly flues standing in his brick cavern, shook my head, and just walked away. Later, when a chimney sweep attempted to clean one of the flues, it collapsed under the mighty weight of the chimney brush. I learned there's no sense in compounding ignorance with timidity.

• Make sure every possible flue has been included in the chimney. If in doubt about a possible furnace or woodstove, put in the extra flue. Retrofitting a chimney would be a mess.

• Make sure the mason is aware of the need for exterior combustion air for all fireplaces and woodstoves. Accommodation for such air passages should be considered a part of the construction of all chimneys and hearths in well-insulated houses. It is accomplished by passing a 4-in.-dia. or 5-in.-dia. galvanized pipe to the outside in the basement. The pipe brings the air to one or several openings in the hearth near the woodstove intake or just in front of the hearth for the fireplace. The air intakes for the fireplace can be hidden by dropping the base of the firebox below finish-floor level by about 5 in.; the air enters just below finish-floor level in the drop.

The chimney also needs to pass through the roof timbers, but this can be a little more difficult to resolve than passing it through the floor timbers (see the drawings on p. 180). First, good geometry is critical. The roof opening must fall directly above the opening in the floor and be the same size horizontally, even though it must be calculated along the roof slope. It's pretty simple math (remember Pythagoras?). Whether the roof system is framed horizontally with purlins or vertically with rafters, there is always the possibility that no special framing will be needed. With luck, the chimney will just slide through the timbers. We always check to see if we can help luck along by changing the layout slightly. If it's close, it's worth a try. For instance, if a rafter or purlin needs to be moved only an inch or two, the change probably won't upset the bearing for materials or compromise symmetry.

When the chimney falls on one side or the other of the roof peak, the header has to span between purlins or common rafters (but never through a principal rafter, which is part of the bent) to create a larger opening. I prefer to see the chimney pass through at the ridge because it leaves less masonry above the roofline and solves some flashing problems. (When a chimney falls below the peak, it needs a roof-shaped water diverter, called a cricket, on the upper side to prevent snow, ice, and water from getting trapped behind the chimney.) When the chimney passes through the peak, the framing is a little more difficult because the header has to be a small duplicate of the top portion of the rafters. This small truss then frames to purlins or rafter headers on either side of the roof peak (see the photo above).

A pair of short rafters headers off an opening for the chimney at the peak of this frame. There are also framed openings for roof windows at the low eave on the left.

EXTERIOR TIMBERS

In modern timber-frame construction, it's perfectly possible to protect the frame completely from the pernicious effects of weather and condensation. With the timbers snug inside the cocoon of warmth and protection offered by the exterior insulation system (typically foam-core panels), the frame (and the building) should last as long as people care enough to keep the roof tight. In our designs we therefore strive to keep all the timbers inside the insulating system, but situations continually arise in which long roof overhangs and exterior porches are important, even critical, to the design of a house.

Framing roof overhangs

In warm climates, long roof overhangs are used to keep the house cool; in wet climates they help protect the siding and windows from excessive moisture. A roof with a long overhang is like a hat with a decent brim. When the roof overhang is created within the insulation system rather than by passing the timbers through it, the limit is about 2 ft., if you're using doublechip foam-core panels (exterior insulation systems are covered in Chapter 5). If one of the alternate insulation systems is employed instead, especially the foam-and-nailer system (p. 102), the length of the overhang would be based on the relative strength of the framing members. For instance, 2x6s cantilevered beyond the frame could probably create an overhang of about 3 ft., depending on the roof load.

What happens when the timbers of the frame have to fall outside the protection of the insulation system? Essentially, there are three hazards. First, where timbers pass through the insulation, wood movement can cause sizable gaps to develop between the timber and the skin of the panels. Even if the gap is only ⅛ in. on both sides of a 6x8 timber, its effect on air infiltration would be comparable to bashing a 1½-in. by 1½-in. hole in the side of the house. In addition to compromising the insulation, the gaps offer a place for condensation to collect, which could cause rot in the frame. These gaps must be caulked at least once a year while the timbers are drying and stabilizing. So important is this detail that I have only half-jokingly considered carving the maintenance instructions into the timbers.

The second problem with timbers passing through the insulation is that the part of the timber that lives on the inside of the house will stabilize, while the part that lives outside will seasonally swell and shrink with changes in moisture content. Even if the joint looks tight on the inside, it should be checked on the outside—there's no way to know if there's a problem unless you climb 25 ft. up a ladder once a year.

The third problem is that the life span of the whole frame is potentially shortened by the life span of that part exposed to the elements.

Having pointed out these drawbacks, I can say that I am well aware that there is no substitute for timbers when it comes to creating a strong, beautiful roof overhang. If, after carefully weighing the options, this detail wins out, here are some things to do to minimize negative effects.

• I would be more reluctant to use a framed overhang in New Hampshire than in Arizona. Hot and dry climates are the most benign to exposed timbers, and houses in these areas suffer the least from air infiltration. Even in my native Colorado, which is sometimes cold but always dry, timbers can be exposed for a long time without significant damage. But in New England, where everything is either frozen solid or fostering fungal growth, it is wise to consider every other alternative before exposing the timbers to the weather.

• Modern timber frames are more protected now than at any time in history, and because of this we can use almost any kind of wood that is structurally sound. But our forefathers in the craft, who infilled between the timbers rather than cladding from the outside (thus exposing them to the elements), chose white oak as the standard in Europe and cypress and cedar in Japan. Think like the Europeans and the Japanese if you are making a frame overhang, and use a rot-resistant wood.

• The roof system should be detailed to protect the frame members in the overhang. Extending the roofing beyond the timber ends as much as possible helps keep moisture out.

• The most protected overhang is one whose timbers cantilever beyond the frame without the need for support from plates or braces. When horizontal timbers support the overhang, they tend to hold moisture; diagonal braces can pull moisture back to the frame through surface tension. But if the overhang is too great, some form of bracing for the rafters will have to be used.

Principal-rafter and common-purlin roofs are the easiest to protect at the eaves for two reasons. First, only a few pieces pass through the skin. For example, in a 36-ft.-long, four-bent building, there would be 8 penetrations at the eaves, whereas a common-rafter system would probably require 20. Second, at the gable end, the common-rafter system requires that a plate be extended from the walls to support the last rafter pair, which causes several more penetrations and a horizontal timber. (This detail was often used on old Swiss chalets. The top of the extended plate would be protected with a small shingled roof.) In the principal-rafter and common-purlin roof, however, the end

This frame employs extended plates and overhung rafters to create welcome weather protection for this northern California climate that is both very rainy in the winter and very hot in the summer.

rafters can be lowered to allow the purlins to pass over the top. We ordered extra-deep rafters for one of our projects so they could be notched across the top. No wood could be removed from the purlins because the complete cross section was needed for shear strength.

• All exterior-exposed wood must be protected with oil or varnish. Homeowners should remember that they will have to make a commitment to caulking the gaps between the timbers and the insulation. This should be done at least once a year for as long as the wood continues to dry and shrink.

Framing porches

Porches are a different situation entirely from roofs because they must be supported by posts, and there isn't a good way to protect exposed posts to the same degree that exposed rafters or purlins can be protected. Therefore, the porch (or at least the posts that support it) simply can't last as long as the rest of the frame. Thus the best solution is to separate the porch completely from the house by isolating it on the other side of the insulation. This also makes it possible to construct the porch with a wood chosen exclusively for its weather-resistance. To make it easy to attach the roof framing to the exterior sheathing, use timbers for the front wall of the porch to support the roof, but build the roof itself with conventional framing members (see the bottom photo at right).

The most difficult part of the porch to protect is the base of the posts. If posts are to be attached to a concrete floor, use the plinth detail shown on p. 128. When the posts will rest on a wooden deck, allow water to drain by cutting any mortises to pass through the sill. (This is not a good situation for a timber sill because it is so difficult to prevent the surface from retaining moisture.) If circumstances demand the use of a timber sill, use the most water-resistant wood available and bevel the exposed top surfaces to ensure that water will run off.

In this Montana project, extended purlins create overhangs on the gable end of the great room at left and on the entry at right.

For this porch, timber-frame elements link the interior and exterior finishes. But the porch frame is not directly connected to the primary frame for fear of the porch deteriorating before the completely protected interior structure in the harsh Nantucket environment. (Design Associates, Architects.)

When you step into the living room in this house, you move from a low, flat-ceiling space to the drama of a soaring cathedral space.

CHANGES IN BUILDING HEIGHT AND WIDTH

For structural reasons, a change in roofline or building dimension almost always has to occur at a bent; for design purposes, the change has to be aesthetically satisfactory, since the timber frame is an important part of the interior space. When one building has two or more roofline heights or any change in width, there should be a structural decision about how to support the upper and lower rafters at the break, as well as design decisions about which timbers will be visible and how to apply the finish and the insulation.

An illustration will clarify the problem. In the frame shown below, the change in building dimension between the living room and the rest of the house re-

CONNECTING TWO SEPARATE FRAMES

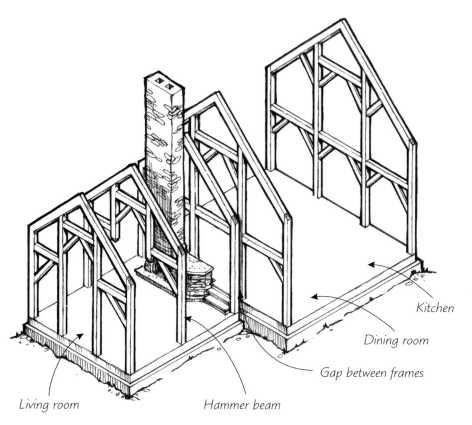

Kitchen

Dining room

Gap between frames

Living room

Hammer beam

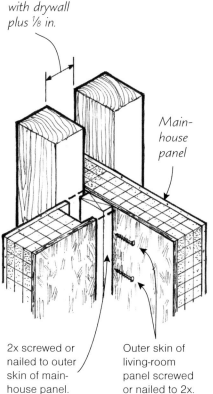

Panel thickness with drywall plus 1/8 in.

Main-house panel

2x screwed or nailed to outer skin of main-house panel.

Outer skin of living-room panel screwed or nailed to 2x.

Frame Details
188

sults in a complete change in volume and feeling. When you take those two steps down to the living room, you move from an area with an 8-ft. ceiling to one with a ceiling that soars to about 20 ft. The three bents in the living room were designed with dramatic hammer beams, while the bents for the rest of the house had function at their core. During design, we were concerned about how the structure would look from both areas and about the transition from the grand cathedral space to the rest of the house.

As it turned out, the most practical solution was to build two independent frames—one for the living room and one for the rest of the house. If we had tried to use a single bent instead of two side by side, we would have needed rafters to support purlins, and posts would have been necessary for the inside corners. Each bent would have lost some distinctiveness. But by creating two separate frames, we were able to define each area completely with

timbers—a design decision that was particularly important in the living room, which had a nice sense of symmetry and unity from the three hammer beams. We left a 5-in. space between the two bents at the building break for insulation and for the finish wall surface of both areas (4½ in. for the typical foam-core panel with drywall on one side and ½ in. for a layer of drywall to be applied to the nail-base sheathing on the other side).

In this example, our biggest concern was to make sure the two frames were securely fastened together. While designed to be structurally independent, they also had to act as a unit. The panels between the two bents are attached to the main house, and the panels on the living-room wing are routed and fitted over a nailer attached to the outside of the main-house panels. The living-room panels are screwed to the nailer and nailed to the main-house timbers (see the detail drawing on the facing page).

The best structural solution is to integrate elements of both bents within a single bent at the point of transition, because it ensures that everything will work as a single unit. But especially when there are internal rafters, building math and bent assembly become pretty tricky. (For that reason, these are referred to as "infernal rafters" in our shop.) There is also a finishing and insulating problem where the gable wall and the lower roof intersect. In the case of the house frame shown on p. 190, we put the lower roof panel on first, with the bottom edge held back ½ in. from the main-house post and routed for a nailer. After the nailer was secured, a 2x4 base plate for the wall panel was precisely located and nailed to the roof panels. The gable-wall panels were cut and routed to fit over the base plate, allowing the wall panel to be secured where there wasn't any nailing area in the frame. Finally, drywall was installed between the post and the panels (see the detail drawing on p. 190).

Here, an internal rafter is framed into a bent to receive purlins from the outer bent (left in photo). Note the 2-in. offset for attaching foam-core panels.

USING INTERNAL RAFTERS TO CONNECT FRAMES

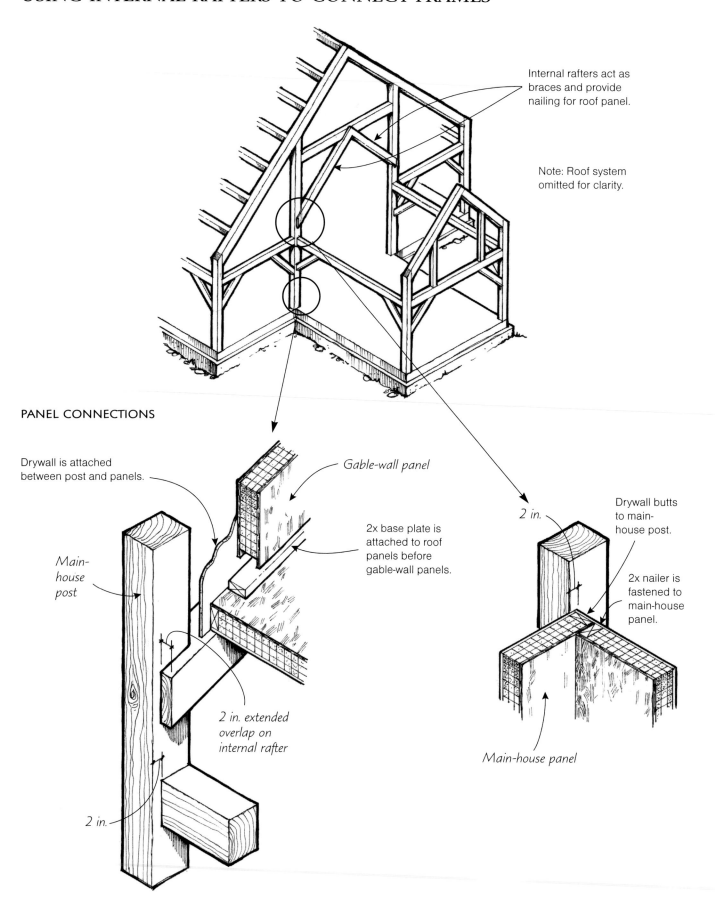

Internal rafters act as braces and provide nailing for roof panel.

Note: Roof system omitted for clarity.

PANEL CONNECTIONS

Drywall is attached between post and panels.

Gable-wall panel

2x base plate is attached to roof panels before gable-wall panels.

Main-house post

2 in. extended overlap on internal rafter

2 in.

2 in.

Drywall butts to main-house post.

2x nailer is fastened to main-house panel.

Main-house panel

VALLEY JOINERY

HIP JOINERY

Principal rafter

Principal purlin

Ridge beam

Mortise aligns with grain of receiving timber.

Tenon

End view of valley peak

Tenon

End view of valley peak

Tenon aligns with grain.

Tenon aligns with grain of timber.

Hip rafter with backing cuts

Valley rafter

Tenon

End view of hip peak

"Backing angles" of roof slopes intersecting

Tenon

End view of valley foot

Mortise aligns with grain and intersects post at corner.

Corner post

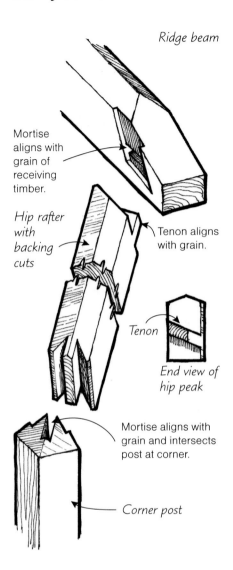

COMPOUND JOINERY

One of the more challenging aspects of timber framing is the execution of the compound joinery necessary for the construction of roof hips and valleys (see the drawings above). For my company, this was a most difficult hurdle in our early years because it was one of the aspects of our craft that we learned with scant historical precedent. Most of what we learned about timber framing came from replication of joinery or details gleaned from house and barn timber frames we were able to examine and use as a standard of procedure and

quality. But when it came to compound joinery, we found ourselves without available examples to use as guidelines. It was not that the examples weren't there; we just didn't find them because surviving high-quality compound joinery in early American timber framing is rare. So we applied all the lessons we had learned from both historical precedent and modern engineering and developed a few guiding principles:

• First of all, the joinery must be functional. Clearly, it would be tempting to

take a shortcut, especially during the steep ascent in the learning curve. Though difficult, the compound joinery should be just as strong and durable as the other joints in the frame.

• Keep it simple. Compound mortise-and-tenon joinery needs no added complexities. The key is to follow the intersection where it leads and do what needs to be done and nothing more.

• Align the mortise and tenon with the grain of their timber. In other words, when making the joints, do not cut across the grain of the wood.

Where the valley rafters and ridge beam join to a principal purlin, one begins to appreciate the complexity and beauty of compound joinery.

Here, two hip rafters terminate into a ridge beam.

The orientation for the tenon is determined by the mortise, but the angle of entry is determined by the tenon. To maintain strength, the two elements are designed to align with the grain of their timbers.

• Place the mortise as close to the neutral axis of the receiving timber as possible. The timber is damaged least by not removing wood from the tension or compression zones of the timber (for more on timber-frame joinery, see Chapter 2).

By following these precepts, compound joinery is really very easy to conceptualize, even when it's difficult to execute. By locating the mortise in the neutral axis and aligning it with the grain of its timber, the tenon follows and is oriented along the grain of its timber, which determines the angle of entry. Those are the two primary determinants of the joint. After that, it is a matter of describing the interface of the two timbers with a housing on the receiving timber.

All of this is not necessarily simple to achieve (and it is not the point of this book to describe this process in detail), but it gets easier quickly and is an essential part of the craft of timber framing. Compound joinery liberates the designer from the constraints of the simpler forms while still not inviting reckless dazzle (see the photos on this page). Break the box, yes, but do only what is needed and honest. Unlike stick-frame construction, timber framing has an opinion.

This hip rafter (middle of photo), along with adjacent common rafters, finishes elegantly at a plate. Compound joinery needs no added complexities to be effective and beautiful.

TIMBERS AND GLASS

In my years as a designer and builder of timber-frame houses, I have talked to at least a thousand people about their dream homes. Only one of them did not list the admission of sunlight as a priority. A shady spot on the north side of a hill would have suited this man just fine; the house would have let in only enough light to cause shadows. I admitted to being concerned about his dim lifestyle, and he confessed to being a hobbit. We didn't build for this guy, and I can only hope that somewhere he was able to find the dark home of his desires.

This fellow would have been perfectly content in the typical home built prior to the early- to mid-1800s, when the use of sheet glass for windows had not yet become widespread. During that time, glass window panes were individually made by craftsmen who would blow a glass bubble and then spin it into a sheet, leaving a crown in the middle. These same glassblowers also created vases and goblets, and the window panes were likewise small and precious. While they admitted light, they did nothing for visibility, for anything viewed through the bubbles would appear distorted. Only the very wealthy could afford much glass. Most houses had a few small penetrations to allow a little light, supplemented by candles, lanterns, and even the fireplace. By day and night, homes were like aboveground caves. The average modern house is a crystal palace by comparison.

There is no doubt we have come a long way, and within the last 15 years alone, significant improvements have practically revolutionized the way we think about glass. For example, by sealing air between two or three panes, windows today can have unheard-of insulating qualities; using argon gas instead of plain air in the cavity can provide an even greater R-value. Large panes can be strengthened to allow spans once requiring structural materials. Low-

Because the glass is mounted in the insulation outside the frame, windows can be designed to allow timber members to be visible from the outside as well as from the inside.

emissivity (low-E) coating, an infrared reflecting surface, is transparent but limits the passage of heat. Ultimate performance is achieved through a combination of technological developments, such as when argon gas is sealed between two layers of tempered, low-E glass. A recent test demonstrated that even with an exterior temperature of 0°F, the interior glass felt warm to the touch. Glazing materials and hardware have also improved over the last few years, and an array of new caulking and gaskets can give site-mounted glass reliable performance.

As a result of this technology, the creative use of glass has become a force in modern architecture. Designers have to balance the aesthetic qualities of expanses of glass against the concomitant heat loss; glass giving better energy performance means the balance shifts toward glass. By using top-shelf, low-E glass and carefully calculating optimum glazing area, significant amounts of glass can now be used without compro-

mising energy performance. These calculations (usually computer generated), consider solar gain, surface area of exterior walls and the roof, house volume, and glass type, among many other factors. The goal is to find the point at which the heat gain from sunny days exceeds the loss from cloudy days and nights. Predictably, the results show that most of the glass should be concentrated on the south side of the building, with modest amounts on the east and west sides to receive light, and as little as possible on the north. Often a solarium is recommended for heat collection.

Glass and timber frames are perfect mates. The spaces between frame members can be filled in with any kind of rigid sheathing material, and glass is such a material. Because the posts carry the entire building load, windows and doors can be mounted just about anywhere in the insulating system. In this section, I'll explore a few aspects of the glass-and-timber relationship, starting with a few notes on integrating manufactured windows and doors into a

In this gable-end wall, white cedar framing creates openings for stock window units, which will be mounted to the outside of the frame along with panels. The timbers will serve as interior trim.

timber-frame house. Then I'll cover solarium design. I'll conclude with several flashing and glazing details associated with mounting glass on timbers.

Integrating manufactured units

Window and door units are mounted in the exterior insulation (foam-core panels), which is in turn secured to the frame, as discussed in Chapter 5. The only relationship between the frame and these window and door units is therefore an aesthetic one, but it is by no means unimportant. In fact, it is critical that the frame and fenestration interact with symmetry and balance.

Design goals can be achieved either by altering fenestration to fit the frame or by changing the frame to suit the fenestration. In several of the houses we have designed, clients have decided that they wanted to see the frame from both the inside and the outside. Instead of mounting the windows between timbers, we located them over

the timbers so that visitors would meet the frame before entering the house. We have also mounted large windows between posts so that the diagonal braces could be seen from both sides. The brace pair can actually enhance the window opening, and it does not interfere with the operation of the window since it is mounted in the insulation outside the frame.

Usually it is best that window and door design coincide with frame design. Fanlight windows, for instance, can be made to fit nicely between the curved arches of knee braces. Another technique is to use timbers to frame window or door openings. The unit is still mounted in the insulation, but the timbers act as the trim. For several of our projects, we have detailed every window and door in the house to be trimmed completely with timbers. Because of the close fit between the fixed dimensions of the manufactured units and the timbers, the wood must be dry

to make a stable connection between the jambs and the timbers.

Designing solariums

A solarium is often thought to be a separate space used to collect heat for distribution to the house. The distribution can be accomplished through doors and windows, fans and ducts, or a masonry mass. But better glass and more intelligent sizing of glazed areas make it possible to build solariums that do not have so much heat loss that they need to be separated from other living areas. The solarium then becomes an inviting place for sitting, reading, and gathering—a place of heat and light, not unlike the hearth in early homes. This is the type of solarium I am most enthusiastic about, even if it sometimes means accepting the compromise that occasionally heat loss will exceed gain.

I came to this preference the hard way. Quite a few years ago we designed a modest-sized house for a site with good solar exposure and correctly judged that we would be able to heat with the sun on days that weren't cloudy. We added a detached solarium to the design, so that we would not lose heat through the glass when sunlight was unavailable. When the solarium was warm and the house cold, a French door and an awning window would be opened to let heat into the house. A fine idea, but we weren't prepared for the fact that since the solarium would not benefit from the house heat, it would get very cold during long cloudy periods. Also, by the time the solarium had been warmed by the sun, the house had also been warmed by solar gain through other windows and heat conducted through the solarium. Because there was no reason to open it to the house, the solarium seriously overheated in sunny periods. (The owner told me the thermometer registered over 140°F right before the mercury popped.) This solarium was either too cold or too hot for use. The solution was to reduce the amount of glass in the solarium, take out the back wall, and incorporate the space into the house.

If a solarium is to be detached and use-ful, it must have a huge amount of mass to store the heat for night and cloudy periods. This type of solarium is usually complicated to build, always expensive, and will still sometimes get too cold. Window insulation (there are many types) is a good idea, but too of-ten it is only an idea. If people don't take the time to operate the insulation, it won't work. One of our clients fig-ured it required five minutes in the morning and five in the evening to pull the insulation over each window. While this doesn't seem that long, it takes more time than the garbage and less than the dishes; just long enough to become another daily chore.

Solariums that are incorporated into the main living space of the house can take many forms, from a simple large window to the common three-sided ad-dition with a large expanse of south-facing fixed glass. Operable window units are mounted on the east and west sides and often on the roof as well, making it easy to vent the solarium when there is too much heat. Because the long side of the building tends to face south anyway, the simplest way to create a solarium is to extend the roofline on the eave side. In essence, the solarium becomes an extension of a bay and is framed by passing the prin-cipal rafters over the outside posts of adjacent bays to the shorter posts at the solarium corners. From a construction standpoint, it is not important that the solarium be in the middle bay; but its placement there is usually more benefi-cial to heat distribution.

Using fixed glass on the south wall is also not a requirement of solariums. If you plan carefully and use stock glass sizes, it is an inexpensive way to develop a large glass area. (Stock glass is generally about one-quarter the cost per square foot of custom Thermopane brand glass.) We use a few different sizes that are commonly available as re-placement panels for sliding glass doors. Unfortunately, the dimensions of the panels of stock glass will proba-

The solarium is often just an extension of the roofline at the eave. Stock glass size helps determine wall height. Dry timbers must be used where the glass will be mounted. The roof window and the operable units on the solarium sides provide ventilation.

This solarium framing, in dry reclaimed southern pine, is designed to accept stock glass sizes.

Frame Details

In this home, increasing the height of the wall provided room for the framing of a three-story window. Two layers of fixed glass were attached to fir timbers, and a custom fan unit, placed on top, was designed to match.

bly not add up to the width of the bay, so unless the bay was designed to accommodate available glass or luck prevailed, there is likely to be some insulated wall on each side of the glass.

The edges of the glass are mounted on the outside faces of the timbers, so any wood that will contact the glass must be dry, even if the rest of the frame is built from green material. Otherwise, you risk disturbing the seal between the glass and the frame or even breaking the glass as the drying wood shrinks, twists, warps, or bows. Because the principal posts carry most of the building load, wood with less structural value, such as cedar and white pine, can be used to receive the glass. The solarium shown in the top photo on p. 195, which has insulated walls extending past the glass to fill out to bay width,

uses a few pieces of dry old-growth southern pine to accept the glass.

The fixed-glass area is framed below the roofline break with a plate (or connecting girt) between principal posts; the vertical members of the solarium are mortised and tenoned to the plate. But if fixed glass is intended for the roof slope as well as for the wall, the position of the plate becomes a problem in that it creates an awkward transition between the sloped and vertical glazing. There are two solutions. One is to eliminate the plate entirely, connecting short rafters to the solarium posts, as shown in the photos on the facing page. A purlin joined to the frame receives the solarium rafters at a point determined by the glass size. The roof glass meets the wall glass at a horizontal 2x2 turned round on a lathe between rafters and left square in section

where it meets the rafters. When the eave is low, and a plate would obstruct the view, this is a nice alternative. The other solution (if a slightly obstructed view is not a problem) is to frame common rafters from a purlin to a plate that rests on top of the solarium posts. The plate is ripped to the roof slope on the top outside edge to serve as bearing for the roof glass.

The plate system is also useful when the solarium spans more than one bay. Using a plate to connect from one corner of the solarium to the other eliminates concern about the location of the bent post, which would otherwise probably interrupt the layout of the glass panels. Solarium posts are framed into the plate at intervals determined by the glass size, and the plate also supports the bent rafters.

There are many ways to design a solarium under an eave. For example, in one contemporary-style house, we increased wall height in the solarium bay to frame a dramatic three-story window (see the photo on the facing page). Two rows of fixed glass were mounted on fir timbers and topped with a custom fanlight. Light penetrates deeply into the house, and the view is visible from a third-floor study. Roof windows operated with electric switches increase light and assist ventilation.

Solariums with gable roofs can also bring sunlight deep into a building and provide a dramatic focal point. But because the compound joinery required is difficult, they are also quite expensive. Gable solariums work best when they are extensions of a single bay, if only to keep the valley framing from bisecting principal rafters. You can bet I learned about this the hard way. A building we did quite a few years ago had a gable-roof solarium that was accessible from three levels. It began at the base with a layer of fixed glass mounted on fir timbers. Then there was a layer of operable manufactured window units, reached by walkways on the second floor. Finally there was a fixed custom fanlight, through which a person on the third-floor balcony could view the outside. The only problem was that the width of the solarium extended past the middle bay into the two adjacent bays, so the valley rafters crossed two bent rafters. It is quite difficult to prefit this kind of joinery, so we generally make careful cuts to mathematical and geometric calculations and then just put it together. Try to imagine the situation. The valley rafter frames into the principal rafter and then picks up on the other side, continuing to the eave where it frames into the outside wall. The math drove us silly, the cutting made us dizzy, and the assembly was nearly impossible physically. But we did it like that... once.

Shed-roof solariums can also be designed at a gable end. The bent that connects to the shed has to have an additional horizontal member to receive

This gable-end solarium, shown from the outside and inside, was planned for a lot of household plants as well as a plant-starting area. Where the sloped glass and the vertical glass connect, a special flashing detail was used instead of a timber plate. A 2x2 plant hanger screwed to each timber rafter helps keep the framing rigid.

MOUNTING VERTICAL FIXED GLASS ON TIMBERS

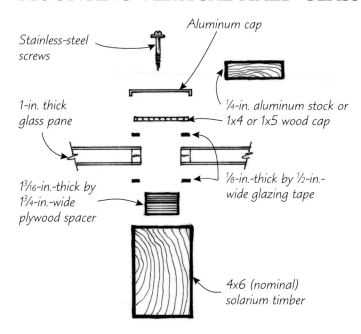

Stainless-steel screws

Aluminum cap

1-in. thick glass pane

¼-in. aluminum stock or 1x4 or 1x5 wood cap

1³⁄₁₆-in.-thick by 1¾-in.-wide plywood spacer

⅛-in.-thick by ½-in.-wide glazing tape

4x6 (nominal) solarium timber

OUTSIDE CORNER WITH INSULATION ON FRONT

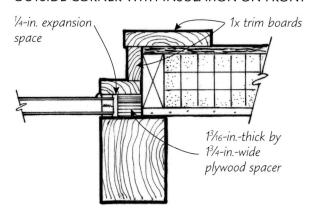

¼-in. expansion space

1x trim boards

1³⁄₁₆-in.-thick by 1¾-in.-wide plywood spacer

OUTSIDE CORNER WITH INSULATION ON SIDE

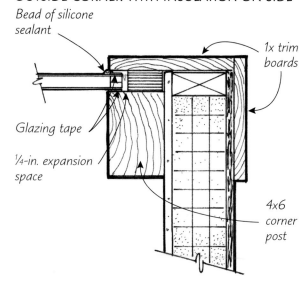

Bead of silicone sealant

1x trim boards

Glazing tape

¼-in. expansion space

4x6 corner post

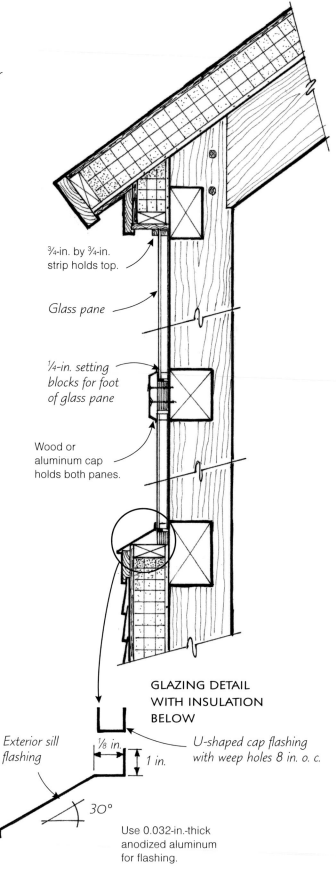

¾-in. by ¾-in. strip holds top.

Glass pane

¼-in. setting blocks for foot of glass pane

Wood or aluminum cap holds both panes.

Exterior sill flashing

⅛ in.

1 in.

30°

GLAZING DETAIL WITH INSULATION BELOW

U-shaped cap flashing with weep holes 8 in. o. c.

Use 0.032-in.-thick anodized aluminum for flashing.

the shed rafters, and there should be posts in the bent to align with the corner posts of the solarium. Otherwise, the framing is no different from an eave solarium. In fact, a shed solarium on the gable end is probably a little easier because the restrictions of bay width do not apply. Stock glass dimensions usually determine solarium width.

Mounting glass on timbers

The first thing to know is that it is not necessary to rabbet the timbers for the glass. Everyone seems to want to do this, but it doesn't really help anything. Along with the insulation, it is better to keep the glass, flashing, and any potential condensation outside the frame. So rabbets are created by nailing plywood spacers to the sides, tops, and bottoms of the solarium timbers just prior to installing the glass. This method is also easier than rabbeting the timbers. After all, you can't exactly pick up a timber and run it through a shaper.

Before getting into the various glazing details, let's quickly review how glass is normally installed. Basically, the glass sits in the rabbets created by the plywood spacers between two layers of glazing tape and is capped by a metal or wood trim piece. The plywood spacers are usually built up of two layers, but if you can't find a combination that works, use a piece of plywood plus a piece of dry lumber. To calculate the correct thickness of the spacers, subtract $\frac{1}{16}$ in. from the thickness of the glass (to ensure a snug fit between the trim and the glazing tape), and add in the two pieces of $\frac{1}{8}$-in.-thick tape. In other words, if the glass is 1 in. thick, the thickness of the spacer would be $1\frac{3}{16}$ in. At least $\frac{5}{8}$ in. of glass should bear on the timber, and there should be an extra $\frac{1}{4}$ in. allowed for expansion, making the depth of the rabbet $\frac{7}{8}$ in. In the plan view of a typical solarium post shown on the facing page, the 4x6 has nominal dimensions of $3\frac{1}{2}$ in. by $5\frac{1}{2}$ in. Because this is a middle post, receiving glass on both edges, you would subtract the $\frac{7}{8}$-in. depth of each rabbet to calculate a spacer width of $1\frac{3}{4}$ in.

The spacers are nailed to the solarium timbers with galvanized ring-shank nails. Each glass panel sits on two $\frac{1}{4}$-in.-thick neoprene setting blocks, which act to level the glass and cushion it from expansion and contraction. The setting blocks are placed in the bottom rabbets positioned at what are called quarter points. To calculate these, simply divide half the width of the glass by two and measure in that far from each edge; for a 4-ft.-wide panel, the quarter points would be 1 ft. in from each edge. If further leveling is required, shim one of the setting blocks with small strips of aluminum.

Once the setting blocks are in, the first layer of glazing tape is carefully applied to the timbers around the perimeter of the opening. The glazing tape is $\frac{1}{8}$ in. thick by $\frac{1}{2}$ in. wide and is preshimmed, which means there are wires embedded in it to keep it from compressing and deforming in hot weather. The tape is applied so that its edges will be flush with the edges of the $\frac{1}{2}$-in.-wide desiccant band between glass panes. It is held back $\frac{1}{8}$ in. to $\frac{3}{16}$ in. from the timber edges to receive a bead of silicone sealant. After the sealant is applied, the glass is set in the opening, and the second layer of glazing tape is positioned so it also aligns with the edges of the desiccant band. Another bead of silicone sealant is applied. Wood or metal trim is positioned over the plywood spacers and the glass edges, applying pressure to the glazing tape and thus to the desiccant bands—it is important that no pressure be put on the glass where it is unsupported by a desiccant band. When the trim is installed, it will force excess sealant to ooze out of the glazing tape. This gets peeled off later.

That's the general scheme. Before proceeding, check with your supplier to ensure that the sealant is compatible with the glazing tape. There are many stories about chemical reactions causing a break in the glass seal.

Getting the water off

The basic theory on treating the bottoms of the glass panes comes from the people who make roof windows. They use battens on the top and sides to hold the glass in place, but generally do not cap the bottom, allowing water to run off freely. On solariums we use trim at the sides and on top to hold the glass to the timbers, but at the bottom we use two different details, depending on whether or not there will be insulation beneath the glass. If there will be insulation, it is necessary to make the transition from the thickness of the glass to the thickness of the insulation. The panel (assuming the use of foam-core panels) would be held beneath the top edge of the bottom solarium beam by about 3 in. This beam is often at or near floor level. A 2-in.-wide plywood spacer is then nailed to the bottom beam, then a block of wood is ripped to slope from the top edge of the spacer to the outside edge of the panel.

This block must be accurately cut and shimmed to fit precisely, because it describes the finished surface. After it is installed, some tricky flashing, generally custom-made by a sheet-metal company, goes down. The exterior sill flashing is installed first, then a U-shaped cap flashing accepts the neoprene setting blocks and the glass. As shown on the facing page, beads of silicone sealant prevent water from entering the assembly.

If the bottom beam of the solarium is on a slab foundation, there is usually no need for insulation below the glass. Thus the glass may rest on a trim board built out to the proper thickness for the glass plus glazing tape. A simple piece of flashing caps the top of the board and runs down about $\frac{3}{4}$ in., as shown in the bottom drawing on p. 201. Then the U-shaped cap flashing is installed as specified previously.

On the corners of the solarium, there are usually two detail options (see the bottom left drawings on the facing page). In one situation, the insulation is mounted to the side of the post because there is no need for it on the front. In the other situation, the insulation is mounted to the front of the post because the wall surface surrounding the glass needs to be insulated. In the side detail, the 1x trim boards must cap not only the corner post but also the insulation. In the front detail, the foam-core panel should be held back on the timber enough to allow for a plywood spacer, as shown. Three pieces of trim then cap the glass and cover the exposed panel edges. The face trim goes on first, side trim is installed second, and the end trim is last. This detail might also occur at the top of the glazing when the glass does not extend all the way to the eave, as in a gable-roof solarium. The only necessary alteration would be to add window-header flashing to the top of the end-trim board. In point of fact, a solarium is a big site-made window; when completely surrounded by the insulating system, the flashing and sealing details are the same as those on commercial windows.

As I mentioned earlier, we often create solariums by extending the roofline on the eave side. We have found that the most consistently available stock glass is 76 in. long, so we commonly design the roof extension to conclude at a height that allows for framing, flashing, and trim of 76-in.-long glass. The solarium shown in the top photo on p. 195 was designed on this basis. The roof was insulated with a typical panel overhang and trimmed as described in Chapter 10. Under these circumstances, the friezeboard at the top of the wall also becomes the top batten for securing the glass, no matter whether the roof trim is based on a flat or sloped soffit. Flashing is not necessary under the eave because the roof overhang solves the moisture problem.

Roof glass

There is justifiable argument over the wisdom of using sloped roof glass in solariums. There is more air movement next to glass than next to an insulated wall, so there are likely to be more convection currents in a solarium than in the rest of the house. These currents carry lots of warm air to the solarium roof. If the roof is glass, expect the heat loss in this area to be significantly greater than if the roof were insulated. Add this to the fact that the heat gain through roof glass in summer is unnecessarily high, and it becomes hard to argue the case in practical terms. So when the design of a house suggests roof glass, I get emotional. I talk about a view where horizon and sky come together, a place to stargaze on a cold winter's night. I mention the effect of warm washes of sun penetrating deeply into the living area. With this out of the way, I should point out that we have used roof glass only about a dozen times on more than ten score houses. Roof glass makes the most sense when there is a relatively small solarium attached to a large living space. Operable roof windows are much more practical because they limit the glass area, provide much-needed ventilation in summer, and are easy to install.

If roof glass will be used, try to reduce its area by keeping the individual panes short. A strategy we commonly employ is to use pieces of full-length stock glass (usually 76 in.) for the vertical glazing and half sheets of the same width for the roof. Keeping width consistent is important to the design, and using a stock size for the vertical glass keeps cost down, even though the half-size glass is a custom order.

Following are several details for the application of roof glass (see the drawings on the facing page). The first thing you might notice is that there aren't any wooden members capping the glass as there are on the wall. Using wood in an area that gets so much heat and moisture is simply an invitation for trouble. Also notice that all solarium roof glass is mounted on rafters instead of purlins. This keeps the glass size manageable and encourages water runoff.

Using a plate to make the transition between the wall and the roof simplifies and strengthens framing and flashing. The plate serves as a good stiffener and connects the entire assembly. It is angled to correspond with the roof slope and creates a bearing surface for both the roof glass and the vertical glass. Give the top and outside face of the plate extra moisture protection with an elastomeric membrane. These membranes have become popular for a number of different roofing applications because they remain elastic despite temperature fluctuations and tend to seal holes that might develop, even around nails and screws. Install the plywood spacers using the method to calculate thickness described on p. 199. Always use a good grade of plywood—it's important that it not absorb moisture and expand. Cut the spacer for the roof glass to fit from the outside edge of the vertical-glass spacer to about 1 in. from the top edge of the plate.

A piece of cap flashing is placed into the rabbet, with its lip bent over the top edge of the timber and securely fastened with ¾-in., #6 galvanized nails every 10 in. Flashing is a bad place to save money, so use as a minimum standard 20-oz. copper or 0.032 anodized aluminum. All the roof flashing should be custom-formed in a shop. The glass is laid into the rabbet using neoprene setting blocks, preshimmed glazing tape, and sealant as described on p. 199, but here the procedure differs. It's a little tricky to lift the flashing enough to allow the glass to sit on the glazing tape and sealant. The problem can be solved by sticking glazing tape to both the top and bottom edges of the glass that will sit in the rabbet. A couple of small wedges on both sides of the glass keep the tape separate from the flashing while it enters the rabbet. After the glass is seated on the setting blocks and before the wedges are pulled out, apply sealant liberally between the flashing and the glass. Install the drip edge next, which is the small piece bent to the roof angle attached to the friezeboard at the top of the wall. The cover flashing is bent at the ends to slip over the top of the cap flashing and over the top edge of the drip edge. With the drip edge, cap flashing, and glass in place, fit the cover flashing over the drip edge, push it forward so that it can engage the cap flashing, then pull it back down the roof slope,

MOUNTING FIXED GLASS ON ROOF TIMBERS

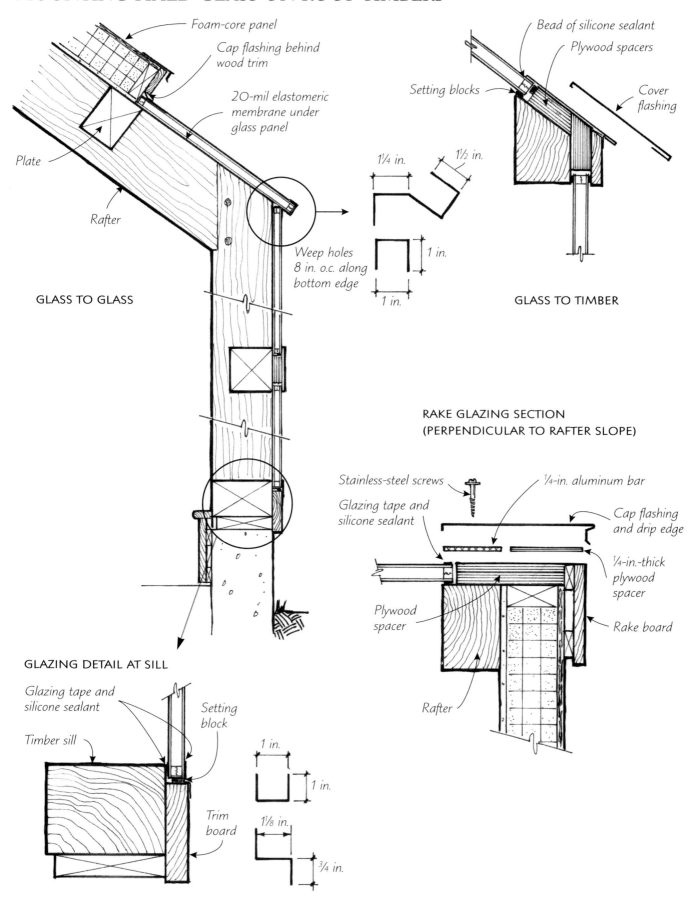

Foam-core panel

Cap flashing behind wood trim

20-mil elastomeric membrane under glass panel

Plate

Rafter

GLASS TO GLASS

Weep holes 8 in. o.c. along bottom edge

1¼ in.

1½ in.

1 in.

1 in.

Bead of silicone sealant

Plywood spacers

Setting blocks

Cover flashing

GLASS TO TIMBER

RAKE GLAZING SECTION (PERPENDICULAR TO RAFTER SLOPE)

Stainless-steel screws

Glazing tape and silicone sealant

¼-in. aluminum bar

Cap flashing and drip edge

¼-in.-thick plywood spacer

Plywood spacer

Rake board

Rafter

GLAZING DETAIL AT SILL

Glazing tape and silicone sealant

Setting block

Timber sill

1 in.

1 in.

Trim board

1⅛ in.

¾ in.

Frame Details

201

In this frame, there are two solariums with fixed glass. One, at the right, is for a sunspace integrated with the primary living area; the other is part of a hallway to the office. All the openings were planned for stock glass sizes.

locking it in place. Obviously, it is quite important that the cover flashing be tight to the glass, and there should be no ridges to trap water. Add more sealant to the drip edge and finish the sealant by beveling the excess with a putty knife to encourage runoff.

Another way to make the transition between roof and wall glass is to frame short rafters to connect with the solarium posts, as shown in the photos on p. 197. The roof glass meets the wall glass with no horizontal framing at the transition; flashing makes the joint leakproof. A 2x2 plant hanger mortised into each rafter serves as the horizontal connection. It is placed about 10 in. from each rafter end and 1½ in. from the inside face. The 2x2 is screwed and plugged to the rafter from the inside.

This detail is more prone to heat loss than the previous one. Because the flashing passes through to the inside, you get condensation in cold weather and ice on the inside of the glass in extreme conditions. Two pieces of flashing are needed, both of which should be made from heavy-gauge material. The vertical glass is installed to stop ¼ in. below the roofline as extended from the timber rafter, to leave room for flashing and to keep the roof glass from contacting the vertical glass. A piece of U-shaped flashing and ⅛-in.-thick neoprene setting blocks, again placed at quarter points, create a cush-

ion should there be any pressure from the roof glass. No flashing tape is needed with this detail. The second piece of flashing is tricky and should be precisely formed by a metal shop. The general dimensions are shown on p. 201, but the angle would change depending on the roof pitch. The weep holes are extremely important. Before the roof glass is installed, setting blocks are positioned to create space for expansion and for any water that might leak into the cavity; a bead of sealant along the top edge inhibits water entry.

Setting the roof glass over the rafters is identical to the procedure for vertical glazing installation, with two exceptions. First, cover the top face of the rafters with elastomeric membrane, and second, use metal for the top cap instead of wood. On the middle rafters, use ¼-in. aluminum bar stock as a stiff batten for the glass, screwing and countersinking it to the rafters 8 in. on center. Take every precaution when installing the glazing tape and sealant—the potential for leakage is great. For a more attractive finish, use anodized aluminum or copper to cap the bar stock. Attach the cap with #6 stainless-steel sheet-metal screws and rubber washers 2 ft. on center.

The detail on the outside edge of the solarium is basically the same as that described previously. It is necessary to cap both the timber and the top edge

of the insulation. The plywood spacer extends to the outside edge of the exterior panels; a ¼-in.-thick plywood strip has to be added after the ¼-in.-thick aluminum batten to keep the top face flush. The flashing must span from the glass to the rake edge and should be custom-formed. Sheet-metal screws are fastened about ¾ in. from the plywood edge on the glass end. Another attachment for the flashing is made by nailing the rake edge of the flashing to the wall. Use 1-in. nails, 12 in. on center, to attach the rake flashing to the wall. Copper nails are best for copper and aluminum for aluminum.

One of the easiest solarium details is at the top of the roof glass, where glass and insulation intersect on the purlin that receives the solarium rafters. Moisture coming off the roof falls away from the intersection, so leaks are prevented. The bottom edge of the insulation stops about 1 in. from the edge of the purlin to leave a bearing surface for the glass. A 20-mil elastomeric membrane strip is first laid into the corner between the top edge of the timber and the spacer. The rest of the installation follows the guidelines discussed earlier; roof trim on the face of the insulation holds the glass in place. Because it is not subjected to as much weather and moisture as it might be elsewhere on the roof, wood trim works fine here.

Interior detailing, whether simple or ornate, should match the quality of the frame.

CHAPTER 10

FINISH DETAILS

To begin this final chapter, I would like to remind readers that the following information, like much of the information presented in this book, is not rigidly prescribed. These are not precise instructions for how to do; rather, look at this chapter as a series of guidelines for how to think about how to do. Let it steer you along, but do not let it stand in the way of individuality and creativity. The chapter starts with trim and stair details; exterior trim and flooring systems are next, followed by interior partitions. I'll end with a discussion of interior surface treatments.

INTERIOR TRIM DETAILS

The process of timber framing is more likely to defy mass production than to embrace it—the timbers are large and unwieldy, their sizes must change to suit structural conditions in the frame, and the joints are numerous and varied. In addition, timber framers themselves tend to be an independent lot. They often do what they do for reasons that are other than monetary, preferring the joy of creativity to the boredom of repetition. As a result, each timber frame takes on an individuality that becomes an important part of the character of the house. It is precisely this individuality that makes the use of stock trim materials one of my pet peeves. For if you go to just about any lumberyard in the United States for trim, you will probably be faced with many racks of trim types but few real choices. They really boil down to two or three types that are used all the time. I have nothing against these designs, just against their incessant and automatic use, which has brought a stifling sameness to houses all over the country.

The economics of using stock trim also bothers me, because you wind up paying a lot more money for a lot less wood than if you were to buy non-machined stock. For instance, a flat 1x4 purchased from a lumberyard is typically ¾ in. by 3½ in.; when it becomes casing stock, it is further reduced to 9⁄16 in. by 3¼ in. The skinny little rounded-over piece of wood sold at about twice the cost of the "full-sized" material it came from is an abuse of wood and, to my mind, an insult to otherwise good construction.

Using plain, flat board stock for casing is less expensive and already more appealing than stock trim, but with surprisingly little effort, flat stock can become distinctive. Start by varying the width and thickness of the pieces. I like to make the head casing for windows and doors heavier than the side casing—the heavier board refers to a structural lintel, and the different dimensions create depth and define each piece (see the photo below). Play around with proportions to fit the circumstances. Consider the species, the intended color and finish of all adjacent surfaces, and the architectural and decorative style. Painted casing will look very different from wood left natural. Large, molded casing imparts a completely different feeling than small, flat casings would. Edges can be refined by molding with a router, a shaper, or a hand plane.

SIMPLE INTERIOR WINDOW TRIM

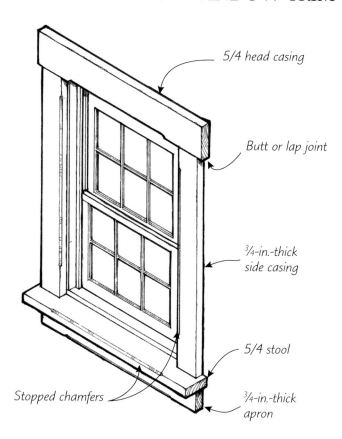

5/4 head casing

Butt or lap joint

¾-in.-thick side casing

5/4 stool

Stopped chamfers

¾-in.-thick apron

With a little effort, flat board stock can become distinctive trim. In this house, standard molding was added to side and head trim to add character and depth.

Simple window trim

My favorite trim detail is based on using 5/4 stock for the head casing and ¾-in.-thick stock for the side casing, as shown in the drawing on the facing page. On windows, the stool is made from 5/4 stock and the apron is made from ¾-in.-thick stock. Widths are variable. The head casing extends past the outside edge of the side casing by about ½ in. to reinforce the idea of a lintel. The casings meet with a simple butt joint, which can be improved with a lap on the back of the head casing. The window stool is rabbeted to fit the sash and also extends past the side casing by ½ in. Below the stool, the ¾-in.-thick flat-stock apron is held back from the stool ends by ½ in. It's a simple scheme and easy to install.

Even left unadorned, this type of trim stands apart from standard trim because it is simple and honest. But it can be made more elegant by adding chamfers to the inside edges of the side and head casings, to the top edge of the stool, and to the bottom edge of the apron. Stop each chamfer 1½ in. before the end or, for the head casing, before it meets the side casing. When the chamfers repeat the embellishment of the timber edges, they can be especially unifying. Beads can also be routed into the face of the casing, stopped usually at the same point as the chamfers. Add a crown molding to the top edge of the header, and the casing takes on more formality. The variations are endless, and that's the very point of using this type of trim. Almost anything you do will be better than the lumberyard offerings, but for less money and not a great deal of work, it is possible to create a truly grand alternative.

Baseboard trim

The timber frame eliminates the need for crown moldings at the intersections of ceilings and walls, so in addition to window and door trim, we are primarily concerned with baseboards. Because the baseboards are a significant trim element, their design should be consis-

INTERIOR BASEBOARD TRIM

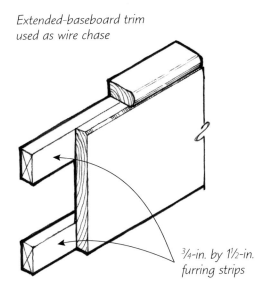

Extended-baseboard trim used as wire chase

¾-in. by 1½-in. furring strips

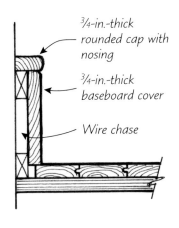

¾-in.-thick rounded cap with nosing

¾-in.-thick baseboard cover

Wire chase

To unify interior trim when extended-baseboard system is used as wire chase, match other baseboard trim to profile of extended baseboard.

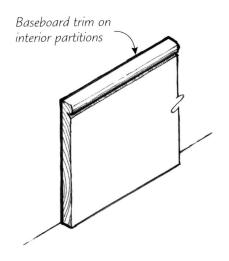

Baseboard trim on interior partitions

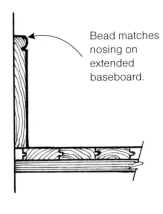

Bead matches nosing on extended baseboard.

tent with the material, style, and detailing of the other trim, and also should match each other where interior partitions meet exterior insulated walls. If the extended-baseboard system is used as a wire chase, as described in Chapter 7, make sure the partition-wall baseboards—which are not built up in the same manner—are the same height as the extended baseboard plus the cap,

and add a bead to match the bead on the extended-baseboard cap (see the drawings above). For an added element of unity, make the same kind of bead on window and door-trim edges. Trim is edge definition; it is always best when it is a consistent pattern of details and materials that are consistent and well executed.

In this home, the bent girt is raised to allow passage at the stair. Newel posts and stair details are designed to match frame details. Note the simple flat-stock trim at the doors. (Photo by Bob Gere.)

STAIRS AND RAILS

During design and construction, seize every opportunity to make the details and material of stairs and rails compatible with the timber frame. Perhaps an existing frame post could act as a newel to receive rails and stringers, or maybe a post could be added for this purpose. At the very least, the edge and end embellishments of the frame can be repeated in the stairs.

Careful planning of stairways is absolutely necessary in timber-frame houses because their openings have to be created in the timber-floor system

when the frame is being constructed. Stairs usually fall between bents, with the normal joist span broken with timber headers. They can also be designed to pass through a bent if necessary, by raising the bent girt in the area of the stair to allow headroom (see the photo above). The plan should detail the exact layout of risers and treads so that the frame openings will fit the stairway. Check the local building code on all stair requirements. Since stairs are a principal means of egress, the codes tend to be quite specific, although not exactly the same everywhere.

In a simple three-bay timber-frame home, the stairs frequently fall in the middle bay. This area is commonly used for passage and transition and so is seldom divided with partitions; sometimes it is even open to the roof. To preserve this spaciousness, we often design open-riser stairs, housing the treads in the stringer and dadoing the balusters into its top edge. At the base and top of the stair, the stringer and the rail mortise into a newel post, which in turn is mortised into the stair header (see the top drawing on the facing page). The newel post has to be projected out of plane toward the stringer so that there will be enough

TWO STAIR DETAILS

OPEN-RISER STAIR

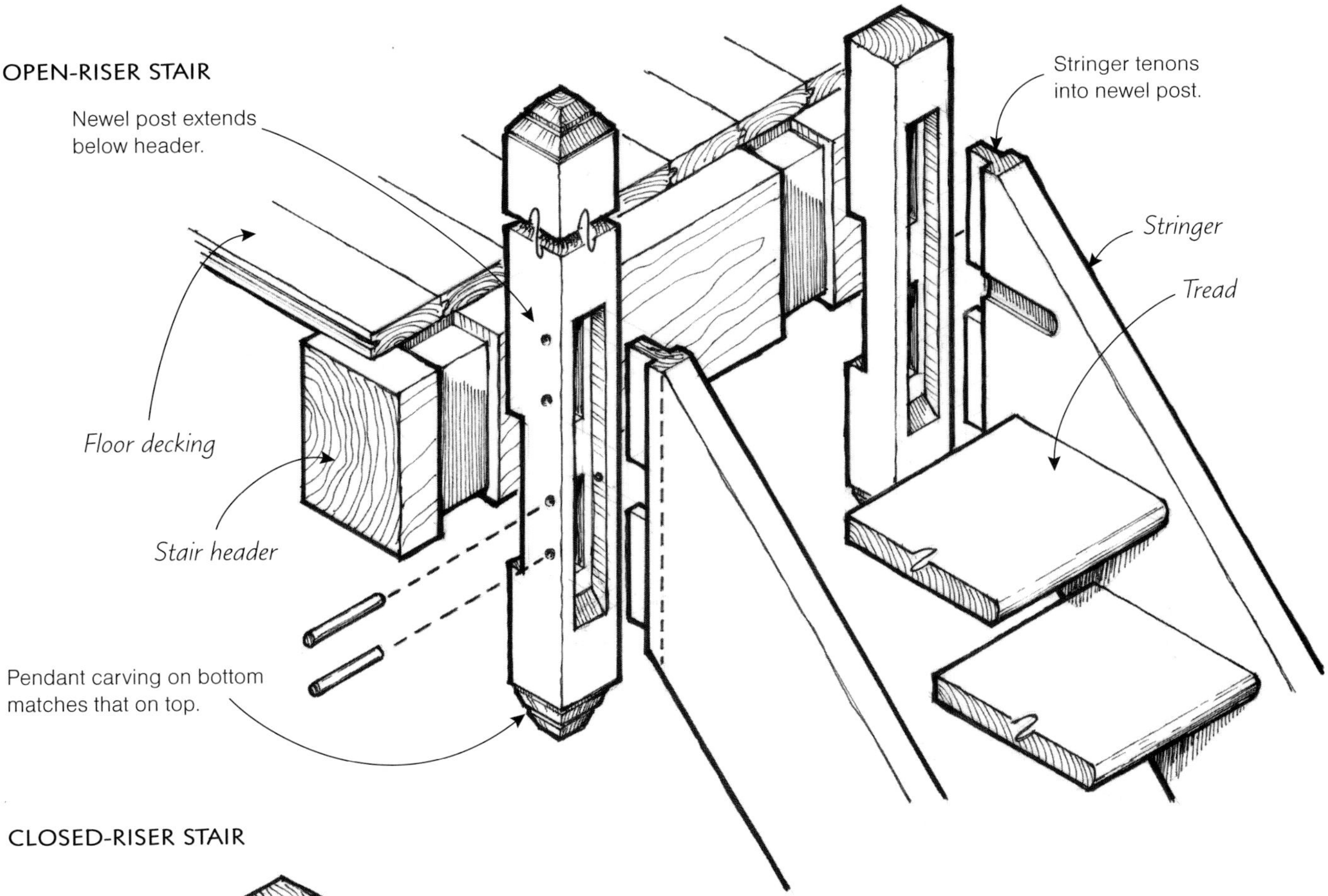

Newel post extends below header.

Floor decking

Stair header

Pendant carving on bottom matches that on top.

Stringer tenons into newel post.

Stringer

Tread

CLOSED-RISER STAIR

Newel post tenons into stair header without pendant drop.

Stringer routed for risers, treads, and wedgings.

Stringer tenons into stair header and newel post.

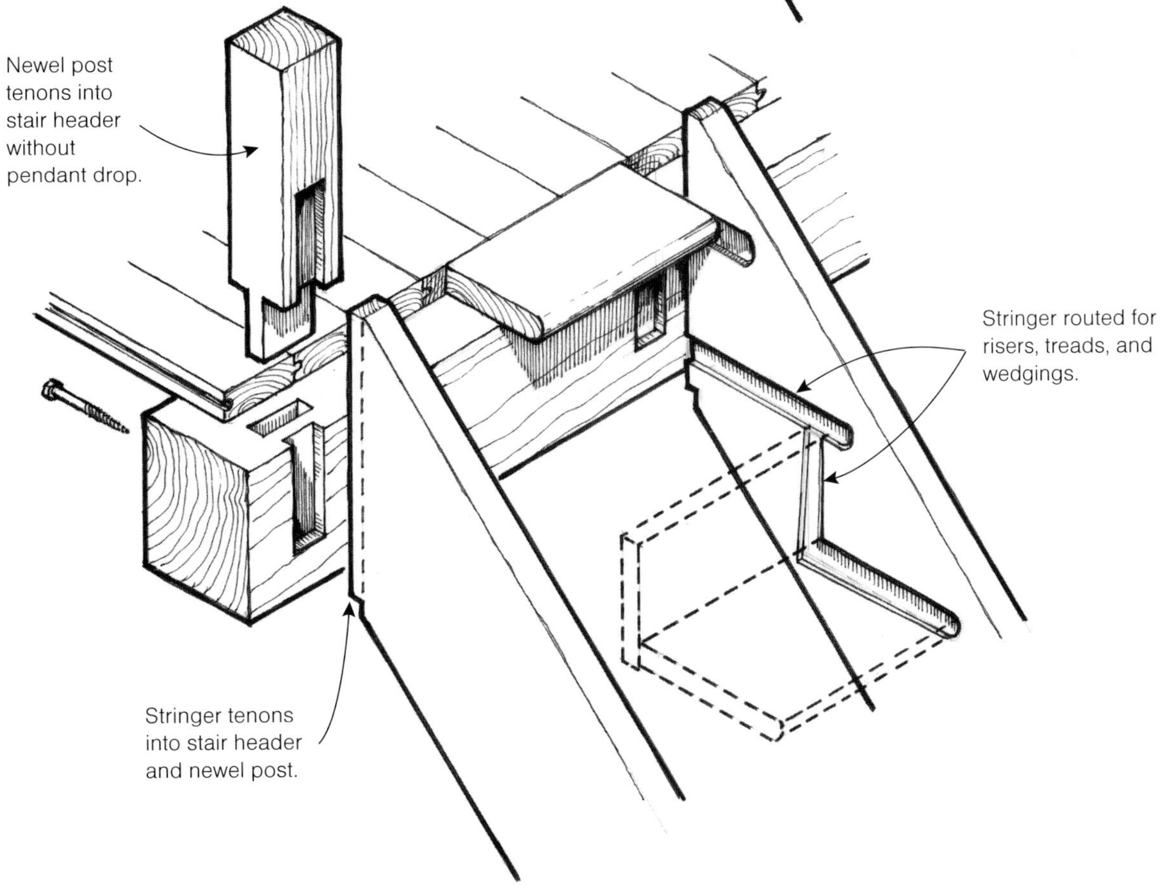

This open-riser stair was designed to complement the frame details. The stringer is mortised into the newel post, and the newel post is mortised into the timber header.

material for a good connection with the stringer. The projected portion of the newel post extends below the stair header and is embellished much like a timber pendant. One great advantage of this system is that the stringer, newel posts, rails, and balusters all can be shop-made and installed as a unit.

Another option is to build a closed-riser stair, in which the newel post is attached to the stair header separately (see the bottom drawing on p. 207). The newel post is designed to align with the edges of the stair header and still receives the tenoned end of the stringer, but the bottom surface of the stringer bears on the face of the stair header. Do not drop the stringer so low that its end grain would be visible from below. Newel-post tenons should be at least 5 in. long to maintain rigidity. It is also important that the stair header be sized to allow the cross-grain mortise of the stringer.

Railings

Railings for catwalks or balconies also can be built into the frame. All that is required is that the railings align with timbers and that their components (upper rail, lower rail, and balusters) be designed into the frame plan. The railing can then be installed when the frame is built, making it stronger and, more important, taking full advantage of the frame as a finish element. The entire contour of rails that join to timbers should be completely housed (by at least ½ in.) to allow for shrinkage.

Balcony railings were built into this frame when it was raised. A housed mortise-and-tenon joint is used between rails and timbers to hide potential shrinkage.

Railings for balconies might also be timbers rather than molded material. Building codes require that stair rails meet a certain profile standard for comfort and safety, but railings at balcony areas can (and perhaps should in many cases) be larger and don't need to match precisely the rail profiles at the stair. If this course is chosen, the balcony railing is easy, natural, and aesthetically integrated into the timber frame.

EXTERIOR TRIM ON FOAM-CORE PANELS

Exterior trim makes a statement about the significance and style of a house. It is a critical design feature, too often ignored or undervalued. If you look at old houses, you will notice that great attention was often paid to the details of exterior trim, especially in the roof. Frequently, the finest woodworking was reserved for elaborate cornices and eaves with multilayered moldings. Contrast this with the modern ranch house, on which any kind of roof trim at all has been practically eliminated. As a result, the building lines are weak and ill defined, which exposes its personality—no pride, no character. Lack of attention to this kind of detail is one reason why modern houses frequently look and feel nondescript.

In Chapter 5 I discussed the foam-core panel insulating system in detail and several enclosure alternatives in general. I didn't go into detail on the alternatives because they are based on conventional building systems and, as such, don't require much more than an explanation of procedure. The panel system, however, is quite different from normal building practice in both theory and execution. This section will therefore touch on a few more details that relate to panels—things we didn't explore in Chapter 5. Most of what follows is a direct result of the fact that typically the panels have less structure for the application of other materials than do standard insulating systems. I should note here that carpenters are by necessity creative people and often are able to deal with the following situations without advice. Indeed, most of the information in this section is comprised of things I have learned from the many carpenters who have worked on my company's houses over the years. The illustrations in this chapter show both typical and doublechip panels because they are both commonly used.

Trim boards

Depending entirely on architectural style and siding, there potentially are

ATTACHING TRIM TO FOAM-CORE PANELS

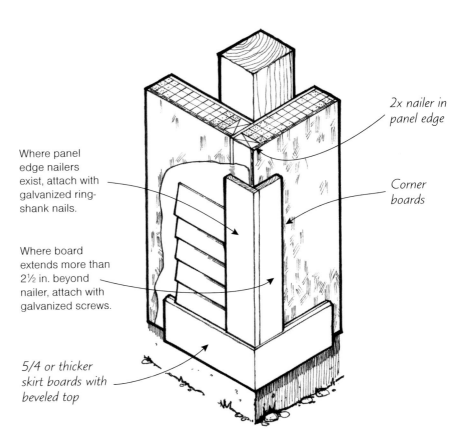

Where panel edge nailers exist, attach with galvanized ring-shank nails.

Where board extends more than 2½ in. beyond nailer, attach with galvanized screws.

5/4 or thicker skirt boards with beveled top

2x nailer in panel edge

Corner boards

quite a few different types of trim boards that might be applied to the walls of a house (see the drawing above). Corner boards are the vertical trim pieces that reach from the base of the siding to the cornice work on the outside building corners. Skirt boards, used only on elaborate trim styles, run around the perimeter of the house at the base. Exterior door and window trim is just like the interior casing except that it gets much more abuse. There are usually a few other miscellaneous trim boards used for mounting such things as light fixtures and electric meters. Despite the relative lack of surfaces to nail to, mounting all these boards can become quite routine once a procedure has been established.

To secure trim boards to a panel where there is not a 2x4 edge nailer, use galvanized self-tapping screws or galvanized ring-shank nails. (Galvanized screws are

used frequently for exterior decks and other applications and are available at most lumberyards.) Screws should be long enough to pass through the panel sheathing by at least ⅜ in. Edges of boards that are 2½ in. or more away from a 2x4 nailer should be secured with screws to prevent cupping. If the board edge is less than 2½ in. away, use ring-shank nails. For instance, there is typically 1½ in. of nailing surface around a typical window or door opening. The trim is mounted onto the unit by at least ½ in., spans the gap between the rough opening and the nailer, and then is nailed to the edge nailer. Under these circumstances, unless the trim for the door or window is at least 4 in. to 4½ in. wide, no screws would be required. Near the ends of boards, always predrill for screws to prevent splitting. I see no reason why the visible head of a screw should be considered less attractive than the head of a nail, but if you disagree, take the trouble to countersink the screws and plug the holes.

Roof trim

Of course there is no standard roof-trim detail that is appropriate for all houses. Trim is designed to fit the style, proportions, and, yes, the budget. We have used numerous roof-trim details, but they fall into two basic categories. One has a sloped soffit at the eave, and the other has a flat soffit.

Applying roof trim to foam-core panels need not be any more difficult than trimming conventional rough framing, but it does require good planning. The easiest way to achieve the roof overhang is to extend the roof panels beyond the wall panels; the trim is attached to the 2x nailers let in to the perimeter of the roof panels. The problem is that the roof panels have a limited load-bearing capacity in this load-bearing cantilever situation. Gen-

erally, the overhang for the standard panel (nonstructural with drywall on one side) should be held to between 8 in. and 12 in. Doublechip (structural) panels usually can extend beyond the wall panel by 16 in. to 24 in. Applying 2-in.-thick tongue-and-groove planking to the roof as the finish ceiling and extending it beyond the wall panel allows the overhang to be increased to 16 in. to 24 in. even when standard panels are used. Before making a decision about the length of the overhang, however, check the roof-load requirements in your area and ask for the panel manufacturer's recommendations about supporting the load.

SLOPED-SOFFIT TRIM

EAVE SECTION

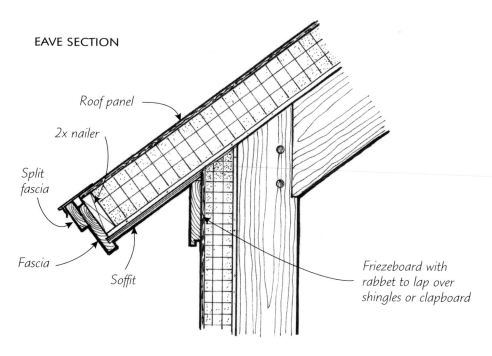

Roof panel

2x nailer

Split fascia

Fascia

Soffit

Friezeboard with rabbet to lap over shingles or clapboard

RAKE SECTION

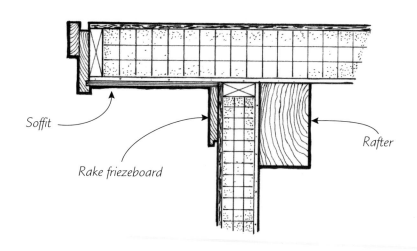

Soffit

Rake friezeboard

Rafter

Sloped-soffit trim

The simplest trim style uses a sloped soffit made of a solid ¾-in.-thick board or, at the very least, ⅝-in.-thick AC exterior plywood (see the drawings at left). One edge of the soffit is ripped to fit against the wall panels, and then the soffit is pushed into place—if the fit between the top of the soffit and the panels is snug, the soffit will hold itself in place temporarily while the bottom is being secured to the nailers in the panel edges. (When standard panels are used, there is no way to screw or nail the top edge of the soffit to the drywall underside of the panel.) The bottom edge of the soffit must fit tightly into a dado cut into the fascia. Assuming the 2x nailers in the panel edges are straight, simply use a combination square to set the dado depth; if the nailers aren't straight, set up a stringline for each run of trim and plan on shimming behind the fascia at the low points. Galvanized nails or galvanized ring-shank nails are usually appropriate for exterior applications.

The friezeboard, which performs the critical function of holding the top edge of the soffit in place, goes on next. The top edge of the friezeboard is ripped to the roof slope, then pushed up until it forces the soffit tightly against the panel, as shown at left. Usually the bottom edge of the friezeboard is rabbeted to hold the last cut of shingles or clapboards. A built-up rabbet

The deep overhang, not the trim, is the focus of this house. Using doublechip panels made it possible to extend the overhang. Cedar 1x6s nailed to the panels form the soffit. Gable-end glass is fixed directly to the timbers of the end bent.

can be made simply by shimming behind the friezeboard with plywood or other material. It will probably be necessary to use some screws (as described in the section on trim boards) to attach the friezeboard to the wall panel, since there is not likely to be good nailing between panel seams.

When installing the rake trim, the lack of an acute angle between the wall and the roof means there is nothing to hold the soffit in place before the friezeboard goes on. Solve this problem by installing the friezeboard first, using an appropriately sized spacer to set the dimension for the soffit. Remove the spacer, push the soffit into place and nail it to the nailers in the panel edges.

Planked-roof trim

When tongue-and-groove (or shiplap) planking is installed as an interior finish before the panels go on, it can be used to create the soffit. On purlin roofs, lay the planking perpendicular to the purlins, running from the eave to the peak (see the top drawings on p. 212). For expediency and accuracy, extend the planking a few inches past

TRIMMING A PLANKED PURLIN ROOF

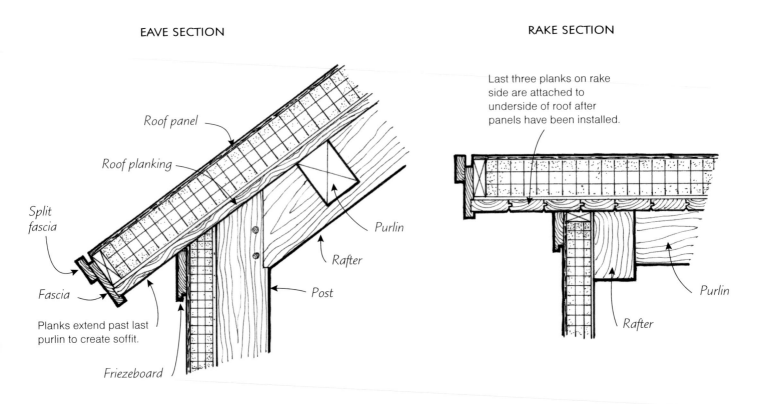

EAVE SECTION

Roof panel

Roof planking

Split fascia

Fascia

Planks extend past last purlin to create soffit.

Friezeboard

Purlin

Rafter

Post

RAKE SECTION

Last three planks on rake side are attached to underside of roof after panels have been installed.

Purlin

Rafter

TRIMMING A PLANKED COMMON-RAFTER ROOF

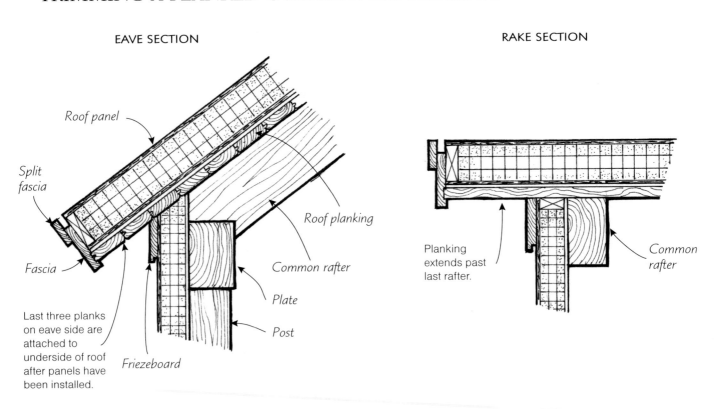

EAVE SECTION

Roof panel

Split fascia

Fascia

Last three planks on eave side are attached to underside of roof after panels have been installed.

Friezeboard

Roof planking

Common rafter

Plate

Post

RAKE SECTION

Planking extends past last rafter.

Common rafter

Finish Details

When blocking out for the trim, it is usually best to make up strips of plywood with blocks attached on the ground and then to put them up as prebuilt units. Note the excess foam from filling the panel joints.

the end of the overhang and cut an entire roof-side of planking to a chalkline. If you're going to do this, there's the potential for an awkward transition between the eave soffit and the rake soffit because of a lack of nailing surface on the rake side. Plan the rake soffit so that a single plank spans from the wall panel to the roof nailer, since there won't be a nailing surface between. To do this, extend the next-to-last plank beyond the last wall panel (which is the last nailing surface) far enough so that you wind up with your last plank at the outside edge of the rake. After the roof panels are installed, the last rake plank can be attached from below.

On common-rafter roofs, the planking is laid perpendicular to the rafters (parallel to the eave). In this case, extend the planking over the gable ends to form the rake soffit (see the bottom drawings on the facing page). Cut the plank ends all at once after they are in place, as you would at the eaves. Plan the soffit at the eave to be a single plank. Extend the first plank that is ap-

plied to the roof surface over the wall panel, as before, so that the matching can continue from the eave to the wall.

An overhang of more than 12 in. implies the use of structural panels, and since structural panels have a nail base on both sides, the problem with soffit attachment is automatically solved. Remember that codes require a fire barrier over the foam, so even if the roof will be sheathed first with planks, it will be necessary to use a material with a 15-minute fire rating (probably drywall) between the planks and the panels.

Fascia

With the friezeboard and soffit in place, the fascia boards can be installed. Cut and nail the fascia boards directly to the panel nailers—the table-sawn dado in the fascia, which receives the soffit, helps with alignment. In a high-quality job, linear splices and corner joints are mitered. When the fascia boards are over 1 in. thick, we have sometimes used finger joints or dovetails at the corners for decoration and

strength. After the fascia board has been attached, cut and nail the split fascia to it to give the trim more depth and a molded appearance.

What makes this type of sloped soffit so easy is that the trim at the eave and rake meet at right angles, resulting in relatively simple cutting and fitting. Changing species, size, and treatment of the components allows the trim to be customized to suit the house. We have used everything from a single, heavy cedar plank to small boards painted in soft colors for both the fascia and the split fascia.

Plumb fascia with sloped soffit

Now let's look at another variety of sloped-soffit trim, used when it is important for the design to have a vertical-eave fascia rather than one perpendicular to the roof slope—for instance, to accept gutter brackets when gutters are to be used. To give the fascia a vertical orientation, it is necessary to create an additional nailing surface after the panels have been installed

PLUMB FASCIA WITH SLOPED SOFFIT

EAVE SECTION

RAKE SECTION

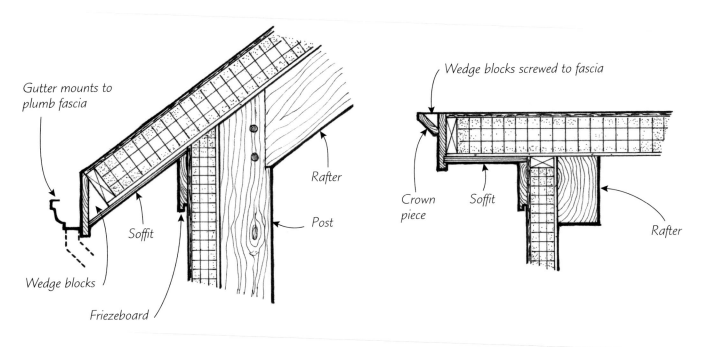

Gutter mounts to plumb fascia

Rafter

Post

Soffit

Wedge blocks

Friezeboard

Wedge blocks screwed to fascia

Crown piece

Soffit

Rafter

(see the drawings above). This can be accomplished either with individual wedge blocks attached to the panel nailers or a single, continuous piece ripped to the correct wedge shape. The problem with the latter method is that a fairly large piece of wood could be required, depending on the roof slope. For example, if the roof pitch were 10-in-12, the smallest leg of the wedge would be about 2½ in. Making individual wedge blocks takes more time, but the pieces can probably be made from scrap. When the fascia is plumb, housing the soffit in a fascia dado is much too complicated, so instead carefully rip the soffit to the plumb line and hold it about $\frac{1}{16}$ in. beyond the wedge block to improve the odds of a good fit. Rake soffits can still be dadoed as described previously.

When a gutter is mounted on the fascia, it adds lines to the detail similar to a crown molding. To keep all of the trim consistent, add a crown to the rake trim. Simply add a wedge strip to the fascia (already fixed to the panel nailer) and nail on a crown.

Flat-soffit trim

In addition to having some aesthetic advantages, flat-soffit trim also provides support for the panel on the eave where the loads are likely to be the greatest. While there are too many possible variations to cover here, they all spring from a few basic procedures. The drawing on the facing page shows a built-up system that we use frequently. Just as in sloped-soffit trim, the eave and rake overhangs are determined by the overhang of the roof panels. For best effect, try to design the detail to include a crown molding that follows the plane of the panel nailer and a soffit located approximately 2 in. to 4 in. below the bottom edge of the overhanging eave panel.

Start on the eave by installing the jet blocks, the soffit, and the fascia. In most cases, the blocks can be cut from 2x4s; a wider fascia might require a 2x6. Each jet block is angled to fit against the underside of the roof slope and has a square front edge to serve as vertical nailing for the fascia. Installation is simplified by nailing a number

of blocks onto a ⅝-in. plywood strip on the ground and installing the assembly as a unit. This also helps ensure a straight line at the fascia, because inconsistencies in the wall surface can be corrected by shimming between the wall panel and the plywood—it is hard to shim one block at a time. Position the plywood along a chalkline snapped on the wall panel, and screw it to the panel with galvanized self-tapping screws. Then toenail the jet blocks to the panel nailer. Shim as necessary between these two pieces to keep the front edge of the soffit level.

The next step is to provide the framing for the corner return, as shown at the left side of the drawing on the facing page. The corner return is optional, but it enhances the richness of the roof trim by creating a visual base for the roof. When the trim is completed, the corner board should fall in the middle of the corner return, giving the whole unit the feeling of a column and capital. Because the corner return allows the eave line to continue at the gable end, the rake can finish to the top of

the return instead of being mitered to the fascia—a procedure that is usually difficult, with results that are not always attractive. Set up the corner return by attaching jet blocks to a ⅝-in. plywood strip. The assembly would fit against the gable end of the building, from the last eave block to the end of the return. This small assembly would be screwed to the eave block, to the panel nailer on the building corner, and to the outside sheathing of the panel beyond the corner. Then the soffit and the fascia are installed along with the eave trim. A solid 2x cap is put on the return, followed by the sloped plywood cap, which has a 15° slope to shed water. Use shims or a nailing strip on the building surface to create the slope. The 2x cap should be ripped to receive a crown at the same angle created by the roof slope on the eave side. The entire top of the corner return should be covered with flashing. It's easiest to make a pattern and have all of the return flashing made by a sheet-metal shop.

To continue the crown on the rake trim, cut a beveled wedge strip to repeat the roof angle at the eave. If possible, this piece should be ripped from a solid piece of wood. If not, install blocks for nailing at least every 24 in.

Begin the rake trim with the soffit and friezeboard. The rake soffit would be attached using the same method described in the sloped-soffit system because of the lack of nailing on the rake overhangs. Fascias are installed after the soffits. The beveled wedge strip is next, and the crown trim is last. Shim to correct alignment, especially on the fascia and crown. Good preparation when installing panels and soffit blocking saves time when the trim is attached. It is not necessary to vent the soffit because there is no air movement through the insulation.

The dimensions of this type of roof trim can be altered according to taste and circumstances. For added depth in the crown, for instance, nail a ½-in.-thick by 1½-in.-wide strip to the fascia

Using only flat boards, this trim detail has a molded appearance in a traditional style. The corner return is centered over the corner board to create a column-and-cap effect. The extra strips on the corner board reinforce the idea of a column.

FLAT-SOFFIT TRIM AT CORNER

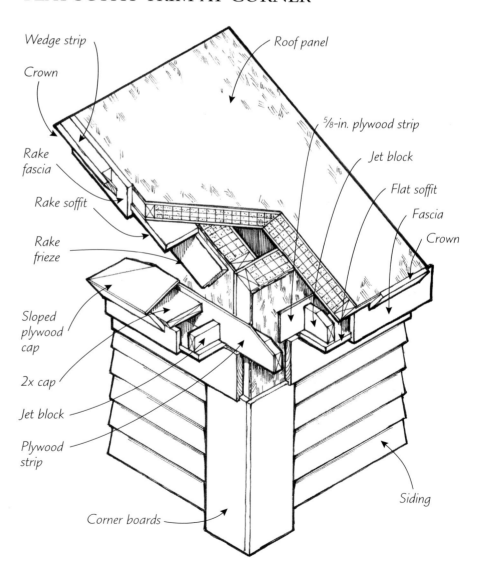

Wedge strip
Crown
Rake fascia
Rake soffit
Rake frieze
Sloped plywood cap
2x cap
Jet block
Plywood strip
Corner boards
Roof panel
⅝-in. plywood strip
Jet block
Flat soffit
Fascia
Crown
Siding

APPLICATION OF FELT OR ELASTOMERIC MEMBRANE ON WARM ROOFS

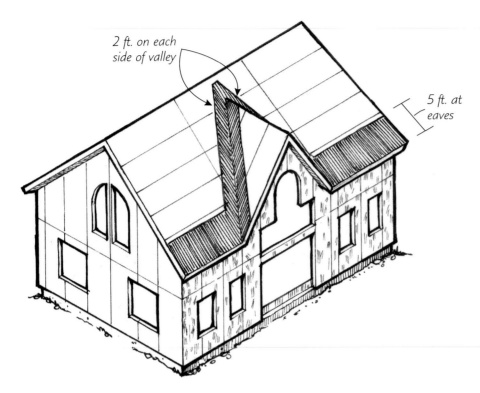

2 ft. on each side of valley

5 ft. at eaves

before the crown. Generally, gutters need a flat vertical face for attachment; if they are required, make the fascia wider by using a larger block and dropping the soffit down to accommodate it. The crown usually remains on the corner return and rake when a gutter is used on the eave.

ROOFING OVER FOAM-CORE PANELS

The typical foam-core roof application is technically a "warm roof," meaning that one side of the panel is exposed to the heated interior and the other to the outside. When warm roofs are used in cold climates, the heat passing through the insulation can cause the snow to melt on the surface of the shingles, flow down the roof, and form an ice dam at the eave; water then backs up behind the dam and leaks through the shingles. A good panel allows very little heat loss, making this problem minimal, but we still like to use 50-lb. felt or

VENTILATED ROOF

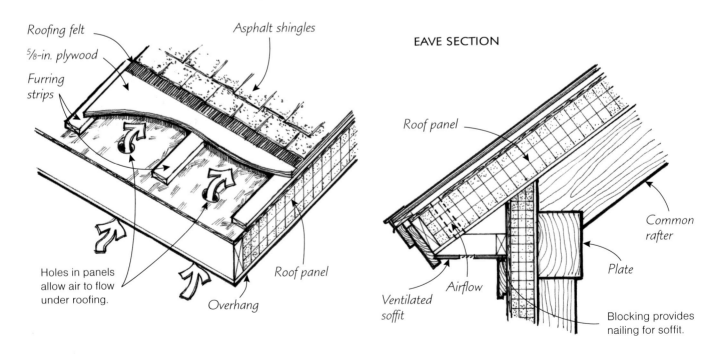

Roofing felt

⅝-in. plywood

Furring strips

Asphalt shingles

Holes in panels allow air to flow under roofing.

Overhang

Roof panel

EAVE SECTION

Roof panel

Common rafter

Plate

Ventilated soffit

Airflow

Blocking provides nailing for soffit.

Furring strips are being attached to this roof surface in preparation for wood shingles. The furring strips will create airspaces to ventilate the roof.

an elastomeric membrane for the first 5 ft. at the eave and for 2 ft. on both sides of valleys (see the top drawing on the facing page).

Since foam-core panels are an effective moisture barrier in both directions, it is possible for moisture to collect on the exterior surface of the panel, under the shingles. This is most likely to occur during extremes of high humidity and heat, or high humidity and cold, and while leakage is improbable, certain kinds of roofing materials might be damaged. The following types of roofing should therefore be laid over furring strips to allow airflow: wood shingles and shakes, slate, tile, and standing-seam metal. (Corrugated metal can be laid directly on the panels.) The airflow keeps the roofing material away from the warmth of the panel, creating a "cold roof." For a real cold roof with airflow from the eave to the peak, it is necessary to cut holes through the panel at the eave overhang to bring air to the space. The soffit is vented to allow air through (see the bottom drawings on the facing page).

Shrinkage and movement of the timber frame cause a certain amount of movement in the panels, and even if it is slight, this movement can cause shingles to wrinkle slightly at the panel seams. For this reason I don't recommend applying lightweight asphalt or fiberglass-based shingles directly to the panels. (If you're going to use these, first nail and glue an additional sheathing membrane, such as ½-in.-thick plywood, to the panels to prevent movement. Of course, this extra cost would greatly exceed the cost of buying heavier shingles to begin with.) Shingles should be the heavily textured architectural type or the heaviest available weight, usually about 310 lb. per square in fiberglass and 350 lb. per square in asphalt. Asphalt shingles are becoming hard to get and are being replaced by those with a fiberglass base.

FLOORING

The issue of flooring in a timber-frame house is a classic case of good news and bad news. The good news is that the floor of one story becomes the ceiling for the story below, making construction efficient and reducing costs. The bad news is that a floor with good sound-deadening characteristics is not as automatic as it is when using conventional construction techniques. It is harder to deaden noise transmission through floors than walls in any event,

because floors are subjected to both airborne and impact sound. The design and installation of floors and ceilings are therefore crucial not only to aesthetics, but also to comfort and privacy.

Plan for noise

It is a very simple, but too often overlooked, observation that proximity to noise is the crux of the sound-transmission problem. In other words, if you expect to find privacy in the library, don't put it underneath your teenager's rock-and-roll headquarters. Such oversights are nearly impossible to rectify during construction. As much as possible, stack rooms that require privacy and those that are public. Let the teenager compete with the blender instead of with Mozart. It is sometimes possible to solve problems of sound transmission during the development of the floor plans by isolating critical areas. But such houses are necessarily large and spread out (read expensive). House plans intended to use space and volume efficiently are the most difficult to insulate against sound. I give special emphasis to this issue because it is not one we have always dealt with well. We didn't forget about noise—we assumed it wouldn't be a problem. Very often the house was being built for a couple not yet with children—people ignorant about the meaning of the word noise. So here is one more suggestion I offer, having learned the lesson the hard way: For the benefit of yourselves or future inhabitants, assume that someday your house will also be home to a tumbling gymnasium and a rock concert, sometimes simultaneously.

Flooring applied over timbers

In timber-frame construction, it makes sense to install the finish floor and ceiling materials over the timber floor—applying the finish floor to one side and the ceiling to the other excludes the possibility of using the frame as finish work. The other alternative, fitting materials between timbers, turns the frame into an obstacle to efficient construction. There's a huge difference between installing flooring over timbers with 5-in. or 6-in. surfaces for fudge

Because this loft is open to the rest of the house, sound-deadening insulation would not have been useful. Therefore, a single layer of planks serves as both the ceiling below and the flooring above.

PLANK FLOOR

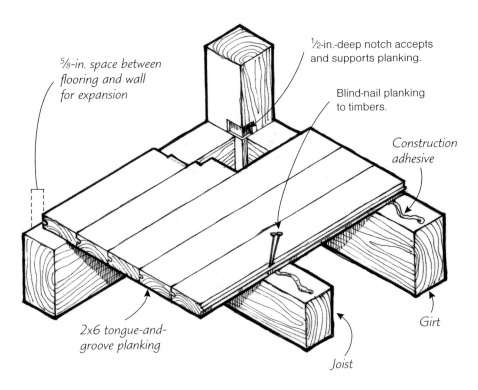

5/8-in. space between flooring and wall for expansion

1/2-in.-deep notch accepts and supports planking.

Blind-nail planking to timbers.

Construction adhesive

Girt

2x6 tongue-and-groove planking

Joist

factors and attempting to scribe materials to fit precisely between timbers 30 in. to 36 in. on center. So, except to solve plumbing problems, we always apply flooring on top of the timber structure.

Plank material

As a general guideline, design timber-floor systems for nominal 2-in.-thick tongue-and-groove planks. The most commonly available planking species are pine and spruce, followed by fir and hemlock. Planking usually comes in an "adequate" grade, but hardly ever "good." It will be called something like "#2 common," which sounds pretty good by the grading book; however, every piece is likely to be as bad as is allowable and probably a little worse. Unless there is a clear demand from the client for a rustic appearance, I prefer to pay the difference for a higher grade of material, or I purchase planking from one of our small, local mills.

Assuming the use of planks or a system with equivalent strength, timber joists ideally should be located about 30 in. on center to keep the flooring stiff. This is about the right spacing for pine planking; it is a little conservative for fir, hemlock, or spruce. (This is not a political discussion. "Conservative" as a structural reference is a good thing for even the most liberal.) Of course, joists ought to be evenly spaced between major beams, so the trick is to find the on-center number closest to 30 in. All timbers still have to be sized to support the floor loads as suggested by the local building codes.

Laminated planking is also available. Although it is expensive, it does have the advantage of greater stiffness, allowing the possibility of spreading the joists out from 4 ft. to 12 ft. on center. This type of planking is normally used for commercial applications and is manufactured in thicknesses from about 1½ in. up to 4 in. Another couple of advantages of laminated material are the ability to choose from a wide range of exposed surface laminates and the ability to end match between joist centers, which cuts down on waste.

Planks on timbers

The simplest floor is a single layer of planks over timbers (see the drawing on the facing page). Although it does nothing to deaden sound, planking is useful in such open spaces as lofts and walkways (see the photo on the facing page). People who wish to build their homes in affordable stages often choose to start with a layer of planks over timbers, adding other materials when they can afford them.

Tongue-and-groove planks usually come with a V-groove on the visible face, which helps to mask shrinkage or an uneven surface by creating a shadow line. For a straight match without the V-groove, just expose the opposite face. Widths of 6 in. or less are easiest to lay and cause the fewest problems with movement.

Wide planks (8 in. or more) are hard to straighten when they are bowed, and because there are fewer joints to absorb movement, seasonal expansion and contraction of the wood will be more noticeable. I know of a building where wide, very dry hardwood planks were laid over timbers late in the winter. When the planks took on some moisture in the summer and expanded, they pushed the walls of the building out as much as 2 in. in some places. This story gave me new respect for narrow softwood planks and reasonable (but not extreme) seasoning. Narrow planks can also be secured by blind-nailing (angling the nail through the plank from just above the tongue), which is much easier than screwing and plugging and much more attractive than face-nailing.

Installation begins by laying the planks perpendicular to the joists at one end of the floor system, using construction adhesive to glue the planks to the timbers. (This helps prevent squeaking and makes the floor stiffer and stronger.) Nails for blind-nailing should be 16d common; if the timbers are oak, the nails should be galvanized to prevent corrosion from tannic acid. When blind-nailing, use two nails directly next to each other on each timber. A

A drywall ceiling laid over the timbers helps to make small rooms feel brighter and larger by reflecting light. A painted background also gives contrast to the frame.

good trick is to hold both nails in your hand and drive them at once; they tend to spiral around each other and provide further locking. Where posts pass through the frame, a ½-in.-deep notch receives the plank. By simply pushing the plank into the notch, scribing is eliminated, and any gaps that might develop when the timbers shrink will be hidden. Leave at least ⅝ in. between the planking and the wall for expansion and contraction. This space will be hidden behind the baseboard and can also be used for running electrical wire.

The ceiling side of the planks can be finished with stain, oil, or both before installation. The floor side can be sanded and finished later in construction. Wall-to-wall carpeting helps absorb noise, especially that caused by impact—kids playing with blocks on a plank floor can make a deafening clatter. If you plan to use carpeting, shop as carefully for the pad as you do for

the carpet, and ask for the one that would be the best sound barrier.

Drywall over timbers

The timber frame itself brings a great amount of wood into the living environment, and adding more exposed wood on the ceiling is often detrimental to design. The alternative is usually a light-colored drywall ceiling, which makes the room brighter by reflecting light and gives the frame more distinction by avoiding wood on wood (see the photo above). My tendency is to use wood planks over timbers for high ceilings and cathedral ceilings (see the photo on p. 220) and to use drywall on low ceilings. Wood can make a large volume seem warmer and cozier. A painted ceiling in a light color makes a small volume feel larger.

To apply drywall over timbers, start by gluing and nailing a 2-in.-wide strip of plywood over the center of each joist, leaving approximately 1 in. of timber

Vaulted ceilings often benefit by having wood ceilings. The wood absorbs light and adds warmth.

DRYWALL AND PLANK FLOOR

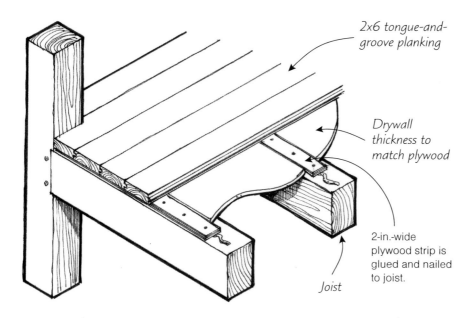

2x6 tongue-and-groove planking

Drywall thickness to match plywood

2-in.-wide plywood strip is glued and nailed to joist.

Joist

on each edge toward the joist bay (see the drawing below). Use ½-in.-thick plywood for ½-in. drywall (which is what we commonly use) or ⅝-in.-thick plywood for ⅝-in. drywall. When the strips are in place, cut sheets of drywall lengthwise to fit between the plywood strips in the joist bays. Since the timbers are approximately 30 in. on center and drywall comes in 48-in. widths, this will mean a large amount of waste. However, by using drywall that is the same length as the joist bay, seams between joists can be completely avoided, and the money saved by not having to tape and spackle seams is greater than the cost of the waste. You can eliminate yet another finishing step by prepainting the drywall before installing it over the joists.

After the drywall is down, glue and nail all the planking to the plywood strips as if they were the timbers. Finally, screw the drywall to the planking from below midway between the joists 16 in. on center. Even if the drywall has been prepainted, it isn't difficult to spackle and touch up the screw heads.

Plaster finish

It's possible to use plaster-based drywall or rock lath instead of standard drywall, with the intention of plastering between the timbers. We don't generally recommend this because it is so much more work, and shrinkage (if the timbers are not dry) eventually pulls the timbers away from the plaster edges, creating a gap. Still, there's nothing like plaster, and it's hard to argue against the warm feeling and natural texture of a good plaster job. If clients choose this option, I encourage them to wait one year before applying the plaster. The problem is that it's hard to wait if you're building on a time-limiting construction loan or if you are simply anxious to move into a finished house. When using plaster-based drywall, don't worry about the seams, because the entire surface will be coated with plaster; try instead to reduce waste.

Sound-deadening floors

Adding drywall to the flooring system does nothing for soundproofing. The interconnected posts and beams of a well-built timber frame are designed for stiffness and assembled under tension, like strings on a guitar; great strength is achieved but so is a great ability to transmit sound. To reduce sound transmission significantly, the sound must be absorbed with a material of less density than the framing members.

We often use a rigid sound-deadening board such as that manufactured by the Homasote Company. Soundboard comes in 4-ft. by 8-ft. sheets and several thicknesses, of which ½ in. is the most commonly used. It has enough compressive strength to support floor loads and enough resilience to absorb some sound. To be effective, the soundboard should be installed in an unbroken layer between other materials, for instance, between the drywall and the planking in the system previously discussed (see the top drawing at right). It goes over everything with no regard for joints. (It is not necessary to join the soundboard seams to timbers—just tack where possible to secure temporarily.) The soundboard is followed with blind-nailed tongue-and-groove planking, but since the nails now must pass through ½-in.-thick soundboard to get to the plywood strips, use 20d nails instead of 16d. To secure the drywall to the planking through the soundboard, use 1¾-in. drywall screws. Probably the biggest problem with installation is to get the soundboard down without stepping through the ceiling. To keep yourself on a solid floor, lay the soundboard and the planking at the same time.

What's lost in this system is the structural advantage of gluing the planking to the framing. But you might want to glue the planking to the soundboard to prevent squeaking.

When soundboard is used in this way, the ceiling does not need to be drywall. Instead, the finished ceiling could be ¾-in.-thick boards (as shown in the bottom drawing above). Soundboard

SOUND-DEADENING FLOORS

FLOOR SYSTEM WITH SOUNDBOARD

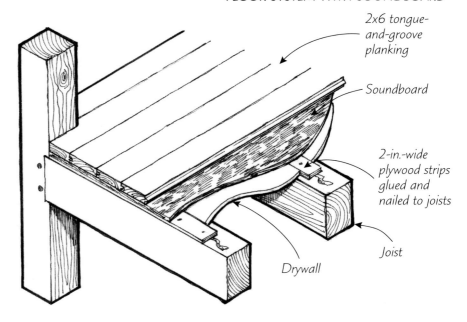

2x6 tongue-and-groove planking

Soundboard

2-in.-wide plywood strips glued and nailed to joists

Joist

Drywall

FLOOR SYSTEM WITH AIRSPACES

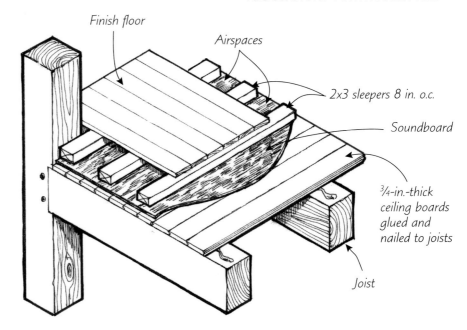

Finish floor

Airspaces

2x3 sleepers 8 in. o.c.

Soundboard

¾-in.-thick ceiling boards glued and nailed to joists

Joist

and planking would then be installed as described previously. In either case, the planking must span from joist to joist. Remember that it is a good idea to notch the entire thickness of the floor assembly into any posts that pass through the floor level to avoid gaps when the timbers shrink.

A floor system with even better sound-deadening characteristics uses the first two steps described previously (ceiling material of drywall or planking plus soundboard) but incorporates an additional step. After the ceiling material and the soundboard are in place, 2x3 sleepers are nailed or screwed 8 in. on center perpendicular to the joists. The

2x3s span the joists and are a nail base for the flooring. Both the airspace between the soundboard and the finish floor and the reduced area of contact over the joists help to increase sound-deadening. If the finish floor will be either carpet or tile, a ¾-in.-thick plywood subfloor is first attached to the 2x3s. This system also creates plenty of space to run wires and is even useful for some plumbing runs.

INTERIOR PARTITIONS

In timber-frame construction, all interior partitions are superfluous as structure. Even partitions as delicate as shoji (light Japanese screens made of a wooden grid overlaid with rice paper) would work. In fact shoji would be perfect for a timber-frame house—light, thin, and movable, offering the ultimate design flexibility. But in most cases, partitions must be of sturdier construction to perform the important duties of providing privacy and blocking sound. As I pointed out in Chapter 4, the design of the timber frame should coincide with the design of the floor plan; rooms should be defined by timbers as well as walls, and therefore most walls will be aligned with timbers. In this section, I will talk a little more specifically about the relationship of walls to timbers and the various ways to install partitions.

For partitions to be integrated successfully with the frame, the designer needs to determine precisely where they will fall in relation to the timbers. Partitions usually consume a total of between 3½ in. and 4½ in., and with this in mind a decision must be made on how much of the timber will be revealed on each side of the wall. To simplify construction, try to hold partitions to one side or the other of the knee braces when possible, revealing the frame to the more public area and concealing it on the opposite side. The alternative—revealing the frame on both sides of a partition wall—requires that individual pieces of framing and drywall be fitted around knee braces—a laborious job.

In a timber-frame house, partitions are not part of the structure; they are spatial divisions only. Therefore, they should be built in a way that enhances the beauty of the frame, yet provides privacy. In this house, the partitions are built with 2x3s and will be sheathed with soundboard. Note the framing to expose the knee braces.

When knee braces are not an obstacle, partition walls can be constructed on the floor and installed as a unit. To the carpenter, the difference between these two methods is extreme. Note that when walls are to be constructed on one side or the other of the knee braces, the designer must specify to the framer that the knee braces be pushed toward the opposite edge of the timber to allow room for the partitions. Edge embellishments must also be considered when planning partitions.

Green timbers will shrink, which is a problem for interior partitions because it is likely that shrinkage will occur after the partitions are in place. It's not just aesthetics at stake here, for even small cracks greatly reduce the ability of the partition to deaden sound. There are only a few solutions to the shrinking-timber dilemma.
• Construct the partitions and put sheathing on both sides but don't finish the walls until the timbers have

stabilized. If the timbers are almost dry or just in need of acclimating to the environment, this might be a reasonable wait of only a few months. However, if the frame was made of green hardwood, the wait could be up to three years.
• Finish the interior walls immediately and plan on filling the spaces with paintable caulking when the cracks appear. As you can imagine, even if this does not seem like the best solution, it is the one most often used. The pleasure of the finished product is not deferred, and caulking the cracks is put off until the next time the walls need painting. Wallpaper should not be put on until the timbers dry because cracks around the edges are unsightly.
• Make the shrinkage a design detail by installing L-bead where drywall meets timber. L-bead is basically a hard metal edge that is attached to the partition before the drywall. The drywall is cut so that it roughly meets the L-bead and is finished after the joint is taped

and spackled. When the timber shrinks, a distinct gap (usually not more than ¼ in.) is left between the edge of the L-bead and the timber—it shows up as a dark space. This works well in situations that will not have to be caulked, such as closet partitions. But on one of our projects, an architect specified that L-bead be used on almost every wall and that a deliberate gap be created from the beginning, which would be filled with dark caulking.

Defining living areas with timbers instead of partitions results in an open floor plan and a feeling of spaciousness that is really a part of the definition of a timber-frame home. But this freedom of movement and of view also allows sound to travel freely. If privacy is a requisite, compensate by sound-deadening all partitions in private areas.

The easiest solution is to use 2x3s to build the partition (see the photo on the facing page) and then apply sound board as the first layer of sheathing on both sides. After the sound board, attach the drywall. The only potential problem with this system is that the electrician may need to use wide, flat electrical boxes to have enough area for wires—standard electrical boxes are too deep for a 2x3 partition.

For even better performance, use a standard 2x4 for top and bottom plates, but use staggered 2x3s as studs. The 2x3s, 8 in. on center, are alternately aligned with either plate edge, giving 16 in. on center nailing for each side (see the drawing below). The advantage is that no stud touches the drywall on both sides, greatly reducing sound conduction through the wall. Half-inch soundboard is then applied to the par-

tition on both sides before ½-in. drywall is installed. Obviously, no sound-deadening system will work effectively without a good seal between the surrounding timbers and the partition. Apply acoustical sealant to the top and bottom plates and to both end studs before fastening. It may still be necessary to caulk after the timbers have stabilized.

Partitions designed not to deaden sound can be made with 2x3s or 2x4s. Because standard electrical boxes are 3 in. or more in depth, 2x4s are more common.

When interior partitions don't align with timber posts, it is important that they be firmly attached to the exterior wall. If a built-up exterior insulation system is used, the problem can easily be solved by providing nailing for the

SOUND-DEADENING PARTITION

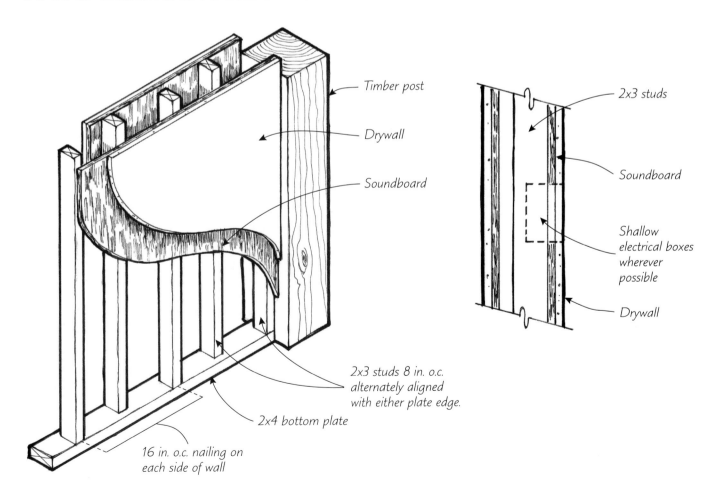

Timber post

Drywall

Soundboard

2x3 studs 8 in. o.c. alternately aligned with either plate edge.

2x4 bottom plate

16 in. o.c. nailing on each side of wall

2x3 studs

Soundboard

Shallow electrical boxes wherever possible

Drywall

stud that meets the exterior wall. But if the exterior wall is a foam-core panel, some advance planning is necessary. Before the exterior siding goes on, screw the stud to the panel from the outside, using galvanized self-tapping screws that are long enough to penetrate the stud by at least 1 in. If this step is omitted, don't bother to tape the corner between the interior partition and the exterior wall, for it will inevitably crack.

SURFACE TREATMENT

While the exterior of the house often must bend to its natural and architectural environment, the interior should be designed to satisfy the inhabitants. Interior decoration has few rules; it is a personal and entirely subjective process. I have a friend who doesn't like things until they reach a state of nearly total decay. When plaster is cracked but still holding on, when paint is faded and beginning to peel, when floor boards are almost worn through from use, when moss is thick on the shingles, she is ecstatic; she thinks things are perfect the moment before disrepair. I know another person who requires that all things have the glitter of newness about them, that the colors be bright, that the brass and stainless steel be maintained with a showroom shine. To him, something used is old, and old things are ugly. We have designed homes to have the look of a barn and some that were intended to have the elegance of a castle, and there's nothing wrong with either. What's important is that a timber-frame home is able to satisfy both requirements. When you hear the words "a timber-frame house," it should conjure an image of a method of construction, not a specific decorative style.

One of the important factors affecting interior style is the treatment of the interior surfaces. The timbers, walls, and ceilings all should be planned carefully in advance to achieve the desired result. The exposed timber frame is an incredibly strong decorative element, and the species should be chosen mostly for its aesthetic value, since engineering should make the frame equally strong no matter what the wood. When deciding, consider that knotty wood of whatever species is more rustic than wood that is free of knots, and straight-grained wood with tight growth rings is more subtle than highly figured wood with widely spaced rings. Oak and southern pine are generally coarser than pine and cedar. To make sure the wood of the frame will not clash with other design intentions, it is important to become familiar with all the options. Each person will bring to this decision personal prejudices and opinions. I once rented a basement apartment from a casket maker, where all the walls and the ceiling were paneled with reject pine from the casket business. The experience left me with very uncomfortable feelings about knotty pine. Another personal opinion I have developed is that the best timber frames are those that are the most subtle, that enhance instead of dictate.

There are two reasons why the timbers in a frame are usually planed and finished. First, it is easier to work timbers planed to specific dimensions rather than deal with varying thicknesses. Second, it is almost impossible to keep the timbers clean from the time cutting starts until the frame is raised. We usually finish-plane or sand the timbers and apply a finish to the interior surfaces just before the raising. The smooth surface also makes it easier to keep the timbers clean in the future. Although there are many possibilities, the most common surface finish is oil. If the timbers are green, it is important to apply a penetrating oil, which will allow the timbers to breathe as they dry.

Some timber framers use a mixture of linseed oil, gum turpentine, and Japan drier with satisfactory results. For dry wood, a thin coat of shellac or polyurethane can be applied as a second or third coat to seal the surface and to keep the mixture from bleeding. Citrus-based oil can also be used as a base, and we have found it a little more durable while the frame is exposed to the

The timbers in the frame are usually planed and oiled, both for appearance and ease of cleaning. After the raising, another coat of clear, citrus-based oil is applied.

Old yellow-pine timbers were resawn to make this frame. The patina of age can't be applied; it is only achieved with time.

weather. It also produces a hard finish without the addition of polyurethane or shellac. Our favorite for durability and appearance is Livos. Tung oil also works well. Your paint supplier can help you mix your own formula or choose among the different brands. One nice aspect of using an oil-based finish is that it is easy to repair marred surfaces, and new coats tend to blend in quite well. It is also possible to buy oil premixed with stain, but before applying any stain, try it on a sample of the same type of wood as the frame. "Medium walnut" (whatever that is), will look vastly different on fir than on pine, and stains are difficult to remove.

In my opinion, the first choice should be to find a wood that will naturally deliver a suitable color and texture with a clear oil finish. If that is not possible, then consider stain. A dark stain is

helpful, for instance, if the frame is to blend with colonial decoration; unstained wood would probably always look too fresh. Still, the first choice might be a wood that would give an old appearance. On many of our projects, we have used timbers resawn from wood salvaged from old buildings (see the photo above). The wood was old, and looked old.

On another of our projects, after the frame went up, one of the owners decided the timbers were too overpowering. She wanted the form and shape of the frame but only as a background. Against my advice, whitewash was applied to the timbers, allowing the grain and texture to show but masking the strong, dark wood. It was a radical solution, but the results were surprisingly good (see the photo on p. 226).

The wall and ceiling surfaces in a timber-frame home serve as a canvas backdrop, helping to highlight the artistic value of the timbers. For this reason, a successful treatment of the surfaces is very often simply a white or off-white paint, a deliberate development of the "negative space" enclosed by the "positive" surround. This is the traditional timber-frame interior style that has been used for centuries around the world. In older buildings, the walls and ceilings are usually plastered, and the wood, having grown dark with age, helps to create the classic "black-and-white" appearance.

There are a couple of other specific uses for white (or very light) surfaces between timbers. They help to reflect light, making the spaces brighter and enhancing the volume. Small rooms and spaces with low ceilings therefore have requested gallery space for specific paintings—a challenge we readily accept, because the timbers seem to function as an additional frame for the artwork, making it quite easy to achieve a satisfying display area (see the top photo on the facing page).

Despite the arguments in favor of simple, light-colored surfaces between timbers, many people choose to use wallpaper with fine results (see the bottom photo on the facing page). Simple print patterns seem to produce less clutter, although some of our creative clients have done striking things with rather extravagant wallpapers. As I have said, there are few rules.

All the exterior wall and ceiling surfaces are usually applied to the outside of the frame as a part of the enclosure system. In most cases, the interior surface is a drywall product. We use a plaster-based drywall, which can either receive a veneer coat of plaster or simply be taped and painted. Taping and painting the drywall is the least problematic because there is a distinct separation between the frame and the wall or ceiling surface.

If the timbers shrink or twist, it isn't likely to cause any major problems. It might be necessary to touch up the paint edges as the timbers dry, but this is a much easier job than having to fill in gaps with spackling or caulking, which is almost certain to be necessary if plaster is applied to the drywall. As the timbers dry, there will be some eventual separation between the frame members and the plaster edges. Therefore, if green timbers are used for the frame, consider not using plaster at all or putting the task off until the timbers have stabilized. This same advice applies to wallpaper. It can be more than a little discouraging to fit paper precisely between the timbers only to find later that the timbers have pulled away from the edges. A better strategy is to paint the walls initially and then apply wallpaper after the frame has dried completely.

When a client decided the natural color of the timbers was overpowering, she decided to whitewash them. The grain and texture of the wood come through, but the dark color was eliminated. (Photo by Brian E. Gulick. Design Associates, Architects.)

benefit the most from having light-colored walls and ceilings. For exactly the opposite reason, large spaces with cathedral ceilings can be made to feel more comfortable and cozy with wood ceilings to absorb the light and to "bring the ceiling down." Another good reason for a white background between timbers is to create a place to hang art. In fact, it amused me to find

fake timbers stuck to the wall in a large art gallery just to develop the feeling that comes naturally to a timber-frame home. The white backgrounds, framed by timbers, become individual focal areas for artwork, and the whole effect can have the atmosphere of a lively gallery. The introduction of artwork is also a great way to bring color into a house. On several occasions, clients

Finish Details

226

Off-white walls between timbers create a good background for a display of art.

Ceilings, whether those of a timber floor or roof system, rarely justify plaster. The drywall is applied over the top, almost always in such a way that there are few, if any, seams. The ceiling surface easily can be finished just with paint. Because the timbers generally fall at the drywall edges, eliminating or reducing the need to tape seams, the drywall can even be painted before installation. Applying plaster on a ceiling is monumentally more difficult than paint because the timbers act as obstacles. There are also more timber edges to worry about while the frame stabilizes. We often encourage clients who prefer plaster to use it on the walls but not on the ceilings. The surfaces are separate enough to have different textures, even if they are the same color. Wood ceilings are easily installed and reduce maintenance. The wood is usually oiled to bring out the grain and color. Future applications of oil will be greatly simplified if the same kind of oil is used on the ceiling boards that was used on the frame. Oil can then be applied to the entire ceiling without extra care being necessary at the edges.

In this home, wallpaper was used along with other surface finishes. Because timbers shrink, it is best to apply wallpaper after the wood has dried.

APPENDIX
SAMPLE BUILDING PROGRAM

PART I

The following will help you consider the pragmatic design aspects of your home. The proposed sizes of rooms, their function, and the needs and activities of the occupants will determine the layout and dimensions of your house. Your answers to the questions below will help to determine design priorities, as well as identify any extras.

1. List projected occupants (family members, relatives).

2. List pets, livestock.

3. Projected time of occupancy of each occupant (life, to 21 years, or seasonal).

4. What transportation vehicles, construction equipment, farm equipment, etc., do you need to store, and what kind of shelter is required?

5. Have you determined the approximate total square footage of required living areas? If so, what is the square footage? How did you arrive at this size (existing situation, family size, number of bedrooms/baths, future needs, furniture arrangements)?

6. List any circumstances particular to you or your family that may affect design (people with disabilities, medical needs, noise considerations, lighting, air quality, temperature control).

7. Should expansion flexibility be a consideration? Do you know what rooms will need to be added and how large they might be?

8. List activities and amount of time to be spent in rooms/spaces below, and approximate space required. Reference to and measurement of the spaces in which you now live may be helpful. Keep in mind furniture, equipment, and storage requirements, among other things (not all of these rooms will apply to your home).

Airlocks _____

Barn _____

Basement _____

Bathrooms _____

Bedroom 1 _____

Bedroom 2 _____

Bedroom 3 _____

Bedroom 4 _____

Breakfast nook _____

Broom closet _____

Closets for clothing _____

Courtyard _____

Darkroom _____

Dining room _____

Dressing room _____

Exterior wood storage _____

Family room _____

Garage/shop _____

Greenhouse _____

Guest room _____

Hot tub _____

Interior wood storage _____

Kitchen _____

Linen closet _____

Living room _____

Mudroom _____

Pantry/storage _____

Patio _____

Playroom _____

Pool _____

Porch _____

Sauna _____

Study/library/den _____

Sunspace _____

Utility/laundry room _____

PART II

This group of questions is intended to help you pinpoint how you would like your life and your dwelling to interact. Try to consider how spaces feel as well as how they look, and remember the flow of people, things, and food through the environment. Indicate that which you find displeasing and the things that have a relaxing effect.

Bedroom

1. Do you like to wake up in a bright and/or sunlit room?

2. Do you like to be able to look outside while lying in bed?

3. Do you prefer the bed to be a particular height off the floor?

4. Do you prefer windows, a fan, or an air conditioner for ventilation?

5. What are the privacy requirements of the bedroom from the outside and from the rest of the house?

6. What are your storage requirements? Give size and general description of items.

7. Do you like a separate dressing area?

8. Does the bedroom also need to function as a study, TV room, or sitting room?

9. What sleeping accommodations will be necessary for other family members or in the future? (Use the first eight questions as guidelines.)

10. Would you feel comfortable if the bedroom had a cathedral ceiling or would you prefer a flat ceiling?

Bathroom

1. What are the special qualities you like in a bathroom? Does it need to be especially bright or roomy?

2. Should there be a bathroom attached to one or more bedrooms?

3. How private should the bathroom be from the rest of the house and from the outside?

4. Do you need a bathroom easily accessible from the outside?

5. Do you prefer fans or windows for ventilation?

6. Do you like to be able to see out a window while showering, washing, or using the toilet?

7. Do you use the bathroom in a hurried or a leisurely manner?

8. Do you prefer showers or baths?

9. When you take a shower or bath, do you use the bathroom to dress?

10. Do you have a preference for a particular brand of fixtures?

11. What requirements do you have for mirrors?

12. What are your storage requirements?

13. What sort of bathing accommodations are necessary for other family members now or in the future? (Use the first 12 questions as a guide.)

Kitchen

1. What times of day and to what extent do you use the kitchen?

2. How many people should be able to use the kitchen at the same time?

3. Will the kitchen be used for eating as well as for food preparation?

4. What appliances are necessary?

5. Is there a particular appliance/fixture arrangement that suits you best?

6. Do you like to be able to look out the window while working in the kitchen? If so, from what area?

7. Do you like a bright or sunlit kitchen?

8. Is it important to have an exhaust fan in the kitchen?

9. How do you prefer to deal with waste and garbage?

10. Where and how would you like to store your food?

11. How much cupboard or drawer space do you need?

12. Do you like pots and pans, dishes utensils, and food to be visible or hidden?

13. Would you use timbers to hang pots and pans?

14. What nonfood items do you store in the kitchen?

15. What other items (such as desk, TV, fireplace) would you like in the kitchen?

16. Should the kitchen be separate from the rest of the house or linked to other areas?

Dining

1. What sort of feeling should the dining area have?

2. Is the dining place a single or multi-purpose area?

3. Is there a need for a guest dining area separate from the normal family dining area?

4. How many people should the dining area accommodate?

5. Is natural or artificial light, or both, appropriate?

6. What is the best way to get food and dishes to and from the dining area?

Living

1. How do you want the living area to feel?

2. Should it be separate or integrated into other living areas?

3. What activities go on in the living room?

4. How many people should it accommodate?

5. Should it have partitions and doors?

6. Should it be bright during the day?

7. What sort of artificial light is compatible with your image of the living space?

8. Is a fireplace desirable?

9. List any equipment you think should be in the living space (stereo, books, video).

10. How do phones and TV figure into your life?

Miscellaneous

1. What should the predominant feeling of the house be (rustic, informal, elegant)?

2. How would you describe the style that makes you feel most comfortable (modern, colonial)?

3. What are the attributes of the timber frame that would help to achieve the above requirements?

4. What other rooms or activity areas are necessary (study, playroom, darkroom, shop)?

5. What guest accommodations are necessary?

6. Is additional storage space necessary?

7. How much interaction between the indoors and outdoors is desirable?

8. Do you like transitional spaces (porches, decks)?

9. Do you see the exterior landscape as formal, casual, or natural?

10. What requirements do you have for outdoor activities and accessory buildings (pool, tennis, gardens, horses, basketball)?

11. What is your attitude toward dirt? Where do you mind it and where is it okay? How do you clean it up and how often?

12. How many vehicles do you have and how do they fit into your life?

13. Do you have pets? How many and what kind?

14. Do you have houseplants? How many? Do they have special requirements?

15. What sort of textures do you like?

16. What colors do you like?

17. List the things you can't do in your present environment that you would like to do in your new environment.

BIBLIOGRAPHY

Alexander, Christopher, Sara Ishikawa, and Murray Silverstein. *A Pattern Language.* New York: Oxford University Press, 1977.

Alexander, Christopher, Sara Ishikawa, and Murray Silverstein. *The Timeless Way of Building.* New York: Oxford University Press, 1979.

Anderson, Bruce and Malcolm Wells. *Passive Solar Energy.* Andover, Massachusetts: Brick House Publishing Co., 1981.

Benson, Tedd. *Timber-Frame Houses.* Newtown, Connecticut: The Taunton Press, 1992.

Benson, Tedd and James Gruber. *Building the Timber Frame House.* New York: Charles Scribner's Sons, 1980.

Brand, Stewart. *How Buildings Learn: What Happens After They're Built.* New York: Viking, 1994.

Brandon, Raphael and J. Arthur. *The Open Timber Roofs of the Middle Ages.* Canada: The Canadian Log House, 1977.

Briggs, Martin S. *A Short History of the Building Crafts.* Cambridge, England: Oxford University Press, 1925.

Brown, S. Azby. *The Genius of Japanese Carpentry: An Account of a Temple's Construction.* New York: Kodansha International, 1989.

Brungraber, Robert (Ben) Lyman. *Traditional Timber Joinery: A Modern Analysis.* Thesis. Ann Arbor, Michigan: University Microfilm, Inc., 1985.

Brunskill, R.W. *Timber Building in Britain.* London: Victor Gollancz, Ltd., 1985.

Coaldrake, William H. *The Way of the Carpenter: Tools and Japanese Architecture.* New York: Weatherhill, Inc., 1990.

Cummings, Abbott Lowell. *The Framed Houses of Massachusetts Bay, 1625-1725.* Cambridge, Massachusetts: Belknap Press of Harvard University Press, 1979.

Downing, A.J. *The Architecture of Country Houses.* New York: Dover Publications, Inc., 1969.

Endersby, Eric, Alexander Greenwood, and David Larkin. *Barn: The Art of a Working Building.* New York: Houghton Mifflin Co., 1992.

Fitchen, John. *The New World Dutch Barn.* Syracuse, New York: Syracuse University Press, 1968.

Foster, Michael, ed. *The Principles of Architecture: Style Structure and Design.* London: New Burlington Books, 1982.

Suzuki, Makoto. *Wooden Houses.* New York: Harry N. Abrams, Inc., 1979.

Futagawa, Yukio. *Traditional Japanese Houses.* New York: Rizzoli International Publications, Inc., 1983.

Grosslight, Jane. *Light.* Englewood Cliffs, New Jersey: Prentice-Hall, Inc., 1984.

Habraken, John. *Supports, an alternative to mass housing.* London: The Architectural Press, 1972 (available from the MIT Press).

Hansen, Hans Jurgen, ed. *Architecture in Wood.* London: Faber and Faber, 1971.

Harris, Richard. *Discovering Timber Frame Buildings.* London: Shire Publications, Ltd., 1978.

Hewett, Cecil A. *English Historic Carpentry.* London and Chichester: Phillimore and Co., Ltd., 1980.

Isham, Norman M. and Albert F. Brown. *Early Connecticut Houses.* New York: Dover Publications, Inc., 1965.

Kelly, Frederick J. *Early Domestic Architecture of Connecticut.* New York: Dover Publications, Inc., 1952.

Kimball Fiske, *Domestic Architecture of the American Colonies and of the Early Republic.* New York: Dover Publications, Inc., 1966.

Langdon, Philip. *American Houses.* New York: Stewart, Tabori & Chang, Inc., 1987.

Langdon, William Chauncy. *Everyday Things in American Life, 1607-1776.* New York: Charles Scribner's Sons, 1943.

Makinson, Randell L. *Greene and Greene, Architecture as a Fine Art.* Salt Lake City, Utah: Peregrine Smith, Inc., 1977.

Mazria, Edward. *The Passive Solar Energy Book.* Emmaus, Pennsylvania: Rodale Press, 1979.

Mullin, Ray C. *Electrical Wiring Residential.* New York: Van Nostrand Reinhold Co., 1981.

SOURCES

Mullins, Lisa C., series ed. *Architectural Treasures of Early America*. 10 vols. Harrisburg, Pennsylvania: Historical Times, Inc., 1987.

Mumford, Lewis. *Roots of Contemporary American Architecture*. New York: Dover Publications, Inc., 1972.

Packard, Robert T., A.I.A., ed. *Architectural Graphic Standards*. New York: John Wiley and Sons, 1981.

Phleps, Hermann. *The Craft of Log Building*, trans. Roger MacGregor. Ottawa, Ontario: Lee Valley Tools, Ltd., 1982.

Poor, Alfred Easton. *Colonial Architecture of Cape Cod, Nantucket and Martha's Vineyard*. New York: Dover Publications, Inc., 1932.

Price, Lorna. *The Plan of St. Gall in Brief*. Berkeley and Los Angeles, California: University of California Press, 1982.

Quiney, Anthony. *The Traditional Buildings of England*. London, Thames and Hudson, Ltd., 1990.

Rempel, John I. *Building With Wood*. Toronto: University of Toronto Press, 1967.

Rybczynski, Witold. *Home: A Short History of an Idea*. New York and Canada: Viking Penguin, Inc., 1986.

Schwolsky, Rick and James I. Williams. *The Builder's Guide to Solar Construction*. New York: McGraw-Hill, Inc., 1982.

Sobon, Jack A. *Build a Classic Timber Framed House*. Pownal, Vermont: Garden Way Publishing, 1993.

Sobon, Jack and Roger Schroeder. *Timber Frame Construction*. Pownal, Vermont: Garden Way Publishing, 1984.

Stickley, Gustav. *Craftsman Homes*. New York: Dover Publications, Inc., 1979.

West, Trudy. *The Timber Frame House in England*. New York: Architectural Book Publishing Co., 1971.

Williams, Lionel Henry and Ottalie K. Williams. *Old American Houses, 1700-1850*. New York: Crown Publishers, Inc., 1962.

Wood, Margaret. *The English Mediaeval House*. New York: Harper and Row, 1965.

Woodforde, John. *The Truth about Cottages*. London: The Country Book Club, 1970.

Wright, Frank Lloyd. *The Natural House*. New York: The Horizon Press, 1954.

The Works of John Burroughs. Vol. 7, *Signs and Seasons*. Boston and New York: Houghton Mifflin Co., Riverside Press, 1989.

Yoshida, Tetsuro. *The Japanese House and Garden*. New York: Frederick A. Praeger, 1954.

To locate foam-core panel suppliers in your area, contact:
Structural Insulated
Panel Association (SIPA)
1511 K Street, N.W.
Suite 600
Washington, D.C. 20005
Phone: (202) 347-7800
Fax: (202) 393-5043

For more information about the craft of timber framing, contact:
The Timber Framers Guild
of North America
P.O. Box 1075
Bellingham, WA 98227-1075
Phone: (206) 733-4001
Fax: (206) 733-4002
e-mail: shargr@aol.com

To locate qualified professional timber framers, timber suppliers, recycled-timber suppliers, qualified timber engineers, or other professionals allied with the timber-frame building industry, contact:
The Timber Frame Business Council
1511 K Street, N.W.
Suite 600
Washington, D.C. 20005
Phone: (202) 783-1100
Fax: (202) 393-5043

Contacting the author:
Tedd Benson
BensonWood Homes
224 Pratt Road
Alstead Center, NH 03602
Phone: (603) 835-6391
Fax: (603) 835-2544
e-mail: tedd@bensonwood.com

INDEX

Page references in italic indicate illustrations.

A

Air conditioning. *See* Cooling system
Aisles:
    defined, 63
    as part of design, 78-79
Architect, floor plans by, 74-75

B

Bathrooms, designing, 84
Bay(s):
    defined, 63
    as part of design, 77-78
Blueprints. *See* Floor plans
Briggs, Martin, *A Short History of the Building Crafts*, 7, 9
Bubble diagram, 72-73
    sample, 71
Building codes, dealing with, 21-22
Building form, 60-62
    intersecting, 62, *62, 63*
    room development of, 62-63, 66-67
Building program, creating, 70
Building shape, framing options for, 64-65
Burroughs, John, 17

C

Casings. *See* Exterior trim. Interior trim
Ceiling, surface treatment for, 225-27
Ceiling joists, framing, 86-88
Chimney, 183-85
    air ducts in, *171*
    framing for, *184*
    planning for, 183-85
Climate, as factor in foundation design, 118-19
Code. *See* Building codes
Cold roof, described, 217
Compound joinery. *See* Joinery, compound
Concrete footing, poured, *121*
Cooling system, 168-71

D

Dead load, defined, 29
Design:
    influence of timbers on, 80-81
    ruling notions of, 69-70
Diagonal braces, importance of to frame, 39-40
Dining room, designing, 81-82
Doors:
    design of, relationship to frame, 194
    framing, *83*
    French, framing, 83, *83*
Dormers, 180-81, 183
    framing for, *181*
Douglas fir, as frame timber, 53
Dovetail, 47-48
Ductwork. *See* Heating

E

Electrical system:
    and floor-system wire chase, 151-53, *152*

horizontal wire chases for, 140-45, 147-48
    extended baseboard wire chase, 140-45, *141, 144*
    timber-sill wire chase, *142*
    baseboard heating unit wire chase, 145, *145*
    cabinet wire chase, 146-47, *146-47*
    sill-plate wire chase, 147-48, *147*
    planning, 137-38
    prewiring for, 138-40
    vertical wire chases for, 148-51
    timber-post wire chase, 149, *149*
    panel-spline wire chase, *149*, 150
Energy audit:
    discussed, 96
    See also Insulation
Energy consumption, reducing, 92
Expanded polystyrene (EPS), as panel core, 113-14
Exterior trim:
    for roof, applying, 210
    sloped-soffit, described, 210-11, *210*, 213-14, *214*
    for a planked roof, 211, *212*, 213
    flat-soffit, 214-16, *215*

F

Fireplace. *See* Chimney
Fixtures, lighting:
    built-in ceiling, planning for, *155*
    mounting between beams, 153
    planning for, 153-54, 156
    recessed, planning for, *155*
Floor, arranging timbers in, 40
Floor deck:
    materials for, 129
    stick-framed, 129, 130, *131*
    timber, 129-30, 134, *135*
Flooring:
    applied over timbers, 217-18
    considerations for, 217-22
    material for, 218-22
    and reducing sound, 217, 221-22, *221*
Floor plans, generating, 74-77, *87*, 88-90, *88, 89*
Floor system, *40*
Foam-core panels, 21, 93-95, *94, 96-97*
    alternatives to, 96-103
    choosing, 103-104
    EPS type, construction of, 114
    installing, 106-109, 111-13
    plan for, 108
    tools for, 109
    joints for 104-106, *105*
    laminated urethane panel type, construction of, 115
    poured urethane panel type, construction of, 115
    roofing over, 216-17
    selecting, 103-105
Footing:
    concrete-block, 122, *124*, 125
    concrete-pier, 128, *128*
    continuous, 122
    grade beam and pier, 125-26, *126*
    insulating, 129
    interior post location in, 128

pier, and deck framing, 130, *130*
    poured, formwork for, *121*
    poured concrete, 122, *123*
    slab-on-grade, 125, *125*
    thickened-edge slab, 126-27, *126*
Foundation:
    factors in designing, 117-20
    slab-on-grade, and floor framing, 132
    stepped, for sloping site, 133, *133*
    systems, 120, 122, 125-28
Frame(s):
    calculating loads for, 26
    connecting separate, *188, 190*
    determining shape of, 60-62
    horizontal members of, defined, 25
    parts of, identified, 25
    raising, methods for, 59-60
    timber species for, 52-53
    vertical members of, defined, 24-25
Frame design, considerations for, 50-67
Free tenons. *See* Spline joinery

G

Geology, as factor in foundation design, 118-19
Glass:
    energy efficiency of, 193-94
    for solarium walls,
        applying *198*, 199
        treating bottoms of panes, 199-200
    for solarium roofs, 200, 201
        applying, 200, *201*, 202
Gutters, installing, 213-14

H

Heating:
    with electric system, 170
    furnace air returns for, *171*
    with hot-air furnace, 169
    with hot-air systems, 169-70
    with hot-water system, 170
Home (Rybczynski), 17
Horizontal members of frame, defined, 25
Horizontal timbers, sizing, considerations when, 29-30

I

Intermediate posts, 38-39
Interior trim, 204-205
    for windows, 204, 205
    for baseboards, 205
Interior partitions, 222-24
    sound-deadening, 223, *223*
    green timbers for, 222-23
Insulation:
    choosing, factors to consider when, 95-96
    development of, 20-21
    and exterior stud system, 98-99, *98*
    fiberglass, 92-93
    foam-and-nailer, for roof, 102, *102*
    and infill stud system, 97-98, *97*
    and horizontal nailer system, 99-100, *99*
    and Larsen truss system, 100-102, *101*
    rigid-foam, for roof, 102, *102*
    R-value of, 95
    See also Foam-core panels

J

Joinery:
  choosing, 42
  compound, principles of, 191-93
    and roof hips, *191*
  mortise and tenon. *See* Mortise-and-tenon joint
  most common used in timber framing, 41-43, 45-49
  spline, 45
  lap, 47-49, *48*

K

King post truss, defined, 27
Kitchens, designing, 81-82, 84
Knee braces, importance of to frame, 39

L

Laminated timbers, as frame timber, 53
Lap joint:
  dovetail, 47-48, *48*
  notched, *48*
  overlap, *48*
Larsen trusses, installing, 100-102, *101*
Lighting. *See* Fixtures, lighting
Live load, defined, 29
Living room, designing, 82

M

Mortise-and-tenon joint(s), 42-43, 45-47
  creating, 6
  designing, for stress, 43
  open, 47, *47*
  sizing, *43*
  strengthening, 44

N

Natural House, The, 92

O

Oak, as frame timber, 52
Open mortise and tenon, 47, *47*
Overhangs, designing, 185-87

P

Pine:
  eastern white, as frame timber, 52
  longleaf, as frame timber, 52
  shortleaf, as frame timber, 52
Plumbing:
  draining system, described, 158-59, *159*
  fundamentals of, 158
  horizontal pipe chases for, 164-67, *165*
  in kitchen,
    sink vents for, 167-68, *168*
    vertical chase for, 168
  layout, example of, *161*
  supply system, described, 158
  vertical pipe chases for, 162-64, *162*
Porches, framing, 187

R

Rafters, supporting, 32
Railings, for catwalks and balconies, detailing, 208
Recycled timbers, as frame timber, 53

Roof:
  cold, described, 217
  common-rafter, 32, *34*
  common-rafter with midspan plates, 32-33, *34*
  principal-rafter and principal-purlin, 33-34, *36*
  principal-rafter and common-purlin, 34-36, *36*
  ventilated, *216*
  warm, described, 216-17
Roofline, changes in, 188-89
Roof overhangs, framing, 185-87
Roof system. *See* Roof
Roof timbers, 36-40
Roof types, described, 31-36
Roof windows, 179
  framing for, *180*

S

Scarf joint, 48-49, *49*
Short History of the Building Crafts, A (Briggs), 7, 9
Site, and influence on design, 73-74
Site conditions, as factor in foundation design, 120
Site plan, creating, 71-72
  sample, 71
Skylights. *See* Roof windows
Solar gain considerations, 71-72
Soil:
  bearing value of, 118
  as factor in foundation design, 117-18
Solariums, 194-97, 199-200, 202
  with gable roof, 197
  with shed roof, 197
  See also Windows
Spline joinery, 45
Spruce:
  Sitka, as frame timber, 53
  white, as frame timber, 53
Stairs:
  closed-riser, *207*, 208
  detailing, 206, 208
  open-riser, 206, *207*, 208
Stress-skin panel. *See* Foam-core panel
Stressed-skin panel. *See* Foam-core panel
Structural insulated pane. *See* Foam-core panel
Study, designing, 83-84
Sunlight, as lifestyle consideration, 193

T

Timber(s):
  availability of, influence on design, 54
  defining space with 81-85, *82, 84*
  design, structural systems analysis of, 55-56
  edge treatments for 173-76, *173*
    when to apply, 175
  end treatment for 176-78, *177*
  green, for interior partitions, 222-23
  green, using in frame, 56
  horizontal, considerations when sizing, 29-30

influence of on timber-frame design, 10, 12
  laminated, for frame, 53
  long, creating, 54
  recycled, for frame, 53, 56
  shrinkage of, 57-59
  sizing, 29-31
  species, for frame, 52-53
  surfacing, 224-27
  under stress, 27
  uninsulated, hazards of , 185-86
Timber frame:
  anatomy of, 24
  forces that bear on, 26-29
  goals in building, 16-20
  major systems of, defined, 24
  typical, *24*
  vertical members, defined, 24-26
Timber frame buildings:
  American style, 12-14
  compared to log buildings, 7-8
  compared to Great Buddha Hall, 5
  compared to Westminster Hall, 5
  early, materials for, 6-7, *6*
  early American house siding for, *13*
  early American style, *11, 15*
  evolution of, 5-15
  focal point of, 5
  during Middle Ages, *9*
  modern, 16-22
  multistoried, development of, 10
  old English style, *11*
  and roof valley, *191*
  saltbox style, development of, 13-14
Tongue and fork. *See* Open mortise and tenon
Trim:
  boards,
    attaching to walls, 209
    types of, 209
  as design feature, 209
  See also Exterior trim. Interior trim
Trusses, 37-38, 100-102
Tying joint, defined 49, *49*

U

Urethane, as panel core, 114

V

Vertical members of frame, defined, 24-25
Vitruvius, quoted, 6

W

Walls, surface treatment for, 225-27
Warm roof, described, 216-17
Windows:
  for admission of sunlight, 193
  design of, relationship to frame, 194
  framing, *83*
Wiring:
  near exterior doors, 150-51, *150*
  partition walls, 148, *148*
  See also Electrical system
Wood shrinkage, dealing with in building, 22
Wright, Frank Lloyd, 92